ENTREPRENEURSHIP SERIES

START & RUN A

CONSULTING
BUSINESS

ENTREPRENEURSHIP SERIES

START & RUN A

CONSULTING BUSINESS

DOUGLAS GRAY

JAICO PUBLISHING HOUSE

Ahmedabad Bangalore Bhopal Chennai
Delhi Hyderabad Kolkata Mumbai

Published by Jaico Publishing House
A-2, Jash Chambers, Sir Phirozshah Mehta Road
Fort, Mumbai - 400 001
jaicopub@jaicobooks.com
www.jaicobooks.com

Published in arrangement with
International Self-Counsel Press Ltd.
1481 Charlotte Road
North Vancouver, BC V7J 1H1
Canada

START & RUN A CONSULTING BUSINESS
ISBN 81-7992-523-4

First Jaico Impression: 2006
Third Jaico Impression: 2008

Printed by Pashupati Printers (P) Ltd., Delhi-95

CONTENTS

INTRODUCTION xix

1 UNDERSTANDING THE CONSULTING BUSINESS 1

  1. WHAT IS A CONSULTANT? 1

  2. WHO GOES INTO CONSULTING? 4

  3. WHY DO ORGANIZATIONS USE CONSULTANTS? 4

    3.1 Temporary assistance 4

    3.2 Objective review 4

    3.3 Third-party request for problem identification and resolution 5

    3.4 Surviving a crisis 5

    3.5 Initiating change 5

    3.6 Obtaining funding 5

    3.7 Selecting personnel 5

    3.8 In-house education 5

    3.9 Dealing with internal personnel difficulties 5

    3.10 Delay tactics 5

    3.11 Executive assistance 6

    3.12 Government regulatory compliance 6

    3.13 Socio-economic and political changes 6

    3.14 Government excess funds 6

  4. REGULATIONS AFFECTING CONSULTANTS 6

2 SELF-ASSESSMENT 7

  1. INTRODUCTION 7

  2. ASSESSING YOURSELF AND YOUR MARKETABLE SKILLS 7

3 SETTING UP YOUR BUSINESS 13

  1. START-UP COSTS AND MONTHLY EXPENSES 13

    1.1 Start-up costs 14

    1.2 Monthly overhead expenses 15

    1.3 Personal expenses 15

  2. SELECTING A NAME 19

    2.1 General considerations 19

    2.2 Fictitious name 19

  3. SELECTING AN OFFICE 20

    3.1 Home office 20

	3.2	Office outside of home	21
		3.2a Office sharing arrangement	21
		3.2b Sharing same private office	21
		3.2c Office rental package	21
		3.2d Occasional office	22
		3.2e Leased space	22
	3.3	Equipping an office	23
		3.3a Computer	24
		3.3b Modem	24
		3.3c Computer software	24
		3.3d Printer	25
		3.3e Copier	25
		3.3f Fax machine	25
	3.4	Office supplies	25
		3.4a Business stationery, cards, envelopes	26
		3.4b Brochures	26
		3.4c Record-keeping documents, invoices, and file folders	26
		3.4d Calendars	26
	3.5	Personnel	26
		3.5a Secretarial staff	26
		3.5b Retaining other consultants	27
4.	SELECTING A TELEPHONE SYSTEM	27
	4.1	A separate phone at home	27
	4.2	Business line terminating at answering service	28
	4.3	Business line terminating at home and answering service	28
	4.4	Overline	28
	4.5	Measured business line	28
	4.6	Shared line	29
	4.7	Interconnect phone purchase	29
5.	SPECIAL TELEPHONE FEATURES	29
	5.1	Call waiting	29
	5.2	Call forwarding	29
	5.3	Three-way calling	29
	5.4	Speed calling	29
	5.5	Phone/fax	29
	5.6	Call display	29
	5.7	Name display	30

	5.8	Call return	30
	5.9	Call again	30
	5.10	Call answer	30
6.	SAVING MONEY ON LONG DISTANCE PHONE CALLS		30
	6.1	Direct distance dialing	30
	6.2	Reduced long distance rates	30
	6.3	Toll-free service number	30
	6.4	Interconnect long distance companies	30
	6.5	Some tips	30
7.	OTHER COMMUNICATION OPTIONS		31
	7.1	Telephone answering devices	31
	7.2	Voice mail	32
	7.3	Toll-free number	32
	7.4	Generic telephone number	33
	7.5	Fax on demand	33
	7.6	Pager	33
	7.7	Cellular phone	34
	7.8	E-mail	34
	7.9	Web site	35
8.	DEVELOPING YOUR WEB SITE		35
	8.1	Pitfalls to avoid	35
	8.2	Keeping the Web site interesting	36
	8.3	How to design an effective Web page	37

4 LEGAL FORMS OF BUSINESS STRUCTURE — 39

1.	INTRODUCTION		39
2.	SOLE PROPRIETORSHIP		39
	2.1	Advantages	40
	2.2	Disadvantages	40
3.	PARTNERSHIP		41
	3.1	Advantages	41
	3.2	Disadvantages	41
	3.3	Partnership agreement	42
	3.4	Kinds of partners	42
4.	CORPORATION		42
	4.1	Advantages	42
	4.2	Disadvantages	44
	4.3	Corporate purposes	44

		4.4	Shareholders' agreement	44
		4.5	Maintaining the corporate protection	45
	5.		S CORPORATION (SUB-CHAPTER OR SUB-S) (UNITED STATES)	47
	6.		LIMITED LIABILITY CORPORATION (LLC) (UNITED STATES)	47
5	**SELECTING BUSINESS AND PROFESSIONAL ADVISERS**			**49**
	1.		GENERAL CRITERIA FOR ADVISER SELECTION	49
		1.1	Recommendations	50
		1.2	Credentials	50
		1.3	Clientele	50
		1.4	Fees	50
		1.5	Technical competence and industry knowledge	51
		1.6	Style and personality	51
		1.7	Confidence	51
		1.8	Communication	51
		1.9	Commitment	52
		1.10	Availability	52
		1.11	Length of time in practice	52
		1.12	Ability to aid growth	52
		1.13	Small firm versus large firm	52
		1.14	Comparison	52
	2.		LAWYER	53
	3.		ACCOUNTANT	53
	4.		BANKER	54
	5.		INSURANCE	55
	6.		CONSULTANTS	55
		6.1	Private consultants	55
		6.2	Consultants subsidized by the government	55
			6.2a Counselling Assistance to Small Enterprises (CASE)	55
			6.2b Service Corps of Retired Executives (SCORE)	56
6	**PREPARING YOUR BUSINESS PLAN**			**57**
	1.		WHY PREPARE A PLAN?	57
	2.		FORMAT	58
	3.		ESTIMATING YOUR START-UP FUNDS	58
		3.1	Assessment of personal monthly financial needs	58
		3.2	Estimated business start-up cash needs	59
	4.		SUMMARY	59

7	**HOW TO OBTAIN FINANCING**	79
	1. TYPES OF FINANCING	79
	1.1 Equity	79
	1.2 Debt	80
	1.2a Short-term or operating loan (demand loan)	80
	1.2b Line of credit	80
	1.2c Term loans	81
	1.2d Trade credit or supplier financing	82
	1.2e Renting or leasing	82
	2. SOURCES OF FINANCING	82
	2.1 Equity	82
	2.2 Debt	83
	2.2a Small Business Administration (United States)	83
	2.2b Business Development Bank of Canada (Canada)	83
	3. COMPETITION BETWEEN LENDERS	84
	4. TIPS ON APPROACHING YOUR LENDER	84
	5. WHY LOANS ARE TURNED DOWN	85
	6. TYPES OF SECURITY A LENDER MAY REQUIRE	86
	6.1 Endorser	86
	6.2 Co-maker	87
	6.3 Guarantor	87
	6.4 Promissory note	87
	6.5 Demand loan	87
	6.6 Realty mortgage	87
	6.7 Chattel mortgage	87
	6.8 Assignment of accounts receivable	87
	6.9 Postponement of claim	87
	6.10 Pledge of stocks or bonds	87
	6.11 Assignment of life insurance	88
8	**KEEPING RECORDS**	89
	1. ACCOUNTING AND BOOKKEEPING	89
	1.1 Separate record-keeping	90
	1.2 Double-entry and single-entry bookkeeping	90
	1.3 One-write accounting system	90
	1.4 Cash or accrual basis for records	91
	1.5 Computer software	91

2. BASIC ACCOUNTING RECORDS 91
   2.1   Sales journal 91
   2.2   Cash receipts journal 91
   2.3   Accounts receivable ledger and control account 92
   2.4   Accounts payable journal 92
   2.5   Cash disbursements journal 92
   2.6   Payroll journal 92
   2.7   General ledger 93
   2.8   Computer software for record-keeping 93
3. NONFINANCIAL RECORDS 93
   3.1   Personnel records 93
   3.2   Tax records 93
   3.3   Service records 94
4. OFFICE SYSTEMS 94
   4.1   Handling new clients and projects 94
   4.2   Time records 94
   4.3   Standard form engagement letters or contracts 94
   4.4   Billing, credit, and collection 95
   4.5   Calendars 95
   4.6   Filing systems 95
   4.7   Computer systems 95

9 HOW TO LEGALLY MINIMIZE PAYING TAX 99
1. TAX AVOIDANCE AND TAX EVASION 99
2. CASH OR ACCRUAL METHOD 100
3. FISCAL YEAR-END 100
4. CORPORATIONS, PROPRIETORSHIPS, OR PARTNERSHIPS 100
5. MAXIMIZING DEDUCTIBLE EXPENSES 101
   5.1   Home office 101
   5.2   Automobile 102
   5.3   Entertainment 102
   5.4   Travel 102
   5.5   Bad debts 103
   5.6   Insurance 103
   5.7   Education and professional development 103
   5.8   Salaries 103
   5.9   Equipment 103
   5.10 Furnishings 104

10 INSURANCE   105

   1. OBTAINING INSURANCE   105

     1.1 Agencies   105

     1.2 Insurance brokers   105

     1.3 Clubs and associations   106

   2. PLANNING YOUR INSURANCE PROGRAM   106

   3. TYPES OF BUSINESS AND PERSONAL INSURANCE 107

     3.1 General liability   107

     3.2 Products or completed operations liability 107

     3.3 Errors and omissions liability 107

     3.4 Malpractice liability   107

     3.5 Automobile liability   107

     3.6 Fire and theft liability   108

     3.7 Business interruption insurance 108

     3.8 Overhead expense insurance   108

     3.9 Personal disability insurance 108

     3.10 Key person insurance   108

     3.11 Shareholders' or partners' insurance 108

     3.12 Business loan insurance   109

     3.13 Term life insurance   109

     3.14 Medical insurance   109

     3.15 Group insurance   109

     3.16 Workers' compensation insurance 109

11 PROFESSIONAL LIABILITY   111

   1. CONTRACT AND TORT LIABILITY   111

     1.1 Contract liability   111

     1.2 Tort liability   112

   2. REASONS FOR CLAIMS   113

     2.1 Counterclaims   113

     2.2 Conflict of interest   113

     2.3 Conflicting interest of clients 113

     2.4 Delegation of part of contract to employee or sub-consultant 113

     2.5 Third party damages   113

     2.6 Unclear expectations by client 113

   3. HOW TO AVOID PROFESSIONAL LIABILITY AND PREVENT LOSSES 113

     3.1 Client control   114

     3.2 Cost estimates   114

	3.3	Carefully drafted contracts	114
	3.4	Free opinions	114
	3.5	Law	114
	3.6	Sub-consultants	114
	3.7	Records, systems, and procedures	114
	3.8	Continuing education	114
	3.9	Quality control	115
	3.10	Communication	115
4.	PROFESSIONAL LIABILITY INSURANCE		115
	4.1	Increase deductibles	115
	4.2	Comparing prices	115
	4.3	Changing the type of coverage	116
5.	PRACTICING WITHOUT INSURANCE		116

12 CREDIT, BILLING, AND COLLECTION   117

1.	DISADVANTAGES OF EXTENDING CREDIT		117
2.	ASSESSING THE CLIENT		118
3.	AVOIDING CLIENT MISUNDERSTANDINGS ON FEES		119
	3.1	Communication	119
	3.2	Written contract	119
	3.3	Invoice	120
4.	MINIMIZING RISK OF BAD DEBTS		120
	4.1	Advance retainer	120
	4.2	Prepaid disbursements	120
	4.3	Progress payments	120
	4.4	Regular billing	120
	4.5	Billing on time	120
	4.6	Accelerated billing	121
	4.7	Withholding vital information	121
	4.8	Holding up completion of important stage of project	121
	4.9	Personal guarantee of principals of a corporation	121
	4.10	Monitor payment trends of clients	121
	4.11	Follow-up of late payments	121
	4.12	Involving client in assignment	121
5.	BILLING FOR SERVICES		121
6.	WHY CLIENTS PAY LATE		122
7.	COLLECTING LATE PAYMENTS WITHOUT LEGAL ACTION		125

8. LEGAL STEPS IF ACCOUNT REMAINS UNPAID 126
    8.1   Collection agency 126
    8.2   Small claims court 126
    8.3   Lawyers 126
9. BAD DEBTS AND TAXES 127

13 SETTING FEES 129
1. DAILY BILLING RATE (PER DIEM) 129
    1.1   Labor 129
    1.2   Overhead 129
        1.2a Fixed and variable expenses 129
        1.2b Indirect and direct expenses 130
        1.2c Calculation of overhead 130
    1.3   Profit 130
2. HOURLY RATE 131
3. CALCULATING A FIXED PRICE QUOTATION 131
    3.1   Determining a fixed price estimate 131
    3.2   Tips on preparing fixed price estimates 132
4. FIXED PRICE PLUS EXPENSES 134
5. CONTINGENCY FEE 134
6. PERCENTAGE FEE 135
7. PROJECT VALUE FEES 135
8. RETAINER FEES 135
9. EQUITY FEES 135
10. UTILIZATION RATE 136
11. VARYING YOUR FEES 136
12. INCREASING FEES 136
13. INCREASING PROFITS WITHOUT INCREASING FEES 137

14 DETERMINING MARKET OPPORTUNITIES 139
1. PRIVATE SECTOR 139
    1.1   Individuals 140
    1.2   Small businesses 140
    1.3   Medium-size businesses 140
    1.4   Large companies 141
2. PUBLIC SECTOR 141
    2.1   Making contacts and obtaining information 141
    2.2   Understanding the government approval system 142
3. GRANT CONSULTING 143

15 MARKETING YOUR CONSULTING SERVICES   145
   1. WHAT YOU NEED TO MARKET YOUR SERVICE   145
   2. MARKETING PLAN   146
   3. MARKETING TECHNIQUES   146
      3.1 Newspaper   147
      3.2 Advertising in trade or professional journals   147
      3.3 Directories   147
      3.4 Brochures   147
      3.5 Direct mail   148
      3.6 Contact network   150
      3.7 Membership in professional, trade, or business associations   151
      3.8 Donating your services   151
      3.9 Attending public and professional meetings   151
      3.10 Lectures   151
      3.11 Teaching   152
      3.12 Seminars and workshops   152
      3.13 Free media exposure   153
      3.14 Radio and television talk shows   153
      3.15 Letters to the editor   153
      3.16 Writing articles   154
      3.17 Writing a book   155
      3.18 Have articles written about you   155
      3.19 Announcement columns   155
      3.20 Newsletters   155
      3.21 Web site   156

16 THE CLIENT INTERVIEW AND CLIENT RELATIONS   157
   1. PURPOSE OF INTERVIEW   157
   2. BEFORE THE MEETING   157
   3. DURING THE INTERVIEW   160
   4. AFTER THE INTERVIEW   161
   5. WHY YOU SHOULD TURN DOWN BUSINESS   161
   6. HOW TO TURN DOWN UNWANTED BUSINESS   162

17 CONSULTING PROPOSALS   163
   1. WHAT IS A PROPOSAL?   163
   2. PRIVATE VERSUS PUBLIC SECTOR PROPOSALS   163
   3. SOLICITED VERSUS UNSOLICITED PROPOSALS   164

	4.	SIMPLE AND FORMAL PROPOSALS	164
	4.1	Simple proposal	164
	4.2	Formal proposal	164
	5.	GUIDELINES AND FORMAT FOR A SUCCESSFUL PROPOSAL	165
	6.	PRESENTING YOUR PROPOSAL	165
	7.	PROPOSAL FOLLOW-UP	169
	8.	WHAT TO DO IF YOUR PROPOSAL IS NOT ACCEPTED	169
	9.	HOW TO AVOID GIVING AWAY FREE CONSULTING	169
	9.1	Potential client interview or discussion	170
	9.2	Analysis of client's need	170
	9.3	Free detailed advice in the written proposal	170
	9.4	Potential future benefit	171
	9.5	Additions to the original fixed price contract	171
	9.6	Free consulting in a follow-up situation	171
	9.7	Relatives, associates, and friends	172
18	**CONTRACTS**		173
	1.	ESSENTIALS OF A VALID CONTRACT	173
	1.1	Offer	174
	1.2	Acceptance	174
	1.3	Consideration	174
	1.4	Competency	174
	1.5	Legality	174
	2.	WHY A WRITTEN CONTRACT IS NEEDED	174
	3.	STRUCTURE OF FORMAL CONTRACT	176
	4.	TYPES OF CONTRACTS	176
	4.1	Letter of agreement	176
	4.2	Letter of agreement with general terms and conditions appended	181
	4.3	Formal contract	181
	4.4	Sub-consulting agreement	181
	4.5	Agency agreement	195
	4.6	Letter of retainer agreement	196
	5.	PREPARING YOUR OWN CONTRACT	196
19	**TIME MANAGEMENT**		197
	1.	KEY STRATEGIES	197
	1.1	Set priorities	197
	1.2	Be organized	198

  1.3 Delegate 199

  1.4 Be decisive 199

 2. AVOIDING TIME WASTERS 199

  2.1 Using voice mail effectively 199

  2.2 Using e-mail effectively 200

  2.3 Too many telephone calls 201

  2.4 Overscheduling/too many things to do 201

  2.5 Too much paper 201

  2.6 Scheduled meetings 201

  2.7 Perfectionism 201

20 EXPANDING YOUR PRACTICE 203

APPENDIXES

 1 CONSULTING AND OTHER ASSOCIATIONS (UNITED STATES AND CANADA) 205

 2 FREE OR NOMINAL COST BUSINESS PUBLICATIONS 206

 3 PROPOSAL EVALUATION CHECKLIST 207

BIBLIOGRAPHY 211

TABLES

1	MAJOR CONSULTING SUBJECT AREAS	2
2	AVERAGE START-UP EXPENSES	14
3	CHECKLIST OF ARTICLES IN A PARTNERSHIP AGREEMENT	43
4	DETAILED CONTRACT CHECKLIST (COMMONLY USED FOR GOVERNMENT CONTRACTS)	192

SAMPLES

1	START-UP EXPENSE CHECKLIST	15
2	MONTHLY EXPENSE CHECKLIST	16
3	PERSONAL MONTHLY EXPENSE CHECKLIST	17
4	BUSINESS PLAN FORMAT	60
5	OPENING BALANCE SHEET (NEW BUSINESS)	72
6	INCOME AND EXPENSE STATEMENT FORECAST (NEW BUSINESS)	73
7	CASH FLOW BUDGET WORKSHEET	74
8	PERSONAL NET WORTH STATEMENT	76
9	STATEMENT OF ACCOUNTS RECEIVABLE	78
10	PROSPECTIVE CLIENT SHEET	96
11	NEW CONSULTING ASSIGNMENT SHEET	97
12	TIME AND SERVICE RECORD	98
13	GENERAL INVOICE	123
14	DETAILED INVOICE	124
16	PROPOSAL FORMAT	166
17	CONTRACT FORMAT	177
18	LETTER OF AGREEMENT (PREPARED BY CONSULTANT)	182
19	LETTER OF AGREEMENT (PREPARED BY CLIENT)	183
20	STATEMENT OF GENERAL TERMS AND CONDITIONS	185
21	FORMAL CONSULTING CONTRACT	187

INTRODUCTION

This book is designed primarily for the beginning or potential consultant, but consultants who have been in practice for a considerable time should also find it helpful. The purpose of this book is to provide essential information and practical step-by-step guidelines to assist you in starting and developing a successful and profitable consulting business. All the information necessary to set up and maintain your own business is included in this book.

The book is organized to reflect a typical consulting business, from getting the original idea to generating income sufficient for your needs and expectations. You will assess your consulting potential and determine your marketable skills in chapter 2. In chapters 3 through 13 you will learn all the basic steps you have to consider before starting your business. Chapters 14 and 15 deal with the marketing techniques essential to success. Without effective ongoing marketing, you simply will not succeed. Chapters 16, 17, and 18 inform you how to negotiate a consulting assignment from the first interview to the proposal to obtaining the contract. Chapter 19 shows you ways of effectively managing your time. Chapter 20 discusses ways of expanding your practice.

The tables, samples, and appendixes have been provided to make the text as meaningful as possible. There are many good reference books that can assist you further; these are listed in the Bibliography and have been divided into various section headings for easy reference by subject area. Directories of consulting associations are listed in Appendix 1. (These directories, which can be found in your local library, contain up-to-date information on addresses and phone numbers.) Consulting is basically a knowledge industry, and access to ways of improving your knowledge should assist you in marketing your skill more effectively.

Each chapter in this book stands independently but is linked to the others. If you know little about consulting or being in business, you should read the chapters sequentially to appreciate the need for dealing with basic business considerations. Understanding and managing the business side of consulting is as essential as performing the consulting service.

Every year the demand for consultants increases as our society becomes more complex. Business, education, health care, government, military, labor unions, social services, churches, and volunteer organizations employ consultants on a regular basis. Consulting in North America has become a multi-billion dollar industry.

Consultants are people who are determined to succeed, who thrive on challenge, and who believe in themselves.

Consultants are entrepreneurs in the knowledge field. Consultants are individuals who believe that they are competent and capable of rendering a worthwhile service to others.

Consulting offers a continual challenge and can present opportunities for freedom, growth, and satisfaction far beyond those of employment or other forms of business. This book increases your chance of capitalizing on the opportunities and assisting your business success.

Note: This book aims to highlight common consulting practices accurately. However, the information is general in nature, and no legal, tax, or financial advice is given. If legal or other expert assistance is required, you should obtain the services of competent professionals.

Laws are constantly changing. Every effort is made to keep this publication as current as possible. However, the author, the publisher, and the vendor of this book make no representation or warranties regarding the outcome or the use to which the information in this book is put and are not assuming any liability for any claims, losses, or damages arising out of the use of this book. The reader should not rely on the author or the publisher of this book for any professional advice. Please be sure that you have the most recent edition.

CHAPTER 1
UNDERSTANDING THE CONSULTING BUSINESS

1. WHAT IS A CONSULTANT?

A consultant is someone who has expertise in a specific area or areas and offers unbiased opinions and advice for a fee. The opinion or advice is rendered exclusively in the interests of the client and can cover review, analysis, recommendations, and implementation. A consultant generally works in conjunction with the resources personnel of the client, but uses employees, sub-consultants, or others as required for the specific project and in accord with the agreement. A consultant is not an employee but an independent contractor, usually self-employed, contracted to perform a short-term or long-term task and paid on an hourly, daily, or project basis or other fee arrangement.

There are numerous consulting opportunities in the private and public sector. Table 1 provides a brief summary of some of the major consulting areas. The consulting profession has grown extensively over the past 15 years and is now one of the major service industries in North America. The outlook for continued growth of consulting is very positive. Demand exceeds the projected supply.

The consulting industry prospers in most economic conditions. The amount of income that a consultant can earn is, of course, related to many factors, including the field of knowledge and level of expertise in that field. The degree of profit is also directly related to how effectively time is managed and how efficiently the business is administered. New consultants spend a large portion of time managing the task, researching their field of expertise, improving on techniques, and marketing their expertise. Most of these tasks are essential but unbillable hours.

TABLE 1
MAJOR CONSULTING SUBJECT AREAS

Acoustics

Actuarial services

Advertising

Architecture

Association management

Audiovisual services

Automation
 – Office
 – Industrial

Building management

Business administration

Business forms and systems

Cable television

Career guidance

Communication
 – Electronic
 – Interpersonal

Community relations

Conference and convention
 planning and management

Construction services
 – Management
 – Heating/ventilating/
  air-conditioning
 – Inspection and estimates

Curriculum development

Data processing
 – Computer hardware
 – Computer software/
  programming
 – Systems analysis

Direct marketing

Economic research, analysis,
 forecasting

Editorial services

Educational services
 – Curriculum development
 – School/camp selection

Electronics

Employee benefit planning
 – Pension planning
 – Profit sharing

Energy management and
 conservation

Engineering
 – Aeronautical
 – Chemical
 – Civil
 – Electrical
 – Electronics
 – Environmental
 – Industrial
 – Marine
 – Mechanical
 – Mining
 – Nuclear
 – Petroleum

Estate planning

Executive development and
 recruitment

Exhibit planning and design

Financial management
 – Banking
 – Budgeting
 – Investment counseling

Food facilities design

Food retailing

Food services

Foreign licensing

Forestry

Franchising

Freight transportation and
 shipping

Fundraising

Furnishings

Government relations
 – Municipal
 – State/provincial
 – Federal

Graphics

Health services administration

Heating

Hospital administration

Hotel and motel management

House publications

Human factors engineering

Human relations

Human resources development
 – Employee selection and
  training
 – Employee surveys
 – Industrial psychology
 – Personnel productivity

Immigration and naturalization

Industrial/manufacturing
 services
 – Industrial classification
 – Industrial development
 – Industrial testing
 – Production management

Information storage and retrieval

Insurance

Interior design
 – Color
 – Furnishings
 – Lighting

TABLE 1 — CONTINUED

International business and trade

Inventory control

Labor relations

Land use planning

Landscaping

Leasing
- Equipment
- Transportation

Library design and services

Licensing

Lighting

Lithography

Mail order

Marketing programs and services

Marketing research and analysis

Marriage and family relations

Material handling

Materials science

Mergers and acquisitions

Microforms

Museum and exhibit planning and design

National security and defense

Naturalization

New product design

New product introduction

Nutrition

Office design

Office management

Operations research

Opinion polls

Organization analysis and development

Packaging

Personal image

Personnel

Planning (long range, strategic)

Political campaigning

Pollution control
- Air
- Noise
- Water

Product design

Professional practice management

Public relations

Publishing

Purchasing

Real estate

Records management

Recreation planning

Reliability and quality control

Religion

Relocation services

Research and development

Safety services
- Accident investigation
- Expert witness
- Fire protection
- Product liability
- Program design and installation

Sales
- Forecasting
- Management
- Personnel recruiting
- Policy and planning
- Retail/wholesale

Salvage and reclamation

Sanitation

Security (investigation and loss prevention)

Shipping

Small business development

Social services

Sports

Standardization

Statistical services

Stockholder relations

Systems analysis

Taxes

Technology transfer

Telecommunications

Television and radio

Traffic and parking

Transportation

Urban renewal

Utilities management

Venture capital

Wage and salary administration

Warehousing

Women's issues and concerns

2. WHO GOES INTO CONSULTING?

Basically, a consultant is a person with a marketable skill, a perceptive mind, a need for independence and challenge, an ability to communicate with others and persuade them to follow advice, a desire to help others in an effective way, and a wish to be an agent of positive change. In general, the people who go into consulting include:

- People frustrated with their current careers, who see the solutions for problems but are unable to effectively influence decision-makers

- People who want a stimulating, dynamic, growing career that satisfies the need for personal development

- People dissatisfied with the lack of challenge, opportunity, or creativity in their existing jobs

- People graduating from school with training but little experience who wish to work for a large consulting firm

- People who are between jobs and seeking new opportunities and careers

- People who see that they may be laid off and wish to establish themselves in a business to earn a livelihood; these people may start on a part-time basis while still employed

- Retired people who have expertise and wisdom to offer

- People who wish to supplement their present income by using their managerial expertise or technical and academic skills

- People with work experience and industry knowledge or other skills who want to combine a family life with work at home

- People who understand government operations and the contract process, or who have built up contacts in government, politics, or industry over the years

3. WHY DO ORGANIZATIONS USE CONSULTANTS?

There are many reasons why the private and public sector need consultants for problem solving. Some of these reasons are discussed below.

3.1 Temporary assistance

Clients frequently wish to supplement skills in their organization by hiring trained, proven, motivated consultants on a short-term or long-term basis. Consultants may be hired on a project, seasonal, or new funding basis.

By hiring consultants, clients do not have to contend with the training, instruction, and long-term commitment for salaries and fringe benefits entailed in hiring a skilled employee. Recruitment costs alone for a skilled employee can be considerable and cannot be justified for short-lived or cyclical need. Consultants are independent contractors and therefore no tax deductions or fringe benefits are involved.

3.2 Objective review

Consultants are retained as impartial advisers without any vested interest in the outcome of the recommendations. Internal staff may not be able to see the problems or may not be sufficiently objective. A consultant can perform a competent and thorough analysis of the issues. It is easier psychologically for personnel to adapt to external advice rather than the internal advice of someone who may be acting out of self-interest.

3.3 Third-party request for problem identification and resolution

Banks are naturally concerned about any signs of a problem that might put their investment at risk. A bank may need to know whether the problems are related to administrative, personnel, financial, market, or product difficulties and how the problems can be solved. Only an outside consultant's opinion would be credible.

3.4 Surviving a crisis

A business owner suffering from serious business problems may seek an outside consultant to investigate the causes and recommend solutions.

3.5 Initiating change

A consultant can act as a catalyst for stimulating ideas in a highly structured organization that otherwise might be resistant to change due to its size, bureaucracy, and institutionalized nature.

3.6 Obtaining funding

Many nonprofit organizations or small- and medium-size businesses need assistance in obtaining grants or loans for their continued survival. They may lack the expertise, ability, or time to research the availability of funding and prepare a persuasive application. Consultants with an expertise in this area act as advisers or agents.

3.7 Selecting personnel

A client might hire a consultant for recruitment of key executives. The consultant is looked upon as being independent and unbiased with the expertise and time to selectively screen and recommend prospective candidates.

3.8 In-house education

Consultants are hired to provide in-house training to keep staff informed of new management and supervisory techniques or technical knowledge and to improve employee morale.

3.9 Dealing with internal personnel difficulties

Outside consultants are retained to review and make recommendations on internal structure, for example, consolidation of departments or services or elimination of redundant employees or executives. The consultant's report provides the rationale for making the decisions. The consultant then leaves and is not affected by the decision.

Consultants can also be used to resolve conflicts between various levels of management. The consultant plays an arbitrating or mediating role that permits frustrations to be expressed so that energy can be directed toward constructive resolution.

3.10 Delay tactics

Consultants can be hired to perform research studies which take the pressure off a company that is being exposed to public or government scrutiny. This also permits the organization to use the excuse of a consultant's study to justify a delay in decision-making. The consultant is frequently asked to be the contact person, which reduces media attention toward the organization concerned.

3.11 Executive assistance

An executive who is aware of his or her personal limitations may request that a consultant review a problem situation, provide advice on how to deal with it, and possibly follow up with implementation.

3.12 Government regulatory compliance

Government regulations at all levels are constantly changing, and companies are frequently not prepared or trained to comply. Consultants may be retained to provide expertise to assist a company in complying economically, efficiently, and with the least amount of trauma to the organization.

3.13 Socio-economic and political changes

Socio-economic and political matters are always in a state of flux. These changes present opportunities for consultants. For example, pollution problems create a need for environmental protection experts, and fuel shortages create a need for energy conservation experts.

3.14 Government excess funds

Consultants benefit considerably from the expenditure of large amounts of government money. The government may be funding the private sector with the hope of stimulating the economy; there may be political reasons before an election; there may be a balance in a department's budget that must be spent before the end of the budget year so as not to reduce the allotment requested by that department the following fiscal year. Governments also frequently hire consultants to assess needs, provide solutions, and to conduct in-house training.

4. REGULATIONS AFFECTING CONSULTANTS

Some professional organizations are empowered by legislation to exercise rights of practice, membership, and discipline. However, there is no government control or regulation of consultants as such. The term consultant is similar to the term accountant: anyone can use the word to describe his or her activity without credentials, experience, competence, or accountability.

There are many organizations for specific areas of consulting, but membership is voluntary. These organizations or associations have little power or authority to investigate complaints.

Management consultants can apply to become a member of the Institute of Management Consultants. This group provides guidelines for professional practice. (You will find the Institute's address in any of the directories listed in Appendix 1.)

The benefits of membership in a consulting association include:

(a) Certification status if the consultant meets minimum acceptable standards of skill and knowledge

(b) Opportunities for self-development in seminars and workshops

(c) Interaction and networking with other consulting professionals

(d) Representation of the membership's areas of interest to government and other professional bodies

(e) A code of ethics and code of conduct

(f) Keeping current on issues in the area of consulting by means of a newsletter or other publication

CHAPTER 2
SELF-ASSESSMENT

1. INTRODUCTION

Many consultants never do a thorough, honest appraisal of their strengths and weaknesses. If you haven't identified your skills, attributes, and talents, how can you determine your specialty areas and the target market? How are you able to package and sell your services and take advantage of opportunities? Without this awareness it is difficult to project the self-confidence necessary to operate your business and respond to questions a potential client might ask you.

Most consultants never go through the steps outlined in this chapter, and that gives you a distinct competitive advantage. To know yourself — your strengths and weaknesses — is to have power and a prescription for success.

2. ASSESSING YOURSELF AND YOUR MARKETABLE SKILLS

The following exercise is important to help you determine the direction you should take in your new consulting business. For the maximum benefit, take all the time you need to complete each stage. Be honest and candid with yourself. The material you are preparing is for your information and benefit only.

After you have completed the exercise, you will have a comprehensive, detailed, and exhaustive guideline for your successful consulting business. Review it, update it, and modify it on a regular basis. If you have taken the time to thoughtfully complete the exercise, you should feel confident that you have developed a realistic framework for the next important stages of your business development.

SELF-ASSESSMENT

1. Summarize your own autobiography. Review and detail all facets of your past, including work positions, projects you have done, education, credentials you have obtained, free time activities including hobbies and sports, family and personal relationships. Include all the work experiences performed during summers, weekends, or holidays. Start with the most current period and work backward.

2. List all areas of your special interest, achievement, knowledge, and personal satisfaction.

3. List all your skills, that is, things that you can do. Skills are developed or acquired abilities such as instructing, administering, researching, and problem-solving.

4. List all your talents. Talents are a natural endowment, often a unique "gift" or special, often creative, attribute. Frequently a talent is a combination of skills. Think of any evaluations that may have been made about you or comments made by your friends in which your talents were observed, for example.

5. List all your attributes. Attributes are inherent characteristics such as an analytical or inquiring mind, intuition or sensitivity. Various studies have found the following attributes essential to successful consultants:

   - Good physical and mental health
   - Professional etiquette and courtesy
   - Stability of behavior
   - Self-confidence
   - Personal effectiveness and drive; that is, responsibility, vigor, initiative, resourcefulness, and persistence
   - Integrity, that is, the quality that engenders trust
   - Independence: The successful consultant must be self-reliant and not conform to the opinions of others. The consultant must be able to form judgments in the areas of his or her competence and experience
   - Intellectual competence
   - Good judgment; the faculty of sound appraisal with complete objectivity

- Strong analytical or problem-solving ability; the ability to analyze, assemble, sort, balance, and evaluate the basic factors of problem situations of different degrees of complexity

- Creative imagination; the ability to see the situation with a fresh perspective

- Ability to communicate and persuade, with above-average facility, in oral, written and graphic formats

- Psychological maturity; the successful consultant is always ready to experience people, things, and events as they really are with their unique individual characteristics; to view them in perspective and to take the action needed in a calm and objective manner without being diverted from a sound, logical and, ethical course by outside pressure

- Skill in interpersonal relationships, including an ability to gain the trust and respect of client personnel, enlist client participation in the solution of problems, apply the principles and techniques of change, and transfer knowledge to client personnel; a receptiveness to new information or points of view expressed by others; and an orientation toward the people aspect of problems

- Technical knowledge, which means an all-encompassing knowledge of the business and also recognizing lack of skill where it exists and seeking to acquire that skill or employing people with that skill

6. List all the skills and attributes you lack that you believe are necessary for a consulting business.

7. List the skills and attributes you lack related to being a consultant that you believe you can improve; write down how that will happen and how long it will take. Prioritize.

8. Of the skills and attributes that you believe you cannot improve, state how that will affect your consulting business choices, if at all.

9. Speak to friends, relatives, or family members who know you well and whose judgment, candor, and goodwill you respect. Ask them to think about your strengths and weaknesses as they see them, and prepare a list. Also ask them to outline the skills, talents, and attributes they believe you possess and those you lack.

10. Update and modify the personal inventories you previously prepared.

11. Review your list of skills, talents, and attributes and provide specific examples where each trait was used that could have a marketing application in providing consulting services.

12. Prioritize the 10 activities that gave you the most pleasure and personal satisfaction. Outline how well you did these activities. Don't over-estimate or under-estimate your abilities.

13. List the top 10 skills or talents, starting with the most important, that you feel are basic to your consulting business.

14. Imagine the type of consulting projects that you would like to do and write them down in detail and why you would like to do them. Then review your notes and identify the skills, talents, and attributes required to successfully complete these projects.

15. Imagine your personal life in the future. What direction are you currently headed in with your family and career, socially, financially, spiritually, and personally? What effect would a consulting business have on your existing lifestyle? Would the long hours and pressure of the first 6 to 12 months create strains on the family? Are you interested in marketing your abilities locally, regionally, nationally, or internationally? What effect will these decisions have on you and the people in your life?

16. Think of all the consulting opportunities that might be available to you. Consultants sell themselves as people who have solutions to problems or needs, so look for problems/need situations. Focus only on existing or potential problem/need situations that relate to your area of interest and consulting expertise.

17. Increase your awareness of additional consulting opportunities by using the following resources.

    (a) The Bibliography in this book

    (b) Consulting newsletters will stimulate your ideas on managing your practice, marketing your skills, determining consulting opportunities and keeping current on events related to the consulting industry. A list of consulting newsletters is in the Bibliography.

    (c) Magazines and newspapers; you should attempt to read everything you can relating to your specialty and general awareness of current events. Subscribe to trade journals related to your area of interest.

Get on all the free mailing lists that are of interest or relevant to your specialty area. Read your local daily newspaper and, in Canada, The Globe and Mail and The National Post; in the United States, The New York Times, The Washington Post, and The Wall Street Journal. There are other newspapers, of course, that you might prefer to read, but these provide a general indication of trends and interpretation of important events, all of which could have a bearing on opportunities for your business. There are numerous excellent business magazines which can stimulate further ideas and sources of contacts and information. Browse through your local international news outlet for an indication of the publications available. Another alternative is your public library.

(d) Consulting and professional associations; contact with the associations will provide you with an opportunity to obtain information related specifically to your specialty from newsletters, publications, meetings, or other consultant contacts. A list of the major consulting associations is in Appendix 2.

If there is a local association of consultants, either of a general or specialized nature relevant to your needs, try to attend a number of meetings and ask a lot of questions.

The reference book *Consultants and Consulting Organizations Directory*, available in public libraries, lists consultants in various specialties throughout the United States and Canada.

The SBA U.S. sponsors SCORE, which is an organization providing consulting for beginning businesses without charge. The BDC (Canada) sponsors CASE, which is a program where consultants at a very normal rate provide expertise and research skills to beginning small businesses. You may wish to take advantage of their expertise to assist you in the business side of consulting.

(e) Government agencies and publications; depending on the area of your interest, you may want to get on the mailing list of government organizations or departments that have regular publications distributed free or at a nominal charge to the public. The government, of course, is the major purchaser of consulting services, and very large sums of money are expended every year directly and indirectly for that purpose. Sources of procurement and contracts information are outlined in Appendix 1.

(f) Public and university libraries; there is a vast amount of information that is current and accessible for you to research or general ideas in your local library or university libraries. Most of the major libraries would have the various directories listed in the Bibliography and Appendix 1.

(g) Continuing education courses and seminars; universities have continuing education courses pertaining to business and related services. The SBA (U.S.) and the BDB (Canada) have small business seminars and workshops on an ongoing basis, as well as numerous publications pertaining to successful small business management.

(h) Competitors; attempt to identify the competitors in your specific field. Determine what their style and method of operation is, how long they have been in business, how they market themselves, what they charge, and who their clientele is, if possible. Try to ascertain why they are successful, if they are, and how you can best distinguish yourself and find your own niche in the market. You want to have your own unique style if comparisons are made between you and your other competitors by a prospective client.

18. Define the consulting service areas that you would like to provide (refer to Table 1 showing the major fields of consulting activity).

19. Identify who you believe could be possible clients and why.

20. Project how you would like to operate your consulting business. List the important stages and time frames of your business over the next year, three years, and five years.

21. List how you intend to market your services; that is, create a demand for your service and make potential clients realize that you exist. This question will be answered in another chapter, but it is helpful to go through the reflective exercise yourself.

CHAPTER 3
SETTING UP YOUR BUSINESS

You have now assessed your skills, attributes, and abilities and have determined your area of interest and expertise. Various administrative matters have to be understood, considered, and dealt with before embarking on your road to success.

This chapter and the next ten chapters deal with the administrative fundamentals. The challenging and fun part — that is, successfully marketing your consulting business — is explained later.

Before setting up your office and opening your doors to the public, many matters have to be considered. Your fee structures, marketing plan, and business plan, which includes your cash flow projections, will all determine how much revenue you must generate to pay your overhead. It is wise to be conservative when estimating anticipated revenue and the lead time it will take

to reach a break-even point. Your legal, tax, accounting, and financial advisers will influence your initial decisions. These important aspects are covered in other chapters.

This chapter discusses how to establish the basics of an office while controlling your expenses. With thorough review and comparison of the costs of the key overhead areas, you should require minimal capital investment and keep your overhead and risk at a safe level. See Appendix 2 for a list of sources of free or nominal cost business publications.

1. START-UP COSTS AND MONTHLY EXPENSES

There are many factors that determine what your costs and expenses are going to be, such as whether you are going to use your own home or rent an office, whether you are going to buy, finance, or lease new or used furniture and equipment, and whether you intend to hire staff or do the typing yourself. Your individual finances and needs and your shrewdness and negotiating ability will clearly affect your overhead.

1.1 Start-up costs

Start-up costs vary widely depending on your choices and circumstances. Table 2 lists average start-up expenses. Sample 1 is a start-up expense checklist for estimating initial costs of your business. It is important to keep a record of your estimated and actual costs for overhead expenses as well as for your cash flow projections during the start-up and first year of operation. The date to pay column should assist you in scheduling your cash flow or other funds to meet the initial expenses. You should be able to fill in the estimated costs schedule after you have done your research thoroughly. Further details on aspects of start-up costs are covered later.

TABLE 2
AVERAGE START-UP EXPENSES

Item	Price Range*			
Business licenses and permits	$ 20	to	$	100
Business announcement or brochures	250	to		500
Supplies and stationery	100	to		250
Equipment (unless rented, then add rental charge)	500	to		3,000
Rental deposit on office (first and last months)	0	to		800
Utility and phone deposits	0	to		250
Insurance	100	to		300
Legal and accounting	500	to		1,500
Professional or business membership expenses	100	to		300
Answering service deposit (first and last months)	100	to		150
Miscellaneous	200	to		500
TOTAL START-UP COSTS	$1,870	to		$7,650

* Low range assumes the use of home office with outside secretarial service.

High range assumes renting an office with one half-time secretary.

1.2 Monthly overhead expenses

Naturally, monthly expenses will vary widely depending on the type of consulting service you are planning to operate. Sample 2 should assist you in planning and budgeting for your possible overhead expenses.

1.3 Personal expenses

Personal monthly overhead expenses obviously influence your cash flow needs and the amount of resources available to invest in your business. When you prepare your business plan (see chapter 6), you will take into account your personal needs. It will be helpful, though, to consider your personal cash flow needs while planning your business expense outlay. See Sample 3 as a guide for detailing your personal expenses.

SAMPLE 1
START-UP EXPENSE CHECKLIST

Expense	Date to pay	Estimated cost	Actual cost
Business licenses and permits	_____	$ _____	$ _____
Business announcement or other initial business development including brochures	_____	_____	_____
Supplies and stationery	_____	_____	_____
Equipment/furniture	_____	_____	_____
Rental deposit on office (if outside home: first, second, and last months)	_____	_____	_____
Telephone installation and deposits	_____	_____	_____
Utility deposits (if outside home)	_____	_____	_____
Insurance (health, life, liability, theft, etc.; unless paid monthly or quarterly)	_____	_____	_____
Legal and accounting	_____	_____	_____
Professional or business membership or expenses	_____	_____	_____
Answering service deposit (first and last months)	_____	_____	_____
Fax machine	_____	_____	_____
Computer	_____	_____	_____
Printer	_____	_____	_____
Cell Phone	_____	_____	_____
Other	_____	_____	_____
Cushion for unexpected costs (contingency)	_____	_____	_____

SAMPLE 2
MONTHLY EXPENSE CHECKLIST

Expense	Date to pay	Estimated cost	Actual cost
Office rent (if outside home)	_____	$_____	$_____
Printing and supplies (not paid for by clients)	_____	_____	_____
Equipment (monthly payment and/or what you need to set aside for future cash purchases)	_____	_____	_____
Preparation of tax return and other accounting expenses	_____	_____	_____
Legal services (projected and prorated)	_____	_____	_____
Typing and secretarial services	_____	_____	_____
Fax line	_____	_____	_____
Telephone	_____	_____	_____
Internet connection	_____	_____	_____
Utilities (if outside home)	_____	_____	_____
Insurance costs (prorated over 12 months)	_____	_____	_____
Retirement contribution if applicable (estimated costs prorated)	_____	_____	_____
Savings (for yourself and your business)	_____	_____	_____
Loan payment	_____	_____	_____
Taxes (including social security or pension plan prorated over 12 months)	_____	_____	_____
License renewal (prorated)	_____	_____	_____
Advertising	_____	_____	_____
Answering service	_____	_____	_____
Subscriptions	_____	_____	_____
Books and reference material	_____	_____	_____
Marketing	_____	_____	_____
Entertainment and promotion	_____	_____	_____
Automobile	_____	_____	_____

SAMPLE 2 — CONTINUED

Expense	Date to pay	Estimated cost	Actual cost
Travel (in town or out)	_____	$ _____	$ _____
Conventions, professional meetings, trade shows	_____	_____	_____
Professional development	_____	_____	_____
Salary (what you need to meet personal expenses)	_____	_____	_____
Miscellaneous	_____	_____	_____

SAMPLE 3
PERSONAL MONTHLY EXPENSE CHECKLIST

Budget for the month of

ITEM	BUDGET	ACTUAL	DEVIATION
Food	$ _____	$ _____	$ _____
Housing:			
Monthly payment	_____	_____	_____
Taxes (if owned)	_____	_____	_____
Insurance	_____	_____	_____
Clothing	_____	_____	_____
Auto:			
Payment	_____	_____	_____
Gasoline	_____	_____	_____
Repairs	_____	_____	_____
Insurance	_____	_____	_____

ITEM	BUDGET	ACTUAL	DEVIATION
Utilities:			
Electricity	_____	_____	_____
Heat (if not electric)	_____	_____	_____
Telephone	_____	_____	_____
Other (water, gas)	_____	_____	_____
Personal spending (gifts)	_____	_____	_____
Credit cards (not covered elsewhere)	_____	_____	_____
Installment and other loans	_____	_____	_____
Life insurance	_____	_____	_____
Taxes	_____	_____	_____
Recreation	_____	_____	_____
Travel	_____	_____	_____
Investment, including saving	_____	_____	_____
Donations	_____	_____	_____
Medical and dental	_____	_____	_____
Education (family)	_____	_____	_____
Miscellaneous	_____	_____	_____
TOTAL	$_____	$_____	$_____

2. SELECTING A NAME

Selecting your name is an important decision both from an image and a legal perspective. It is essential to be aware of the implications of selecting your name from the outset.

2.1 General considerations

Many consultants do business under their own names: for example, "David R. Jones, Educational Consultant." The business card and letterhead stationery would also show the address and telephone number (with area code) and a brief description of the service. The description could read, for example, "Research studies and project management."

Many consultants prefer to use their own name because they are offering a personal service and promoting and selling themselves. The drawback of using your name is that it implies a one-person operation; this could cause a client to doubt your capacity to complete a project if you are ill or injured. For this reason, and by personal choice, some consultants prefer to use the phrase "and Associates" after their names. This implies a business with more than one person and a resource base of skilled consultants.

Many consultants contract with subconsultants as required, depending on the job project. This cuts down on overhead, provides depth and flexibility, and expands consulting contract opportunities. Other name variations include "Jones Educational Associates" or "Educational Consulting Associates."

It is important to describe the nature of the services you are offering and not limit the future development of your consulting service. For example, if you are a hospital consultant, you may not want to state on your letterhead or business card "specializing in personnel development" if you could receive other spin-off consulting work outside the limits suggested by personnel development. Don't use the word "freelance," as it may not project the professional image you want to create.

Some consultants prefer not to use their own name in the firm's name for a number of reasons. One reason is that the consultant does not want an employer to be aware that a consulting business is being operated part time. Another reason is that if goodwill is developed under a company's name rather than an individual's, a higher price might be obtained if the consulting practice is sold.

If you decide to incorporate your business, you must have the name approved by the responsible government department and the name must end in Ltd. or Limited, Inc. or Incorporation, or Corp. or Corporation. Advantages and disadvantages of forming a corporation are discussed in chapter 4.

2.2 Fictitious name

If you are operating your proprietorship or partnership business under a name other than your own, you are required in most jurisdictions to register your fictitious name. Filing for fictitious names does not apply to corporations.

The procedures vary from area to area. The costs generally range from $10 to $75. Ask your lawyer about the requirements for your area. The procedure generally is to fill out forms disclosing the people behind the name and, in some cases, to place an ad in the local newspaper or legal gazette outlining the information in the filing documents.

3. SELECTING AN OFFICE

Most beginning consultants operate out of their homes. As the business grows, the decision might be made to move into outside office space.

Normally consultants go to the client's office, but occasionally clients wish to meet the consultant at the consultant's place of business.

3.1 Home office

There are several advantages to operating out of your home. You save money on gas and rent. The stress of commuting to work is reduced. You are able to deduct from income tax the portion of your home you are using for business purposes. (The tax deductions you can use when you have a home office are covered in chapter 9.)

Being close to the family is an important consideration for some consultants.

There are also disadvantages to having a home office. You may be distracted by your family members during the work day, or your presence may be distracting to family members. The mix of home and office dynamics could negatively affect your private life. You could turn into a workaholic due to the proximity of your office. Your home might be distant from your clients' offices, which would make it difficult for your clients to visit you. If clients come to your home office on occasion, you would want

your home to present a positive impression and not to detract from your professional image. Your home address on your stationery and business card could present a questionable image to prospective clients who may wonder about your business competence. Clients may view you as a freelancer and be more likely to question your fees.

Due to the limitations of working out of your home, you may wish to consider a professional identity package provided by various office service businesses. This includes a mail drop address and telephone answering service, as well as other features you may desire.

The mail drop means having an address that is recognizable as a business and, depending on the location, as a prestigious address. The staff at this location are able to receive or send out courier packages for you and receive envelopes or messages from clients who may stop by "your" office.

These services can generally be found under "Secretarial Services" or "Stenographers — Public" in the Yellow Pages telephone directory. A post office box number has a negative effect in terms of your credibility and business reliability, and should be avoided if possible. However, if you look in the Yellow Pages under "Mail Box Rentals" you will see companies providing a wide range of other services such as fax transmissions, e-mail, courier, word processing, desktop publishing, photocopying, etc. If you work out of your home, it may be an advantage to rent a mail box. For security and marketing reasons, you may prefer to keep your home address confidential.

Having a personalized telephone answering service connected to your telephone at home lets you know your telephone calls are being handled in a professional manner whether you are at home or out making calls. By keeping the answering service informed of your schedule for the day, your callers will receive the appropriate response and know when the call might be returned.

Generally, it's not a good idea to use an answering machine; it doesn't present a professional image, callers get the impression that you are a one-person operation (which, of course, you are), and you may be perceived as a freelancer, which has a negative connotation to some.

3.2 Office outside of home

You may wish to get an office outside your home when circumstances and finances justify it. Having your own office address increases credibility and stature when dealing with clients or prospective clients. Studies have shown that consultants are able to collect higher fees for performing the same work when operating out of an office.

When considering an office location, factors such as expense, image of business address, your proximity to clients, and referral possibilities should be examined.

Try to look at your long-range goals over two years and imagine what your office needs might be. It is costly to pay for new office stationery and other start-up costs, and several moves may create an image of instability.

3.2a Office sharing arrangement

You may wish to look for an office with complementary professional or business tenants and prospective business clients. You have your own office and generally supply your own personal office furniture, but the rent expenses of the office and the receptionist's salary are shared on a proportional basis by the tenants. The secretarial expenses are negotiated depending on use.

If you do seek out a pooling arrangement, try to have a minimal notice period to leave the premises. You may wish to leave due to expansion, inability to pay the rent, or personality conflicts. It is fairly common to have a three-month notice provision. Make sure that the terms of your rental relationship are in writing and signed by the necessary parties before you begin your relationship.

As a general caution, avoid sharing space with a client. You could have a falling out or the client could attempt to use your time for free or look on you as staff.

3.2b Sharing same private office

Two or more people may use the same office space. The parties agree on the costs of furnishing the office, unless it is already furnished, and an agreement is worked in terms of the hours and days of use. Costs of this arrangement are negotiated on a per use basis.

3.2c Office rental package

There are firms in the business of renting packaged office space. There can be anywhere from 5 to 50 tenants or more. Each tenant has a private office, and there is a common reception area.

The office package arrangement is a good source of potential contacts for networking or prospective clients, depending on the mix of the tenants.

Telephone answering and office furniture are frequently included in the package price as well as a nominal number of hours of secretarial time per month. The rental arrangement may be a minimum two- or three-month notice to vacate, or a six-month or one-year lease arrangement. Prices and terms of various office package arrangements may be negotiable if there is competition in that marketplace in your community.

There are several other advantages of an office package arrangement. Other services that might be available to save you considerable money on staff and equipment include:

(a) Street mailing address — not a post office box number

(b) Postage metered mail for prompt delivery and a professional appearance

(c) Typing and desktop publishing — a variety of typestyles available on computer for letters, reports, invoices, statements, etc.

(d) Secretarial services, including letter composition and editing using correct business language and form

(e) Photocopying — a bond copier with various features including collating could be available to produce quality copies on your letterhead, transparencies, or address labels

(f) Word processing services with the advantage of speed, efficiency, and storage and retrieval capacity

(g) Data management and bookkeeping

3.2d Occasional office

You can rent a board room or an office for as short a time as an hour, a half day, or a day. The cost is negotiable. The occasional office space can be found through office rental package services described earlier. Some firms require that you have a telephone answering or professional identity package arrangement with them before you are able to rent occasional office space.

3.2e Leased space

Leasing space does have its advantages, and it is most important that you consult your accountant and a competent lawyer familiar with commercial leases before signing anything. You should shop around for space to make sure you have the best arrangement for your needs and to assist you in negotiating.

Leases are generally for a period of one to five years. There are three basic types of lease payment formulas. The terminology may vary, but the concepts are the same. The first type, called a "net" lease, means that the base rent is the total rent. In other words, the flat negotiated rate is the only monthly payment you have to make.

The second type of rent, "double net," is similar to the first except you have to pay a pro rata share of any tax increases over the base tax period outlined in your lease. If the taxes increase substantially, you could have extra overhead you had not anticipated.

The third type, "triple net" rent, can be very expensive. The base rent is just the beginning. All other landlord costs, such as taxes, insurance, maintenance, repair, improvements, management, and administration fees, are passed on proportionately to the tenants. This could increase your monthly rent by 50% to 100%. The other problem with this type of rent structure is the resulting uncertainty when you try to budget for your rental overhead expenses.

A variation of this third formula involves paying the landlord a percentage of your gross revenue. Naturally, for a professional consultant, this is an unacceptable arrangement.

Some of the clauses to be wary of when you are considering a lease include ones that restrict your ability to sublet or assign your lease, that restrict the use you intend for the premises, or that limit alterations or improvements to the premises; clauses setting out liabilities and duties of the landlord and tenant; acceleration clauses in case of a default; and clauses requiring your personal guarantee if you are doing business as a corporation.

If you are still interested in signing a lease, attempt to negotiate as many attractive features as possible. All leases are negotiable and there are no standard clauses. Your lawyer can properly advise you and possibly negotiate the lease on your behalf. The following tips will help when you are negotiating your lease:

(a) Rather than negotiating a three-year lease, for example, try to negotiate a one-year lease with two additional one-year options. This way you minimize the risk in the event you cannot afford the lease, or in case you need to expand or the premises are otherwise unsuitable for your needs.

(b) Consider offering the last two or three months as a deposit. If you default the lease and leave before the end of the term, the deposit monies go to the landlord and you are free of any further liability.

(c) Put in the lease that alterations or improvements you intend to make will be at the landlord's expense.

(d) Attempt to get the first few months free of rent as an incentive for you to lease the premises.

(e) Try to get out of paying the last month's security deposit rent if possible. If it is not possible, try to negotiate with the landlord to pay you interest at a fixed rate on the security deposit money.

Another factor in leasing space is the additional expense for furniture and equipment for your office and reception area, plus the additional costs of a secretary or receptionist. All these additional costs have to be carefully factored out to ensure there is sufficient cash flow to justify the commitment.

3.3 Equipping an office

Equipping an office is not too expensive if you buy secondhand furniture. You can obtain good used business furniture from bankruptcy sales, auction sales, or through the classified section in the newspaper. The type and quality of furniture that you select naturally will relate to your type of consulting clientele and the image that you want to project.

There are certain basic things you need for your office, including desk, chairs, tables, lamps, bookcases, file cabinet, calculator, telephone answering device (optional), tape recorder (as a dictaphone, to record meetings, to record consulting or marketing ideas), card file and/or address file, clock, postage meter, and briefcase. You will probably also need a computer, printer, photocopier, fax machine, and other communications equipment.

Here is an overview of some of the main types of communication equipment you should consider.

3.3a Computer

It is likely you are already computer literate and possibly have your own personal computer (PC) at home. Your computer is an essential tool that will maximize your consulting capabilities.

Computer hardware refers to your computer, monitor, and keyboard, as well as your printer and modem. A basic desktop computer and/or a portable computer, such as a laptop, may be all you need. Producing documents, giving presentations to clients, working with graphics, maintaining lists of clients or other records, bookkeeping and accounting, or doing other financial calculations such as budgets or forecasts are all tasks that can be accomplished on your computer.

In addition, you may want to use your computer to keep track of appointments and scheduling information, to do project management or estimates, or for access to various online information services (e.g., Internet).

When deciding on what computer to buy, investigate the manufacturer's customer support services and consider the following:

- Is there a three-year limited warranty on parts and labor, with a one- or two-day turnaround policy?
- Does the manufacturer offer one year of free on-site service, extendible for an additional fee?
- Is there lifetime technical support, 24-hours a day, seven days a week, including holidays, via a toll-free number?
- Does the manufacturer offer free remote inspection of your system via modem?

To comparison shop, attend computer trade shows, check out various computer stores that offer a wide range of brand names, and read consumer computer magazine reviews of computers. There are many basic computer books available at computer or software stores. Most colleges and school board adult education programs have a range of computer courses available during the evenings and weekends. As a basic rule of thumb, first decide what type of software you need and then purchase a computer that is compatible with the software.

3.3b Modem

A modem is a device connected to your personal computer that allows you to send data to and receive data from computers anywhere in the world over telephone lines. A fax modem is a device that lets you send and receive faxes from your computer.

3.3c Computer software

As you are probably aware, there is a wide range of software available to meet all your consulting business needs, whether it be for word processing, data or list management, mailing lists, desktop publishing, graphic design, billing and accounting, project management, scheduling, information access, or financial projections and spreadsheets. There are new products being released on an ongoing basis, so be sure to comparison shop at software stores. There is an extensive array of highly sophisticated software available at modest cost to save you time, money, and effort. All of this will reinforce the professional image you wish to create and maintain.

3.3d Printer

Your printer is probably one of the most important components of your computer system because the quality and appearance of any documents you produce for your clients reflect your expertise. In general, high print quality and high speed mean a more expensive printer. Color printers are also available. Resolution measures the print quality in dots per square inch (dpi). The higher the dpi, the higher the resolution and the better the print quality. Laser printers have the highest resolution, followed by ink jet and dot matrix printers.

3.3e Copier

There are many types of copiers available including color and small portable copiers to meet your growing business needs. Look for features such as length of warranty, service contract options (on-site or designated repair outlet), paper size (letter, legal, ledger), enlargement or reduction capacity, quality of resolution, automatic or manual feed, speed (measured in copies per minute), duplexing (two-sided copying), size of paper trays, etc.

3.3f Fax machine

A fax machine is an essential part of your communication equipment. You can transmit documents, diagrams, photographs, etc. through the fax machine to an existing or prospective client for instant communication. You can also buy a portable fax if that would be valuable for your type of business.

There are many fax features available, and competition has brought prices down. Fax machines can print on plain paper, with or without a telephone attached. Some features to consider include transmission speed, quality of resolution, contrast levels, and stored memory capacity. This last feature is helpful in case your machine runs out of paper in the middle of a transmission. Other desirable features include —

- automatic redial,
- stored telephone directory of most commonly used numbers,
- broadcast capability (sends to multiple preprogrammed numbers),
- delayed transmissions for cheaper long distance rates,
- fax/phone switch, and
- management reports (activity reports, message confirmations, error logs, etc.).

3.4 Office supplies

The basic supplies you need include business cards, letterhead, stationery and printed envelopes, brochures, records for bookkeeping, invoices, filing folders, and various types of calendars.

3.4a Business stationery, cards, envelopes

Your business stationery is very important as it represents you, your image, and your business. It should present a professional and conservative image. It should state your name, your business name, the type of consulting (if applicable), address, postal/zip code, telephone number with area code, fax number with area code, e-mail address, and Web site address (if applicable).

All your stationery should correspond with the format and image of your business card. Choose a good quality paper stock. Purchase blank pages of your letter stock so that your second page will match the color of the first. Neutral shades such as beige, ivory, or white create a professional impression. You have a choice between litho (flat) or thermo (raised) ink. The raised, glossy appearance of thermo creates a richer effect. The cost of raised letter is not much more than flat, but extra time is required for printing. Because the printing business is very competitive, be sure to compare rates.

Some consultants prefer to have a logo on their business card. Have a graphic artist or desktop publisher design and prepare the logo and other customized material.

3.4b Brochures

Depending on the type of consulting practice you have and the nature of the clientele you wish to attract, brochures may be part of your marketing plan. You may choose to have a promotional writer assist you in preparing the text for a brochure that will effectively outline the services you provide for your specific clientele or market. Consider having your brochure designed on a desktop publishing program. Often writers provide desktop layout and design services as well as writing and editing. Such services can be found under the "Sales Promotion Services" section of the Yellow Pages. For printing, check for competitive rates and allow yourself considerable lead time to obtain the best rate. One color ink on colored stock is less expensive than two inks and can be just as effective. Naturally, brochures are less expensive by quantity.

3.4c Record-keeping documents, invoices, and file folders

These items are necessary for the orderly maintenance of projects, systems, and good business management. The types of record-keeping documents are outlined in chapter 8.

3.4d Calendars

For recording appointments, telephone calls, and deadlines you should have a desk calendar, a wall calendar, and a daily diary that you carry with you. The time that you spend on client files must be recorded in detail for proper billing and for your protection in the event of a dispute.

3.5 Personnel
3.5a Secretarial staff

Most beginning consultants do not have the workload or cash flow to justify hiring a secretary. Some consultants prefer to type the documents and correspondence themselves, but even if you are a good typist, you will make more money consulting or finding new clients than you will typing. Some consultants have a family member do the typing, but this can cause strains on the family relationship.

It is far more cost efficient and practical to "rent" a secretary. In many cases, the typing costs related to a client file can be billed directly to the client, in addition to your fees. You then have verification from the typing service if there is any question on your account.

Find a professional typing service that offers temporary or one-time service. Ask how much lead time is required, what the turnaround time is, and what other services they offer. Interview several professional typing services and ask to see sample copies of their reports, newsletters, and correspondence so that you can judge the professional quality of the work.

It is essential that word processing services be available. As a consultant, you will be producing large quantities of material that requires neat, clean, and correctly styled typing. A word processor can produce this quality and store your contracts, proposals, form letters, reports, and mailing lists for retrieval.

A professional secretarial service can also look after all your correspondence and document needs including preparing invoices and reminder letters for your receivables. You can ask the secretarial service if one staff member will work on your file so that person will become familiar with your style. A dictaphone tape for transcription is a considerable benefit in terms of consistency and time saved when one person gets accustomed to your methods.

3.5b Retaining other consultants

Employing another consultant as an independent contractor — in other words, a sub-consultant — is a common technique to reduce overhead and increase your resource base and efficiency. There are times when you might need specialized skills or additional help to be able to satisfy a potential client contract. Try to develop a subcontracting network of consultants you can call on when needed. Many consultants take on projects they could not complete themselves and subcontract portions to another consultant.

It is important to maintain your position with your client as the main source of information and communication. Your client need not know that you have subcontracted out a part of the job.

4. SELECTING A TELEPHONE SYSTEM

Your telephone, in many ways, is your lifeline to a successful consulting practice. Many consultants start out using their home telephone number and a telephone answering device, but there are problems with this. Inexpensive alternatives exist. The important consideration is the impression your telephone system gives your clients or prospective clients and how effectively you receive incoming messages.

4.1 A separate phone at home

Many consultants operating out of their homes prefer to have a separate line for their consulting practice apart from their personal line. This saves the frustration caused by children answering your phone or family members tying up the phone with their personal calls.

4.2 Business line terminating at answering service

You may wish to have an office number that does not go to your home, but terminates at your answering service. Your answering service could then phone you at home (if those were your instructions) and advise you of a phone message.

Alternatively, you could telephone the answering service from time to time to pick up messages. You could then return calls on your personal line. The advantage of this system is that you save on the monthly line charge for a business telephone installed in your home, but still have a telephone answering capacity.

When selecting an answering service, it is very important to consider the personal aspect of the service. An answering service that has only 40 to 60 lines will generally be more attentive, know your business better, and personalize the responses so that the caller is unaware it is an answering service. Compare various answering services and ask for references from their clients.

The quality of your answering service is vital to the reputation and goodwill of your business. In many cases the person answering the phone will be the first representative of your firm to the caller. A drawback of the larger answering service companies with trunk lines and hundreds of customers is that the switchboard operators are frequently very busy and therefore unable to personalize your phone messages. Another factor is the turnover that can occur in personnel. With the larger answering services, it is very difficult to hide the fact that it is an answering service.

4.3 Business line terminating at home and answering service

Your business line can pass through an answering service's switchboard. All calls may be intercepted by the answering service if those are your instructions, or, with a switch on your phone unit, you can decide to answer the phone yourself for certain periods of the day. The answering service staff can be told the appropriate procedures for incoming phone calls. There are additional monthly line charges for this system.

4.4 Overline

An overline feature allows an incoming phone call to come through on a second line while you are on the first line. This is an appropriate feature if you have only one phone. Too many busy signals give a negative impression and may result in the loss of a prospective client. Another technique is to give out your business telephone number for incoming calls and use your personal phone for outgoing calls.

4.5 Measured business line

A measured business line can reduce your monthly phone charges for service in half. The reduced business rate has a limit of 50 outgoing phone calls per month. No limit is placed on the number of incoming calls. If you make more than 50 outgoing calls in a month, you are charged an additional fee per phone call (approximately 11¢, but it varies).

If you make many outgoing phone calls, this system is not economical. Some people use the measured line system for incoming calls and their personal phone for outgoing calls.

4.6 Shared line

A number of people may agree to share a common telephone number. Usually it is a feature offered by a telephone answering service for one of its unused lines. Telephone expenses are reduced considerably. The phone is answered "4444," "Suite 100," or some such nondescriptive phrase, or it can be answered "consulting office" if there are two or more consultants receiving calls on the same line.

4.7 Interconnect phone purchase

Private telephone equipment companies are now able to compete using the main telephone circuits. Rather than renting or leasing your phone from your telephone company, you have the choice of purchasing your phone. You still have to pay the monthly service charges and long distance charges, but you do not have to pay the monthly equipment charges. Your decision is a matter of comparing the break-even point in purchasing your phone over renting your phone.

5. SPECIAL TELEPHONE FEATURES

There are many invaluable telephone feature options available to create an impressive and positive professional business image. They will also save you time and money and improve your efficiency. Ask your telephone company for a current list.

5.1 Call waiting

The call waiting feature emits a beep when you are on the phone to tell you another caller is trying to reach you. If you have a custom phone, it allows you to put one call on hold, answer the second call, and switch back to the first caller.

5.2 Call forwarding

Call forwarding allows you to send your calls to another phone number or pager, either automatically, if not answered within three rings, or if your line is busy. You never miss incoming or expected phone calls.

5.3 Three-way calling

This is similar to a conference call feature. It allows you to talk to people at two or more locations at the same time.

5.4 Speed calling

This feature allows you to place a call with a one-digit code.

5.5 Phone/fax

A combination phone/fax provides a separate number for your fax machine, even though it uses the same telephone line. You still have your regular phone number. The phone and fax cannot be used at the same time. Your fax machine, if attached to your regular phone line, can identify that a fax message is being transmitted. If you are using a fax frequently, you may want to have a separate line, otherwise you will frustrate your clients. In addition, if you have a home office, a separate fax line solves the problem of your telephone ringing in the middle of the night because of a fax transmission.

5.6 Call display

Call display shows you an incoming caller's number on an electronic display screen before you answer the phone.

5.7 Name display

This is an added option to call display that identifies the name of a caller.

5.8 Call return

Call return lets you know when a busy line is free and lets you return the last call placed or received at the touch of a button.

5.9 Call again

The call again feature keeps trying a busy number for you for up to 30 minutes. It rings when the busy number is free.

5.10 Call answer

This feature automatically answers calls if you are on the phone or unavailable.

6. SAVING MONEY ON LONG DISTANCE PHONE CALLS

There are many occasions when consultants wish to make long distance phone calls for which no reimbursement can be expected from the client, for example, in marketing efforts, prospective client contacts, or a fixed price contract where your costs are built into the contract. Some of the ways of saving money on long distance calls are mentioned below.

6.1 Direct distance dialing

By dialing a number directly rather than asking for operator assistance or third-party billing, you save quite a bit. The amount of savings varies but can be obtained from your telephone company.

6.2 Reduced long distance rates

There are specific times, which vary in different regions, when long distance rates are one-third to two-thirds less than the regular daily rates. This saving can be considerable especially when the time zones allow you to telephone at the cheapest rate but still during the business hours of the long distance call recipient. Telephone companies as well as interconnect companies also offer attractive discount programs based on volume usage.

6.3 Toll-free service number

There are many companies, including prospective clients, that have 1-800 or 1-888 service. This system allows the caller to make a free long distance call to the toll-free number. A directory which lists the firms that have 800 or 888 numbers can be obtained through the phone company.

6.4 Interconnect long distance companies

These companies don't offer local telephone service, but purchase long distance at a bulk rate from a telephone company and offer a discount rate on business and residential long distance usage. The result is intense competition in long distance rates, so be sure to comparison shop when you sign up for long distance service.

6.5 Some tips

If you are placing long distance phone calls on behalf of a client, ask the operator to call you back with time and charges. This will allow you to record the call in your record system so that the expenses can be passed on to your client directly on the next bill. If you do not adopt this system, you won't be able to render an account to a client for various long distance phone calls until you receive your telephone bill.

To limit your overhead for long distance phone calls on behalf of the client, you may wish to ask the client (and confirm it in writing) for the authority to third-party bill to the client's phone number any calls pertaining to your contract or consulting project.

A technique for saving money on long distance phone calls that are being done for information or marketing purposes is to place a long distance phone call person-to-person at 12:30 p.m. in the time zone of the recipient. In most cases, senior people are not in their offices at this time; a message is left by your operator with the recipient company, giving your name and phone number and operator call back number. Also leave a message through the operator about the time and day that you will be in to receive the phone call. State the recipient's time to eliminate confusion.

It is very rare for the recipient caller in government or industry to return your call on a collect basis. You can make sure that you are in your office or home when the incoming call is expected, and you won't have to pay the long distance phone charges.

7. OTHER COMMUNICATION OPTIONS

7.1 Telephone answering devices

The purpose of a telephone answering device (TAD) is to help you avoid losing critical calls if you are away from your office. It also acts as an efficient office screening agent. The TAD answers the phone, gives a message, and accepts a message from the caller on your behalf. After you have dictated your message into the machine, dial your own number so you can critique your message.

There are six basic kinds of answering machines. Due to the intense competition in this market area, comparative pricing is recommended if you are in the market for a TAD.

(a) Announce only answers the telephone with one or more prerecorded announcements up to several minutes long.

(b) Announce/record gives a prerecorded message and allows the caller to leave a message.

(c) Call screening helps you avoid unwanted calls. By turning the volume higher, you can listen to a caller's message without his or her knowledge. If you wish, you can pick up the telephone, interrupt the regular answering cycle, and talk to the caller.

(d) Record can record a conversation. This is useful if you need proof that you have communicated important information to another party. In many jurisdictions you are obliged to notify the other party that the call is being recorded. For this reason, some of these machines may emit a tone at intervals to remind both parties that the conversation continues to be recorded.

(e) Dictation allows you to dictate messages for subsequent transcription.

You bypass the normal use of the telephone answering machine and use features exactly like those of an office dictation machine.

(f) Remote control allows you to transmit a signal from any other phone by means of a remote device. The machine will automatically respond and play back over the phone any messages that have been recorded. This is convenient if you are out of town but expect calls at your office.

As mentioned earlier, telephone answering devices have their limitations. They can create an impression that you are very much a beginner in business and still struggling. Some callers find it very annoying to talk to an answering machine; others refuse to leave a message or leave a message that is unclear. Therefore, you may prefer to consider other options, such as voice mail or an answering service.

7.2 Voice mail

This is an effective means of communicating for many businesses. It is similar to a telephone answering machine in various limited aspects, but is far more versatile.

Most telephone companies offer this feature, although generally with just a few menu options for the person phoning. Each menu option involves a separate voice mailbox that is interconnected. There are voice mail companies that can customize features and create new options for you (e.g., pushing a specific number on the phone to be connected to your associate, to receive a fax, to have you paged, etc.).

You can also buy your own computer software voice mail system. Many profes-

sional ID plans offered through a packaged office service also provide this option. The following are some of the key benefits of voice mail:

- Operates all the time, 24 hours a day, seven days a week.

- You can call-forward your regular phone number to the voice mail numbers so that it connects automatically. The advantage of this is that you won't have your sleep interrupted by someone phoning you in the middle of the night, as you would if you had a regular answering machine. For example, you may have international clients who live in different time zones.

- Reduces frustrating games of "telephone tag" because it gives the caller the opportunity to leave a message.

- If you are out of town, you can phone your voice mail in the evening to benefit from lower long distance rates when you retrieve messages.

- Voice mail can be connected to your pager or cellular, or be programmed to phone you at your regular phone number or at another phone number if a message is left. (See Chapter 19 for additional tips and benefits of voicemail service.)

7.3 Toll-free number

You may want to consider obtaining a toll-free 1-800 or 1-888 telephone number if the nature of your business involves existing or potential clients phoning you long distance. For example, if you offer public seminars across the country, people prefer to phone a toll-free number rather than incurring long distance charges. You could have the number directed to a 24-hour, seven-day answering service that will take the registration details and charge card information. In many cases, telephone companies charge a nominal basic monthly fee of about $10 for the number, and in addition you pay only actual usage charges with no minimum charge. Basic long distance rates could be from 30¢ to 40¢ a minute, depending on where the caller is phoning from. However, you are also entitled to time-of-day discounts as well as volume usage discounts. The net effect could be affordable, efficient, and profitable, depending on your needs. When you obtain a toll-free number, it is reserved for you and accessible throughout the United States and Canada. However, you can limit access to certain area codes if you prefer, depending on your marketing objectives.

7.4 Generic telephone number

Some business cards have more numbers than a lottery ticket. The caller may not know the right number to reach you. Are you available at your office phone number, pager, voice mail, or cellular number?

Many telephone and other companies offer a single phone number that can direct calls anywhere you want them to go, for example, your office, home, car, cellular, voice mailbox, out-of-town hotel number, or anywhere in the world. If you are busy or unable to take a call, your caller can leave a message. There are also other features available such as call screening (you receive only the calls you want), call connection (caller waits on the line while you are paged to any touch-tone phone), and call director (gives your caller a choice of destinations, for example, "Touch 1 to speak to the receptionist, 2 to speak to customer service, or hold the line to leave a message"). Some generic numbers also have a fax mail feature that can automatically recognize a fax transmission and store it for future confidential retrieval from any fax machine.

7.5 Fax on demand

This feature allows you to program an option onto your outgoing voice mail message that lets the caller activate an immediate fax transmission. The caller inputs his or her fax number on a touch-tone phone and your fax message is sent to the caller's fax machine. You can store any number of pages for transmission on your computer. If you have a consulting business that sells products or gives seminars, for example, you can save time by sending out current information for routine enquiries. To save money, check to make sure you are billed on the basis of 6-second transmission increments minimum, not 30 or 60 seconds.

7.6 Pager

Pagers can be an ideal way to be notified when someone is attempting to reach you by phone. You can buy, rent, or lease pager units. They are small, light, easily attached to your belt or your pocket, and can notify you that you have a message with an audio tone or a beep, or with a visual or vibrating alert. Pager services are available through telephone or private pager companies. There are three main types of pagers.

(a) An alphanumeric pager can receive and display complete text messages of a phone call and up to 40 messages of 80 letter or number characters each.

(b) The numeric pager displays the caller's telephone number and allows you to screen calls for immediate call back when necessary.

(c) The voice pager provides full audio messages with hands-free operation, thereby reducing the need for call back.

7.7 Cellular phone

You may want to consider a cellular phone for your business needs. Due to intense competition in this industry, prices have gone down as the number of features available have gone up. There are also many airtime volume discount packages available. To save money, make sure you are billed based on a minimum of 6-second usage intervals, not 30 to 60 seconds. Rather than giving a client direct access to your cellular number, you may want to have a pager that records messages left on your cellular or telephone voice mail and then notifies you. This is effective for urgent messages or time-sensitive callers. Alternatively, you could call up your voice mail from time to time to retrieve messages from your cellular. That way you control cellular time usage and costs more effectively. You also minimize unexpected or unwanted interruptions. For example, you may decide to return a client's call from a regular phone or pay phone. Cellular phone features that are available include —

- call forwarding,
- call waiting,
- three-way calling,
- transfer to a voice message center

and/or voice mail if no answer on your cellular,

- microphone attachments for your car to permit hands-free use, and
- detailed billing.

You can also buy cellular phones that have the compatibility to support two-way data and fax communications. Such a cellular phone could be connected to a portable fax machine or computer with a fax and/or computer modem to send and receive data.

7.8 E-mail

With your computer, you can transmit messages over the phone lines to someone else's computer through electronic mail (e-mail). You need to know the recipient's e-mail "address" or password to access his or her computer. The message you send remains stored in computer memory until he or she retrieves it. Conversely, you need to provide your own password so that the person you have e-mailed can reply. Many people have their e-mail address printed on their business cards. Communicating via e-mail can be appropriate in certain consulting situations because it is speedier than letters, faxes, couriers, or telephone. In addition, you can attach documents easily to the e-mail. However, since the work you do for many clients requires confidentiality, for liability reasons you may not want to use e-mail for all your client communications. If you are considering using e-mail, it would be beneficial to have a highspeed Internet connection, which can be provided by your telephone or cable company. (See Chapter 19 for a discussion on additional uses and benefits of e-mail.)

7.9 Web site

The Internet is an online computer network that links many other networks. This "network of networks" is estimated to join millions of computer users worldwide, and it gives its users access to an incredible amount of data and information. The Internet is a cornucopia of information, not all of it useful. There are research, communication, and marketing opportunities on the Internet. If you aren't already acquainted with it, you should at least explore the possibilities. Refer to the Self-Counsel publication *Low-Budget Online Marketing for Small Business* for further information.

To fully utilize the massive marketing benefits of the Internet, you should consider developing your own Web site. The next section will discuss some of the issues about developing your own Web site.

8. DEVELOPING YOUR WEB SITE

For marketing and professional image purposes, you may wish to develop your own Web site.

Think carefully about two things: the nature of the medium, and your audience. If you are designing a Web site, or evaluating a competitor's site, you should consider the following points:

- Who are the readers?
- Why would they visit the site?
- Do they have common questions, needs or concerns?
- How can you best communicate with them?
- What would make them come back?

As an exercise, it might be useful to write down an answer to each of the above questions, and keep your responses in mind when evaluating your own site.

8.1 Pitfalls to avoid

What would make you not return to a Web site? Would you re-visit a site where —

- the page crashed your browser?
- the screen was difficult or impossible to read?
- the design or content was ugly or offensive?
- the information was useless or inappropriate?
- the content was stale or obsolete?
- the site was difficult to understand or navigate?

What annoys you tells a lot about you. Did your own list of objections focus on page elements that annoy you: blinking text, too many advertisements, distracting animations, or whatever? Or, did you concentrate on the nuts and bolts of content delivery issues, such as bandwidth limitations and performance issues, or compatibility problems with other software issues?

There are general principles that can help steer visitors to your site in the direction(s) you want them to go:

(a) Most people will follow the first link that appears interesting and, in turn, follow other interesting-sounding links from it as they go. While this seems pretty obvious, it means that you ought to position your "important" links first. Apparently, Web surfers are an easily distracted lot.

(b) Many people have trouble dealing with pages that rely on "helper applications." A link to a help page doesn't seem to help too much.

(c) Very few people are willing to "sign up" to gain access to a page that requires some form of registration, no matter how interesting the content.

(d) The number of complaints about frames (a type of Web page constructed from different, simultaneously loaded page elements, arranged in two or more panels) has diminished greatly, as the computer systems are more streamlined and loads more quickly. Many people still don't like frames, as they feel they clutter and distract the viewer from the viewing image.

(e) Many people don't like non-black text on a colored background, no matter how aesthetically pleasing it may seem to you. Although there's the obvious subjective issue of whether they like your choice of colors or not, there are occasional technical issues too. The problem is that you can never be sure of how many colors or how many pixels the user has on his or her display.

(f) Web surfers generally use Microsoft Internet Explorer and/or Netscape Navigator browsers. Be sure to test your Web site to make sure it works with both these browsers, at the very minimum.

(g) The perceived lack of speed of your Web page can be a major source of complaints. Be sure to test your site's Web pages from a computer running a 28.8 modem, which statistically still represents a significant share of the Internet-using audience.

(h) Opinion seems divided on how often you should change your Web site's design. Some advocate changing design substantially once or twice a year, to keep the look "fresh" and current. However, even if you never redesign your site, it is imperative that you update your site often — preferably, weekly or monthly, depending on your client expectations and the nature of your consulting practice. On the Web, nothing is as stale as yesterday's news. Fresh content will also encourage visitors to "bookmark" your page, for later visits.

The above considerations are all worth thinking about. Of course, you can't please everyone. However, after a few months' worth of feedback from visitors to your site, or from a well-chosen "focus group" of testers who can critique the site before it is unveiled to the public, you will have received enough feedback to get a sense of what works and what doesn't.

8.2 Keeping the Web site interesting

On business-oriented Web sites, there are a few categories of content that are consistently popular:

- fresh news,
- timely coverage and in-depth analysis of almost any topic, and
- answers to frequently asked questions (known as FAQs).

For example, your site might provide details of new products or services, a few thought-provoking or informative articles (both your own and from trade journals or popular media), an FAQ section related to your field of consulting, and any upcoming public seminars you might be giving. In addition, you could have a partial list of clients and some client testimonials.

8.3 How to design an effective Web page

Keep it short. You only have a few seconds to catch a reader's eye. Color helps. A short list of your top attractions or newest products is better than a long list of everything under the sun.

(a) Short headlines. Keep headlines to six words or less. Keep lists to 10 items or less.

(b) Make it interesting. Involve the reader. A description of a product's benefits is always more effective than a list of its features. Remember: explain, don't just describe. Make them think. Invite action and always avoid passive-tense phrases.

(c) Great pictures. In order to get quality pictures to illustrate Web pages, the Web designer needs to have access to some type of scanner, and a good-quality original.

(d) The big pictures. Don't fall prey to "clip art syndrome," where amateur designers litter their pages with several small images. In design work, the secret is to be bold. Make the design stand out and take command of the reader's attention.

(e) Focus attention. When designing a logo or headline, pick the most important word and emphasize it. Make it bigger, bolder, or, if you will be printing in color, make it stand out.

(f) Simple typefaces. Limit the use of exotic typefaces or, in the case of Web pages, graphics that look like typefaces. If angled, warped, stretched, shadowed, or italicized text isn't essential to the message you are trying to convey, resist the urge. Never use an exotic typeface as body text. Don't use more than three or four typefaces in a single page.

(g) Contrast is the key to a successful web design. All emphasis is no emphasis. Never use all capitals in body text. It's okay for short headlines but quickly becomes tiring to read, and never use all caps in cursive script font.

(h) White space helps. Don't crowd every inch of your page with text. Let the headlines breathe. It's especially important to leave plenty of white space around all sides of your page, unless it contains an image that bleeds off the page. As a rule of thumb, leave a white space zone equal to about one-tenth of the size of the design — minimum. It often works well to surround this "white zone" with a dark border. Research shows that people will look at a page with more white space longer.

(i) Contrast is good. If you are using tables (boxes), follow the rule of thumb about borders in the last tip. Don't overcrowd text in a box that's too small. When legibility, comprehension and retention go up, your page's message is more effective.

In summary, make sure you comparison shop and get quotes from at least five Web site designers before you make your selection. You need that benchmark comparison and learning curve experience. Do your research of other sites with features you like, so you can tell the designers before they give you a quote. Make sure you have a "back-end" functionality as part of your Web site design. That is, you can easily make content changes to the site yourself. Also, your web designer can use existing Web site template software programs, and customize a site to meet your needs, and save you money in the development process.

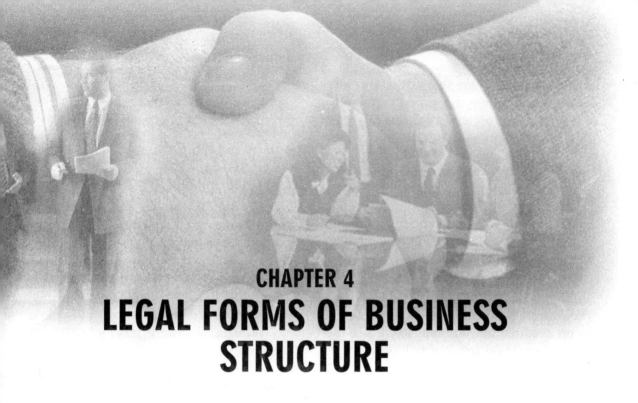

CHAPTER 4
LEGAL FORMS OF BUSINESS STRUCTURE

1. INTRODUCTION

There are basically three forms of legal structure: proprietorship, partnership, and limited company. You should seek competent legal and accounting advice before deciding on your business structure, as there could be distinct advantages or disadvantages to each depending on your situation.

Many consultants start out as a sole proprietor, as that is the easiest way to start a business. If additional skills or personnel are required on a specific project, sub-consultants may be retained as independent contractors by the proprietor.

In the field of consultancy in particular, a healthy ego is essential to sell yourself and your skills. Because of this, conflict is likely to occur when two or more consultants set up a partnership and share joint decision-making but have individual dreams and goals. It is common for such arrangements to have problems and dissolve.

Forming a corporation is a third option. The corporation can be owned by just one person (similar to a proprietorship) or two or more people (similar to a partnership).

This chapter discusses the factors that you and your professional advisers should examine when making a decision about your business structure.

2. SOLE PROPRIETORSHIP

A sole proprietorship is a business owned and operated by one person. To establish a sole proprietorship, you need only obtain whatever local licenses you require and open your business. It is the simplest form of business structure and operation.

2.1 Advantages

Ease of formation: There is less formality and few legal restrictions associated with establishing a sole proprietorship. You can start almost immediately. There are no complex forms to complete and no documentation required between you and any other party. In most jurisdictions, all that is legally necessary to operate as a sole proprietorship is to register the business and obtain the proper licenses. Licenses can be required by various levels of government.

Cost: Registering the business and obtaining licenses involves minimal costs. There are no partnership or corporate agreements required by you because you are the sole owner. Legal fees are reduced accordingly.

Lack of complexity: A sole proprietorship is straightforward. Unlike other forms of business, there is little government control and, accordingly, fewer reports are required to be filed with government agencies and departments. The owner and the business are taxed as one.

Decision-making process: Decisions are made exclusively by the sole owner, who has complete authority and freedom to move. The owner does not have to obtain approval from partners or shareholders or a board of directors.

Sole ownership of profits: The proprietor does not have to share the profits with anyone. The profits generated by the business belong to one person. The sole owner decides how and when the money will come out of the business.

Ease of terminating/sale of business: Apart from legal responsibilities to employees, creditors, and perhaps clients, you can sell the business or close it down at your will.

Flexibility: You are able to respond quickly to business needs in day-to-day management decisions as governed by various laws and common sense.

2.2 Disadvantages

Unlimited liability: The sole owner's personal assets, such as house, property, car, and investments, are liable to be seized if necessary to pay for outstanding debts or liabilities. As mentioned earlier, the proprietor and the business are deemed to be one and the same in law.

Less financing capacity: It is more difficult for a proprietor to borrow money than for a partnership with various partners or a corporation with a number of major shareholders. A lender, when looking for security and evidence of outside resources, can turn to other people connected with the business rather than just the one person in a proprietorship. A partnership or corporation can give an investor some form of equity position, which is not available in a proprietorship.

Unstable duration of business: The business might be crippled or terminated upon the illness or death of the owner. If there is no one appropriate to take over the business, it may have to be sold or liquidated. Such an unplanned action may result in a loss.

Sole decision-making: In a partnership or a corporation, there is generally shared decision-making or at least input. In a proprietorship, just one person is involved; if that person lacks business ability or experience, poor decision-making can cause the business to suffer.

Taxation: At a certain level of profit there are tax disadvantages for the sole proprietor.

3. PARTNERSHIP

A partnership is usually defined as an association of two or more persons to carry on a business in common with a view to making a profit. The partnership is created by a contract, either verbal or written, between the individual parties.

3.1 Advantages

Ease of formation: Legal formalities and expenses in forming a partnership are few compared to incorporating.

Pride of ownership and direct rewards: Pride of ownership generates personal motivation and identification with the business. The profit motive could be reinforced with more people having a vested interest.

Availability of more capital: A partnership can pool the funds of a number of people compared to a sole owner who has only his or her own resources to draw upon, unless loans are obtained.

Combination of expertise and talent: Two or more partners, by combining their energies and talents, can often be successful where one person alone would fail. This is particularly true if the business demands a variety of talents such as technical knowledge, sales ability, and financial skills. It is important that working partners bring complementary skills to the business, thereby reducing the workload of each partner.

Flexibility: A partnership may be relatively more flexible in the decision-making process than a corporation, but less so than a sole proprietorship.

Relative freedom of government control and special taxation: Compared to a corporation, a partnership is relatively free from many restrictions and bureaucratic red tape.

3.2 Disadvantages

Unlimited liability: The major disadvantage of a partnership is the unlimited liability. This unlimited liability is much more serious than in a proprietorship because all the partners are individually and collectively liable for all the debts and liabilities of the partnership. Each partner's personal assets are liable to be seized if necessary to pay for outstanding business debts.

Unstable duration of business: Any change in the partnership automatically ends the legal entity. Changes could include the death of a partner, or the admission or withdrawal of a partner. In each case, if the business is to continue, a new partnership agreement must be written.

Management of difficulties: As mentioned, when more than one owner assumes responsibility for business management, there is a possibility that differences of style, priorities, philosophy, and other factors will arise. If these differences become serious disputes and are unresolved, the partnership may have to be terminated, with all the financial and personal trauma involved. It is difficult for future partners to foresee whether or not personalities and methods of operating will clash.

Relative difficulty in obtaining large sums of capital: This is particularly true of long-term financing when compared to a corporation.

Partnership agreement problems: The larger a partnership becomes, the more complex the written agreement has to be to protect the rights and identify the responsibilities of each partner. This can result in additional administration and legal costs.

Difficulty of disposing of partnership interest: To withdraw capital from the business requires approval from all other partners. This takes time and involves legal and administrative expenses.

3.3 Partnership agreement

A partnership agreement, sometimes called articles of partnership, is absolutely necessary in a partnership relationship. The agreement normally outlines the contribution of each partner in the business, whether financial, material, or managerial. In general, it defines the roles of the partners in the business relationship.

Some of the typical articles contained in a partnership agreement are shown in Table 3.

If you are considering a partnership relationship, complete the checklist headings and then see your lawyer and accountant. By the time you have completed the checklist with your prospective business mate, the engagement could be off.

3.4 Kinds of partners

An *ostensible partner* is active in the business and known as a partner.

An *active partner* may or may not be ostensible as well.

A *dormant partner* is inactive and not known or held out as a partner.

A *secret partner* is active but not known or held out as a partner.

A *silent partner* is inactive and not known or held out as a partner.

A *nominal partner* (partner by estoppel) is not a true partner in any sense, not being a party to the partnership agreement. A nominal partner, however, holds himself or herself out as a partner, or permits others to make such representation by the use of his or her name or otherwise. A nominal partner, therefore, is liable to third parties as if he or she were a partner.

A *sub-partner* is a person who is not a member of the partnership but contracts with one of the partners to represent that partner by participating in the firm's business and profits.

A *limited or special partner* risks only his or her agreed investment in the business assuming that statutory formalities have been complied with. As long as he or she does not participate in the management and control of the enterprise or in the conduct of its business, the limited partner is generally not subject to the same liabilities as the general partner.

4. CORPORATION

A corporation is a legal entity, with or without share capital, which can be established by one or more individuals or other legal entities. It exists separate and distinct from these individuals or other legal entities. A corporation has all the rights and responsibilities of a person with the exception of those rights that can only be exercised by a natural person.

4.1 Advantages

Limited liability of shareholders: Shareholders' personal assets are separate from the business and cannot be seized to pay for outstanding business debts incurred by the

TABLE 3
CHECKLIST OF ARTICLES IN A PARTNERSHIP AGREEMENT

1. Name, purpose, and location of partnership
2. Duration of agreement
3. Names and character of partners (general or limited, active or silent)
4. Financial contribution by partners (at inception, at later date)
5. Role of individual partners in business management
6. Authority (authority of partner in conduct of business)
7. Nature and degree of each partner's contribution to firm's consulting services
8. Business expenses (how handled)
9. Separate debts
10. Signing of checks
11. Division of profits and losses
12. Books, records, and method of accounting
13. Draws or salaries
14. Absence and disability
15. Death of a partner (dissolution and winding up)
16. Rights of continuing partner
17. Employee management
18. Sale of partnership interest
19. Release of debts
20. Settlement of disputes; arbitration
21. Additions, alternations, or modifications to partnership agreement
22. Noncompetition in the event of departure

corporation. There are exceptions, dealing primarily with the issue of fraud.

Flexibility for tax planning: Various tax advantages are available to corporations that are not available to partnerships or proprietorships. Tax planning must be undertaken with the help of a professional accountant.

Corporate management flexibility: The owner or owners can be active in the management of the business to any desired degree. Agents, officers, and directors with specified authority can be appointed to manage the business. Employees can be given stock options to share in the ownership, which can increase incentive and interest.

Financing more readily available: Investors find it more attractive to invest in a corporation with its limited liability than to invest in a business whose unlimited liability could involve them to an extent greater than the amount of the investment. Long-term financing from lending institutions is more available since lenders may use both corporate assets and personal guarantees as security.

Continual existence of corporation: A corporation continues to exist and operate regardless of the changes in the shareholders. Death of a shareholder does not discontinue the life of the corporation. Continual existence is also an effective device for building and retaining goodwill.

Ownership is readily transferable: It is a relatively simple procedure to transfer ownership by share transfer unless there are corporate restrictions to the contrary.

Draw on expertise and skills of more than one individual: This feature is the same concept as in a partnership, where more partners (shareholders) contribute diverse talents. However, a corporation is not required to have more than one shareholder.

4.2 Disadvantages

Extensive government regulations: There are more regulations affecting a corporation than a sole proprietorship or partnership. Corporations must report to all levels of government.

Activities limited by the charter and bylaws: Depending on the jurisdiction, charters can be very broad or can severely restrict a company's activities.

Manipulation: Minority shareholders are potentially in a position to be exploited by the decisions of the majority of the company.

Expense: It is more expensive to establish and operate a corporation due to the additional documents and forms that are required compared to a proprietorship or partnership.

4.3 Corporate purposes

Some jurisdictions require that the articles of incorporation include a statement of the purposes of the corporation. When you provide a list of the purposes of the corporation, make sure that you define them expansively. Do not restrict the activity of your corporation. A general clause should be included allowing the corporation to expand into any business activity permitted by law. A competent lawyer can assist you in preparing this document to enable you to maximize your corporate options.

4.4 Shareholders' agreement

A shareholders' agreement involves the same concepts of protection as a partnership agreement. Many of the provisions outlined in the partnership agreement are also included in the shareholders' agreement. There are additional provisions frequently covered in the shareholders' agreement, including:

- A restriction on transfer of shares

- A buy-sell provision that sets out the formula for buying and selling shares in the company

- A provision on personal guarantees of corporate obligations

- A provision on payback by corporation of shareholders' loans

- A provision giving all shareholders the entitlement to sit as a director or nominate a director as their representative. This protects minority shareholders from lack of managerial information and provides them with a directorship vote or veto on corporate decisions. If you intend to be a majority shareholder, you may not wish to volunteer this provision.

Many shareholders believe that corporate bylaws set out the recipe for resolving problems within the corporation and between the shareholders, directors, and officers in some magical fashion. In most cases, the bylaws only cover formulas for resolving disputes in a few circumstances. It is the shareholders' agreement that expands the protections to resolve fairly any disputes between shareholders.

If you intend to incorporate and have one or more additional shareholders in your corporation, it would be wise to obtain your lawyer's advice on a shareholders' agreement to protect your interests.

4.5 Maintaining the corporate protection

One of the advantages of operating through a corporate entity is the protection against personal liability for the debts and liabilities of the corporations. This is assuming, of course, that you have not signed personal guarantees. However, there are situations that could cause you to be personally liable for corporate debts. Generally, if it can be shown that a fraud was perpetrated through use of the corporation, or the director totally disregarded the corporate formalities, the advantage of the "corporate veil" can disappear.

When a court treats the corporation as a sham and imposes personal liability on the shareholders or directors, it is said to "pierce the corporate veil." Here is a list of precautions to follow to prevent personal legal attack.

- *Meetings:* A corporation acts only when its employees (officers, directors, and shareholders) act. If a corporation holds no directors' or shareholders' meetings, the corporation may not really exist. Therefore, every corporation should hold at least one shareholders' and one directors' meeting annually and have that fact documented.

- *Corporate name:* A business operating in the corporate form must let the general public know that it is a corporation with limited liability by attaching either "Inc." or

"Incorporation," "Corp." or "Corporation," or "Ltd." or "Limited" to its name, depending on the form you selected at incorporation. You must specify the corporate designation everywhere the company name appears.

- *Acting as agent:* When a shareholder/employee executes a document or engages in a transaction, the person must make it clear that it is being done on behalf of the corporation. That is, when you sign a check or contract, you should write your corporate office title (i.e., president, secretary, etc.) after your name.

- *Tax returns:* The corporation must file an annual tax return and observe the rules for withholding on payroll taxes. You must make sure that all periodic reporting requirements are satisfied and that there is never any failure to pay to the taxing authorities all sums paid by or deductions from the corporate employees. Any sales tax collected must be remitted within the appropriate period.

- *Adequate capitalization:* If a corporation is inadequately capitalized so that there is insufficient capital investment to meet the claims by creditors, the courts may impose personal liability on the corporation's shareholders or directors for its business obligations. You should, therefore, be careful that your "equity" in the corporation does not become too diluted by loans from yourself and from third parties. As an arbitrary rule of thumb, a debt to equity ratio not exceeding 8:1 is reasonable. However, what is truly "inadequate" depends on the extent of actual corporate liabilities and the extent of assets to satisfy those liabilities.

The laws in Canada and the United States and within the individual provinces and states vary; these cautions may not be necessary or applicable in your area. Your lawyer can advise you properly.

- *Separate accounts:* Many shareholders of closely held corporations treat the corporation's assets as their own. They combine personal and corporate funds, use corporate funds to pay personal expenses including medical bills and taxes, and generally disregard the corporate "formalities." By doing so, however, they run the risk that a court may also disregard the formalities and hold the person liable for the company's debts. The shareholders and directors, therefore, should maintain separate corporate and personal accounts and use the company funds only for business needs.

- *Filing annual corporate forms:* Most jurisdictions require an annual report to be filed. The form requires that you list the shareholders, officers, directors, and current business address of your company, as well as other incidental information. This document must be filed on time to avoid penalties and possible involuntary dissolution. This dissolution could mean that you would be held personally liable for debts of the corporation.

5. S CORPORATION (SUB-CHAPTER OR SUB-S) (UNITED STATES)

As a consultant, you may wish to consider the advantages of structuring your business as an S corporation in the United States. The purpose is to permit a small business corporation to treat its net income as though it were a partnership. One objective is to overcome the double-tax feature of taxing corporate income and shareholder dividends. Another purpose is to permit the shareholders to have the benefit of offsetting business losses incurred for the corporation against their income.

Only closely held corporations, that is with 35 or fewer shareholders, may make the S election. All shareholders must consent to the S election, and only one class of outstanding stock is allowed. A specific portion of the corporation's income must be derived from active business rather than passive investments. No limit is placed on the size of the corporation's income and assets.

At some future point you may wish to revert to a full corporation for tax advantage reasons. This is permitted, but the corporation may not be able to reelect the S vehicle for several years once the S election is reversed. This is to eliminate small corporations from changing frequently to maximize tax advantages. Since S forms of incorporation are not recognized in all states, you should obtain further information from your professional advisers.

6. LIMITED LIABILITY CORPORATION (LLC) (UNITED STATES)

A limited liability corporation (LLC) is a form of doing business that combines the limited liability for loans and lawsuits of a corporation with the "pass-through" tax benefits of a partnership. Pass-through taxation means that the business is taxed only once — at the member/shareholder level — rather than at both the member/shareholder and LLC/corporate level.

S corporations are also eligible for pass-through taxation, so why form an LLC instead of an S corporation? Because certain limitations are placed on S corporations that do not affect LLCs. For instance, an S corporation must not have more than 35 shareholders, and the shareholders must be individuals, estates, or certain types of trusts. Corporations, partnerships, LLCs, and nonresidents may not be shareholders in an S corporation. All these entities, however, can be members in an LLC. Another limitation placed on S corporations is that they may have only one class of stock. As a result, the financing options are limited. S corporations are not good tax shelters because deductions for losses are limited to the shareholder's basis in the corporate stock.

LLCs have an advantage over S corporations when it comes to foreign investors. Because an S corporation cannot take on nonresidents as shareholders, it is unable to have much interaction in the fast-growing international business market. Also, LLCs, unlike S corporations, are not subject to additional partnership tax status qualification requirements. LLCs must simply meet partnership tax requirements. LLCs need not elect partnership tax status and then be continually vigilant in order to retain such status as S corporations must.

For more information refer to the Self-Counsel book *How to Form and Operate a Limited Liability Company*.

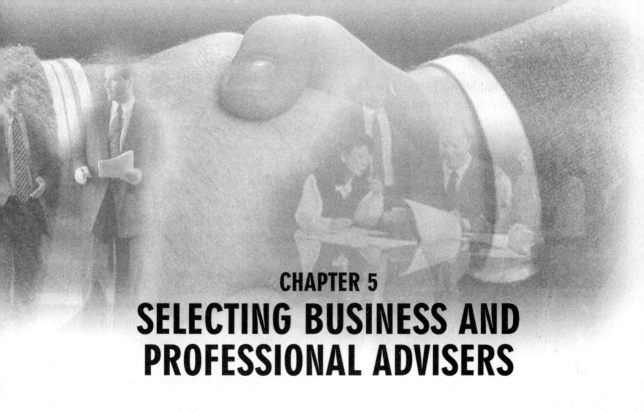

CHAPTER 5
SELECTING BUSINESS AND PROFESSIONAL ADVISERS

Since you may be operating on your own, or with a few associates, you will need an extended management team to advise you in specialized areas where you lack knowledge, ability, or interest. Your advisers are, in effect, your employees and associates and should be considered an integral part of management decision-making.

Every business decision involves a legal decision or implication. Every business decision involves accounting, bookkeeping and, at times, tax considerations. The fatality rate of small businesses is enormously high. Statistically the odds are practically ten to one that your small business will not be in business three years after you begin your practice.

This chapter discusses the benefits of the effective use of business and professional advisers, with sections on how to se-

lectively evaluate them and how to use their skills to your advantage.

1. GENERAL CRITERIA FOR ADVISER SELECTION

How well you select your professional and business advisers will have a direct bearing on your business success. Poor advisers or no advisers will almost certainly lead to your business downfall. Your main advisers are your lawyer and accountant, followed by your banker. You should see at least three different people from each of these three professions before you make your selection. It is important to have the comparative assessment.

The following general guidelines should assist you in the careful search and selection of your advisers.

1.1 Recommendations

One of the most reliable methods of finding an adviser is by a personal recommendation from your existing advisers or friends in business whose judgment and business sense you trust. Bankers and business advisers who deal on a regular basis with professional advisers are in a good position to pass judgment based on their business dealings. When lawyers, accountants, or bankers refer to each other, it implies a good working relationship and mutual trust.

Don't rely completely on any referral; make your own cautious assessment. You might also want to try the lawyer referral service in your area. For a nominal fee you can see a business or corporate lawyer for an initial consultation.

1.2 Credentials

In Canada, all lawyers have an "LL.B." designation. In the United States, lawyers have either an "LL.B." or "J.D." designation.

Accountants in Canada have a professional designation such as "C.A." or "C.G.A." In the United States, look for the designation "C.P.A." The training requirements and public practice background of C.A.s and C.P.A.s are similar if not identical.

Certification and credentials only ensure that the individual has passed minimum standards of education. They do not ensure that the person is a dynamic, innovative, or creative business adviser with a specific amount of experience relevant to your needs.

1.3 Clientele

Most professional advisers have a homogeneous client base. Some advisers have many small business clients, others emphasize personal clients, while others go after corporate business. An adviser with a good base of small- to medium-size commercial clients will probably be the most appropriate for your business needs.

1.4 Fees

Fees will often vary by the size of the community in which the professional practice is operated, the size of the practice, and the volume of business. You may find that advisers who charge fees in the middle range, edging toward the higher end of the scale, are often quality practitioners in high demand who are still aggressive and innovative in their business practice.

Advisers who are at the low end of the fee scale can be entrepreneurial types, but cut-rate pricing may also indicate a cut-rate, high-volume approach to business which will not suit your objectives. Low prices are sometimes an indicator of low quality, low esteem, or little experience.

Very high-priced advisers tend to be more conservative, less aggressive, and less willing to spend the necessary time with small business clients because their priorities lie with the big firms. Fees vary and many professionals will negotiate them.

In a smaller or medium-size community, a realistic hourly rate for a lawyer or accountant is approximately $75 to $100 per hour. Advisers in larger cities will be more expensive, perhaps $100 to $150 per hour or more. If you are given an estimate by your lawyer or accountant and that estimate is exceeded, it is not uncommon for your adviser to reduce the fee as a gesture of goodwill in order to keep your ongoing business. Lawyers in general are more agreeable to charging a fixed fee. In some jurisdictions a lawyer can charge a contingency fee. For example, a lawyer may sue on your behalf and recover $100,000 owing to you and receive a fee in the form of a percentage, say 35%, of that amount.

It is important to be very open when discussing fees and payment expectations.

1.5 Technical competence and industry knowledge

You must satisfy yourself that your advisers are competent in the areas of your greatest need. Ask them how much experience they have had, and how comfortable they are, with your field.

A specific understanding of the problems, needs, and issues of your type of business can enable your advisers to provide the exact assistance you require. This is different from technical skill competence. It has more to do with experience in a particular type of industry. If the adviser has provided guidance to other small business owners in similar situations, there is an increased possibility that the adviser will be able to provide you with more reliable assistance. For example, if you are a hospital consultant, a lawyer who specializes in or is very familiar with health or hospital law could be an asset to you.

1.6 Style and personality

A critical factor in the selection of advisers, beyond simple compatibility, is style. You can have greater confidence in the aggressive adviser who takes the initiative and offers advice before you request it. This style indicates an initiator rather than a reactor, a person who anticipates and performs before

matters become serious. It also indicates a creator, an entrepreneur, and a person who can empathize with your problems and concerns. This kind of adviser is more likely to come up with creative solutions to problems and be a complement to your planning function. This type of adviser will not only be a sounding board, but a true part of the management team.

1.7 Confidence

You should feel a sense of confidence when relating to your adviser, whether it be in the general sense or in dealing with a specific problem or issue. You should have a certain amount of personal compatibility with your adviser. If you don't, you will probably end up rejecting a fair amount of advice. In other words, if you do not feel that good chemistry exists with an adviser, seek a replacement as soon as possible. If you do not relate well to the adviser, you may hesitate to ask for advice, which could result in some poor management decisions.

Never allow your advisers to treat you in a condescending or paternalistic manner. You should consider them as equals with special knowledge offering a service in the same manner that you are offering a service to your clients.

1.8 Communication

You should select an adviser who communicates well, openly and free of jargon. Your adviser should explain the necessary concepts to you so that you understand the issues involved and the decisions that have to be made. Effective communication also means that your advisers forward to you any correspondence sent or received through their offices relating to your business.

1.9 Commitment

It is important to sense that your adviser is committed to your best interests and your success. An adviser who is involved with clients that are larger, more important, or higher paying than you are may become indifferent to your needs. You should be alert to this.

1.10 Availability

It is important for your advisers to be available when you need them. You are spending time and resources to develop a relationship that will enhance your business decisions. If your adviser is frequently out of town or, in the case of a lawyer, in court on a regular basis, you may not have the immediate access you need. Of course if the adviser is of exceptional quality and ideally suited to your type of practice, some allowances should be made.

1.11 Length of time in practice

There is naturally a correlation between the degree of expertise and length of time in practice. You should therefore ask directly how many years of experience your adviser has in the area of your needs.

1.12 Ability to aid growth

A good professional adviser will have a history of assisting growth in other clients. The adviser should be able to anticipate growth problems in advance and provide guidance to deal with them.

1.13 Small firm versus large firm

Choosing a small or large firm is in many ways a matter of your own personal style

and the type of firm you relate to most comfortably. Larger firms tend to be in the central area of the city, which may involve parking problems. Their fees are higher. Generally, the larger firms do not have a small business orientation in their marketing and service priorities. The larger firms do have highly specialized advisers and a resource base of associate personnel. This degree of depth may or may not be necessary in your situation. It is not uncommon in larger firms to have small business clients passed over to junior associates or students in training as the more senior advisers handle larger clients.

Smaller firms generally deal with and relate to small business entrepreneurs. Selecting an adviser in a small- or medium-size firm of three to ten people provides you with a resource base if you need it. An adviser who is a sole practitioner may be very busy, too generalized in his or her areas of practice, and lacking a referral resource base within the firm.

1.14 Comparison

Make sure you check out at least three advisers before making a final decision. The more selective you are in comparing the personalities, styles, competence, and attitudes of prospective advisers, the more likely it is that you will find someone with whom you can establish a good relationship. Prepare questions for your potential advisers and compare their answers. Assess the quality of answers to your questions, then decide who will be the most benefit to you. Most initial consultations are free; be sure to confirm this when you set up the meeting. The more interviews you conduct, the greater your knowledge base and the greater your confidence that you will choose the right person or firm.

2. LAWYER

There are basically two types of lawyers that you should consider as your advisers. The same lawyer might be able to assume both roles.

You need a lawyer who specializes in small business. A lawyer who cares about small business clients assumes the same role and attitude toward your business health and survival as your physician to your personal health.

The other type of lawyer you need is one who specializes in contract law. You will need to have several "boiler plate" contracts prepared depending on the type and style of service you are providing. There are times you will need to have a specialized contract made up by a lawyer or have the lawyer review and advise you on a contract that has been prepared by the client.

If your business lawyer does not have the expertise in contract law, request that you be referred to someone within the firm or outside who does. For continuity and efficiency, you want to maintain your business lawyer for all matters that don't require additional expertise. You should be able to phone your lawyer as your needs arise and feel confident that the unique aspects of your business are known and understood.

For your protection, you should retain a lawyer before you start up your business, as there are many legal pitfalls that can be encountered. There is a temptation to save money on legal fees in the beginning stages of the business when cash flow is minimal.

Some people do their own incorporation to save on initial start-up expenses, but then continue the saving by never obtaining legal or accounting advise, an unfortunate example of false economy and bad judgment.

3. ACCOUNTANT

An accountant is the other essential business adviser on your management team. It is very important that you retain a qualified accountant with the designations described earlier. A bookkeeper is not an accountant and, in most jurisdictions in Canada and the United States, there is no restriction on anyone's using the name "accountant" and purporting to provide accounting services without any qualifications or training.

There are many essential services that an accountant can provide. An accountant can advise on all start-up steps of a new business, including the tax and accounting considerations of various types of business organization. Normally an accountant will communicate with or coordinate work with your lawyer. The accountant considers important matters such as when your fiscal year-end should be and whether you should use cash or accrual method in keeping your books.

An accountant can advise on preparing a business plan for a loan application. This includes recommending the type of loan you should consider and how it is to be paid. Documents such as a profit and loss statement, a balance sheet, and a financial statement can be prepared by the accountant. He or she may refer you to a banker, which can have a positive effect on your loan application if the banker knows and respects the accountant.

An accountant can advise on all aspects of tax planning and tax-related business decisions which occur from time to time, as well as file your tax returns.

An accountant can advise how to set up your office bookkeeping system. The accountant can have the bookkeeping done by someone in his or her firm at a negotiated fee or you can hire an independent bookkeeper. Your accountant should be able to recommend some bookkeepers.

An accountant can analyze and interpret your financial information, point out areas that need control, and recommend ways of implementing the necessary change.

An accountant may be aware of various government grant programs that could be of interest to you.

An accountant can coordinate your personal and business affairs and advise you on investments, tax shelters, income splitting, and other matters.

An accountant can advise and assist you if you want to change your proprietorship or partnership into a limited company at some point. If the transfer is done correctly, you can minimize any negative tax consequences.

4. BANKER

Your relationship with your bank and banker is your financial lifeline. The process of selecting a bank and banker is a critical one, and substantial comparative shopping is necessary to obtain the optimal combination of personality and knowledge.

The qualifications of the banker should be considered along with his or her specific experience with your type of business, specific reputation for taking risk, and the demands that are made for security and for reporting results.

Find out the amount of the banker's loan approval limit. If your needs are less than the limit, the loan can be approved by that individual without further review by another loans officer. This means you only have to convince one person to approve your loan request, not additional anonymous people behind the scene. How well your relationship develops with the banker and how successful you are getting your loans approved will depend largely on the factors outlined in chapter 7 on how to obtain financing.

There are specific danger areas that can affect your banker's relationship with you. When the bank's manager changes, there is always a period of risk and uncertainty. The new manager does not want to have any medium- or high-risk loans on the books to taint his or her record. During the first three or four months after a new manager takes over, outstanding loans are reviewed and categorized within the criteria set by him or her. This is the time when loans can be called or additional security requested or interest rates increased. You should develop a personal relationship with the manager when you take out a loan. If you hear that a new manager has taken over, make a point of quickly introducing yourself and briefly discussing your business in a positive way.

Bank policies change from time to time and your type of business could be looked upon as increasing in risk. For example, if real estate is in a slump in your region, the bank could make a policy decision to be very cautious about existing or pending loans related to real estate. If you are a real estate consultant, that decision could affect your loan. If you think the bank is concerned, prepare a realistic assessment of how you intend to deal with the situation in advance. You may have diversified consultancy, not just related to real estate, or you may have other options available to that you could explain to your banker.

Ask your accountant and lawyer which bank and banker they recommend. This is probably one of the most effective introductions. If the banker has an ongoing relationship with a professional who is advising you as a client, a less impersonal relationship will exist and there is a better chance that decisions affecting your loans and your business will be made more carefully.

5. INSURANCE

It is important to select a professional insurance broker with experience and knowledge in the areas of insurance you require. An insurance broker can have various professional qualifications, and you may wish to find out what those credentials are. Insurance is covered in detail in chapter 10.

6. CONSULTANTS

6.1 Private consultants

You may wish to approach a practicing consultant for advice to assist you in your business. As previously discussed, consultants are not restrictively licensed like other professionals. To protect yourself, you should inquire about their expertise, qualifications, and length of experience. Obtain references and contact them. Apply the general criteria for adviser selection. You will want to satisfy yourself that the consultant is person-

ally successful. If the consultant has not been successful, how can he or she possible offer advice that will help you? Consultant fees may range between $50 to $150 per hour or more, depending on many variables.

6.2 Consultants subsidized by the government

Both the Canadian and U.S. governments have consulting services available for small business.

6.2a Counselling Assistance to Small Enterprises (CASE)

In Canada, the federal government, through the Business Development Bank of Canada (BDC), sponsors consultants in CASE. The counselors are retired and active business experts who wish to be mentors or provide other assistance. They are able to identify areas of opportunity, solve problems, and help people manage more effectively. Businesses starting up, expanding, closing, or just not making the kind of profit expected can benefit from the help of an experienced business person.

The requirements of the clients are matched with the background and expertise of available counselors. The CASE coordinator selects the appropriate counselor, reviews reports outlining recommendations submitted by the counselor, and follows up on assignments. The hourly fee for the counselor's time is modest compared to the fees charged by private consultants, and includes meeting with the client, doing necessary research, and outlining recommendations in a written report to the client. Further information can be obtained from a local BDC office.

The BDC also sponsors small business management seminars and workshops, strategic planning, and other services, as well as various forms of financing. Contact your local branch to obtain further information and to place your name on the mailing list.

6.2b Service Corps of Retired Executives (SCORE)

This American program is similar to the Canadian program, and is sponsored by the United States Small Business Administration (SBA). SCORE is composed of retired and active executives who share their knowledge, experience, and business counseling for a modest fee. Further information can be obtained from a local SBA office.

The SBA also sponsors small business management seminars and workshops. Contact your local branch to obtain further information and to place your name on the mailing list.

CHAPTER 6
PREPARING YOUR BUSINESS PLAN

1. WHY PREPARE A PLAN?

Most consultants prefer to be a consultant first and a business owner second. But planning and good management skills are vital to business success. Those who do not plan run a very high risk of failure. If you do not know where you are going in your personal or business life, there is little prospect that you will arrive. A business plan is a written summary of what you hope to accomplish by being in business and how you intend to organize your resources to meet your goals. It is an essential guide for operating your business successfully and measuring progress along the way.

Planning forces you to think ahead and visualize; it encourages realistic thinking instead of overoptimism. It helps you identify your customers, your market area, your pricing strategy, and the competitive condi-

tions under which you must operate. This process often leads to the discovery of new opportunities as well as deficiencies in your plan.

Having clear goals and a well-written plan aid in decision-making. You can always change your goals, but at least with a business plan you have some basis and a standard comparison to use in evaluating alternatives presented to you.

A business plan establishes the amount of financing or outside investment required and when it is needed. It makes it much easier for a lender or investor to assess your financing proposal and to assess you as a business manager. It inspires confidence in lenders and self-confidence in yourself to know every aspect of the business when you are negotiating your financing. If you have a realistic, comprehensive, and well-documented plan, it will assist you greatly in convincing a lender.

Having well-established objectives helps you analyze your progress. If you have not attained your objectives by a certain period, you will be aware of that fact and can make appropriate adjustments at an early stage.

Spending three or four hours each month updating your plan will save considerable time and money in the long run and may even save your business. It is essential to develop a habit of planning and reassessing on an ongoing basis as an integral part of your management style.

2. FORMAT

The business plan format shown in Sample 4 is a starting point for organizing your own plan. The comments following the subheadings should help you decide which sections are relevant to your business situations.

The business plan format normally consists of four parts: the introduction, the business concept, the financial plan, and the appendix.

The plan starts with an introductory page highlighting the business plan. Even though your entire business is described later, a crisp one- or two-page introduction helps capture the immediate attention of the potential investor or lender.

The business concept, which begins with a description of the industry, identifies your market potential within your industry and outlines your action plan for the coming year. Make sure your stated business goals are compatible with your personal goals and financial goals, your management ability, and family considerations. The heart of the business concept is your monthly sales forecast for the coming year. As your statement of confidence in your marketing strategy, it forms the basis for your cash flow forecast and projected income statement. This section also contains an assessment of business risks and a contingency plan. Being honest about your business risks and how you plan to deal with them is evidence of sound management.

The financial plan outlines the level of present financing and identifies the financing sought. This section should be brief. The financial plan contains pro forma (projected) financial forecasts. These forecasts are a projection into the future based on current information and assumptions. In carrying out your action plan for the coming year, these operating forecasts are an essential guide to business survival and profitability. It is important to refer to them often and, if circumstances dictate, rework them. Samples 5, 6, and 7 show forms you might want to include in your business plan.

The appendix section contains all the items that do not naturally fall elsewhere in the document, or which expand further on the summaries in the document. These might include a personal net worth statement (Sample 8) and a statement of accounts receivable (Sample 9).

3. ESTIMATING YOUR START-UP FUNDS

3.1 Assessment of personal monthly financial needs

Personal expenses will continue in spite of the business and have to be taken into account when determining monthly cash flow needs. It is important to calculate personal expenses accurately so that appropriate decisions can be made in terms of funding and the nature of the start-up practice — whether it should start out on a part-time or full-time basis, using the home as an office or renting an outside office. Refer back to Samples 2 and 3 in chapter 3 to review this important information.

3.2 Estimated business start-up cash needs

An estimate of the start-up cash required can be calculated by referring to Table 2 in chapter 3. Naturally, each consultant's situation can vary considerably and therefore the worksheet is a guide only.

During your first few months you will probably not have enough sales revenue to finance your short-term costs. This usually occurs for one of three reasons: your sales are below projection, your costs rise unexpectedly, or you have not yet been paid for consulting work already performed (overdue accounts receivable). Many professionals experience accounts receivable problems during the early months of operation because clients tend to pay professionals after they have paid other outstanding bills. Your conservative cash flow analysis prepares you for this situation and enables you to plan your cash needs.

4. SUMMARY

Before presenting your business plan to a lender or investor, have two or three impartial outsiders review the finished plan in detail. There may be something you overlooked or underemphasized. After your plan has been reviewed by others, take it and your financial statements to your accountant for review. You should also discuss with your accountant all the personal and business tax considerations that might be involved. You may wish to have your accountant come with you to the bank when you discuss your loan proposal. This is not uncommon and can create a very positive impression.

Discuss with your lawyer the security you are proposing. Your lawyer should explain fully before the plan is submitted the effect of your pledging collateral security and what the lender could do if you default. You should also seriously evaluate whether the security pledged is too excessive for the loan or risk involved and whether the risk is too great to pledge your personal assets.

Your familiarity with your business plan will increase your credibility and at the same time provide you with a good understanding of what the financial statements reveal about the viability of your business.

1. Introductory page

    (a) Company name

        - Include address and telephone number

    (b) Contact person

        - Consultant's name and telephone number

    (c) Paragraph about company

        - Nature of business and market area

    (d) Securities offered to investors or lenders

        - Outline securities such as preferred shares, common shares, debentures, etc.

    (e) Business loans sought

        - For example, term loan, operating line of credit, mortgage

    (f) Summary of proposed use of funds

2. Summary

    (a) Highlights of business plan

        - Preferably one page maximum

        - Include your project, competitive advantage, and "bottom line" needs

3. Table of contents

    (a) Section titles and page numbers should be given for easy reference

4. Description of the industry

    (a) Industry outlook and growth potential

        - Outline industry trends — past, present, and future — and new developments

        - State your sources of information

    (b) Markets and customers

- Estimated size of total market, share and sales, new requirements, and market trends

(c) Competitive companies

- Market share, strengths and weaknesses, profitability, trends

(d) National and economic trends

- Population shifts, consumer trends, relevant economic indicators

5. Description of business venture

(a) Nature of consulting service

- Characteristics, method of operation, whether performed locally, regionally, nationally, or internationally

(b) Target market

- Typical clients identified by groups, present consulting patterns and average earnings, wants and needs

(c) Competitive advantage of your business concept

- Your market niche, uniqueness, estimated market share

(d) Business location and size

- Location relative to market, size of premises, home or office use

(e) Staff and equipment needed

- Overall requirement, capacity, home or office use, part- or fulltime staff or as required

(f) Brief history

- Principals involved in the consulting business or proposed consulting business, development work done, resumes and background experience of principals, resumes of key consulting associates if applicable

6. Business goals

(a) One year

- Specific goals, such as gross sales, profit margin, share of market, opening new office, introducing new service, etc.

(b) Over the longer term

- Return on investment, business net worth, sale of business

7. Marketing plan

(a) Sales strategy

- Commission sales staff, agents, sub-consultants
- Sales objectives, sales tools, sales support
- Target clients

(b) Sales approach

- Style of operation and techniques

(c) Pricing

- Costing, mark-ups, margins, break-even

(d) Promotion

- Media advertising, promotions, publicity appropriate to reach target market
- Techniques of developing exposure, credibility, and contacts

(e) Service policies

- Policies that your consulting practice will adopt with regard to cred it and collection, bidding, nature of clients, etc.

(f) Guarantees

- Service performance guarantees or other assurances will vary depending upon nature of consulting practice and type of contractor client

(g) Tracking methods

- Method for confirming who your clients are and how they heard about you

8. Sales forecast

(a) Assumptions

- One never has all the necessary information, so state all the assumptions made in developing the forecast

(b) Monthly forecast for the coming year

- Sales volume, projected in dollars

(c) Annual forecast for the following two to four years

- Sales volume, projected in dollars

The sales forecast is the starting point for your projected income statement and cash flow forecast.

9. Costing plan

(a) Cost of facilities, equipment, and materials (as applicable)

- Estimates and quotations

(b) Capital estimates

- One time start-up or expansion capital required

10. Operations

(a) Purchasing plans

- Volume discounts, multiple sources, quality, price

(b) Inventory system

- Seasonal variation, turnover rate, method of control

(c) Space required

- Floor and office space, improvements required, expansion capability

(d) Staff and equipment required

- Personnel by skill level
- Fixtures, office equipment

(e) Operations strategy

11. Corporate structure

(a) Legal form

- Proprietorship, partnership, or incorporation

(b) Share distribution

- List of principal shareholders

(c) Contracts and agreements

- List of contracts and agreements in force

- Management contract, shareholder or partnership agreement, service contract, leases

(d) Directors and officers

- Names and addresses, role in company

(e) Background of key management personnel

- Brief resumes of active owners and key employees

(f) Organizational chart

- Identify reporting relationships

(g) Duties and responsibilities of key personnel

- Brief job descriptions — who is responsible for what

12. Supporting professional assistance

(a) Professionals on contract in specialized or deficient areas; would include lawyer, accountant, banker, insurance agent, etc.

13. Research and development program

(a) Product or service improvements, process improvements, costs and risks

14. Risk assessment

(a) Competitors' reaction

- Will competitors try to squeeze you out? What form do you anticipate any reaction will take?

(b) List of critical external factors that might occur
- Identify effects of strikes, recession, new technology, weather, new

com- petition, supplier problems, shifts in consumer demand, costs of delays and overruns, unfavorable industry trends

(c) List of critical internal factors that might occur
- Income projections not realized, client dispute or litigation, receivables difficulties, demand for service increases very quickly, key employee or consultant quits

(d) Dealing with risks
- Contingency plan to handle the most significant risks

15. Overall schedule

(a) Interrelationship and timing of all major events important to starting and developing your business

16. Action plan

(a) Steps to accomplish this year's goals
- Flow chart by month or by quarter of specific action to be taken and by whom

(b) Checkpoint for measuring results
- Identify significant dates, sales levels as decision points

17. Financial forecast

If a business has been in operation for a period of time, the previous two or three years' balance sheets and income statements are required

(a) Opening balance sheet
- The balance sheet is a position statement, not an historical record; it shows what is owned and owed at a given date. There are three sections to a balance sheet: assets, liabilities, and owner's equity. You determine your firm's net worth by subtracting the liabilities from the assets.

- Your balance sheet will indicate how your investment has grown over a period of time — investors and lenders typically examine balance sheets to determine if the company is within acceptable assets to liability limits

- See Sample 5

(b) Income and expense forecast statement (profit and loss)
- The income and expense forecast can be described as the operating statement you would expect to see for your business at the end of the period for which the forecast is being prepared
- For a new business, the forecast would show what revenue and expenses you expect the business to have in its first year of operation
- It is very useful, of course, to prepare a forecast for a period longer than one year, so you might want to prepare a detailed forecast for the next year of operation and a less detailed forecast for the following two years
- Preparing an income and expense forecast for a new business is more difficult than preparing one for an existing business, simply because in a new business there is no historical record to go by. For this reason the preparation of the forecast is an even more essential, interesting, and rewarding experience than doing it for an existing business, despite the time and effort required. This analysis exercise will answer the question of whether a profit will be made.
- The income statement (sales) is the most difficult because it is the most uncertain at the commencement of business; it is essential that a figure be projected on a conservative estimate
- The main concern is to account for expenses accurately and in as much detail as possible; this will then provide a target or break-even figure toward which to work
- Some headings may not be appropriate for your type of consulting practice; other headings should be added
- See Sample 6

(c) Cash flow forecast
- A cash flow budget measures the flow of money in and out of the business. It is critical to you and your banker.
- Many business operate on a seasonal basis, as there are slow months and busy months. The cash flow budget projection will provide an indication of the times of a cash flow shortage to assist in

properly planning and financing your operation. It will tell you in advance if you have enough cash to get by.

- A cash flow budget should be prepared a year in advance and contain monthly breakdowns
- See Sample 7

(d) Cash flow assumptions

When reviewing the cash flow plan, certain assumptions should be made:

- Sales: monthly sales (consulting service fees) that are expected to materialize
- Receipts: cash sales represent cash actually received; receivables collected represents the collection of amounts due for goods sold on credit; rental income is rent that will be collected in advance at the beginning of each month
- Disbursements: accounts payable to be paid in month following month of purchase
- Accounting and legal: to be paid upon receipt of bill, expected to be in the spring or after your fiscal year end financial statements have been completed
- Advertising: anticipated to be the same amount each month and paid for in the month the expense is incurred
- Automobile: anticipated to be the same amount each month and paid for in the month the expense is incurred
- Bank charges and interest: anticipated to be the same amount each month and paid for in the month the expense is incurred
- Equipment rental: to be paid for in monthly payments
- Income taxes: amount for taxes of the prior year and to be paid in the spring
- Insurance: annual premium to be paid quarterly, semi-annually, or annually in installments of equal amounts
- Loan repayment: amount is the same each month and paid in accordance with the monthly schedule furnished by the lending institution

- Office supplies and expenses: to be paid in month following receipt of invoice and supplies to be purchased on a quarterly basis

- Taxes and licenses: to be paid for upon receipt of invoice, expected to be in January and July

- Telephone: to be paid for in month following the month the expense is incurred; amount expected to be the same each month except in the last quarter when rates are expected to increase

- Utilities: expected to fluctuate with weather conditions and to be paid for in the month following the month the expense is incurred

- Wages and benefits: wages to increase at the beginning of the year; amount considered to be the same each month and paid for in the month the expense is incurred

- Miscellaneous: expected to be the same each month and paid for in the same month the expense is incurred

- Bad debts: varies

(e) Break-even analysis

- The break-even analysis is a critical calculation for every consulting business. Rather than calculating how much your firm would make if it attained an estimated sales volume, a more meaningful analysis determines at what sales volume your firm will break even. An estimated sales volume could be very unreliable as there are many factors which could affect revenue. Above the break-even sales volume it is only a matter of how much money your business can generate; below the break-even level of sales, it is only a matter of how many days a business can operate before bankruptcy.

- A break-even analysis provides a very real and meaningful figure to work toward; you may need to update it every few months to reflect your business growth

- The break-even point is where total costs are equal to total revenues

- The calculation of total costs is determined by adding variable costs onto the fixed costs

- Total costs are all costs of operating the business over a specified time period

- Variable costs are those that vary directly with the number of consulting services provided or marketing and promotion activities undertaken. These typically include automobile expenses, business travel expenses, supplies, brochures, etc. Variable costs are not direct costs which are passed on to the client in the billing.

- Fixed costs are costs that do not generally vary with the number of clients serviced. Also known as indirect costs, these costs typically include salaries, rent, secretarial service, insurance, telephone, accounting and legal supplies.

18. *Financing and capitalization*

(a) Term loan applied for
- The amount, terms, and when required

(b) Purpose of term loan
- Attach a detailed description of the aspects of the business to be financed

(c) Owner's equity
- The amount of your financial commitment to the business

(d) Summary of term loan requirements
- For a particular consulting project or for the business as a whole

19. *Operating loan*

(a) Line of credit applied for
- A new line of credit or an increase, and security offered

(b) Maximum operating cash required
- Amount required, timing of need (refer to "cash flow forecast")

20. *Present financing (if applicable)*

(a) Term loans outstanding
- The balance owing, repayment terms, purpose, security, and status

(b) Current operating line of credit
- The amount and security held

21. References

(a) Name of present lending institution
- Branch and type of accounts

(b) Lawyer's name
- Lawyer's address and telephone number

(c) Accountant's name
- Accountant's address and telephone number

22. Appendix

The nature of the contents of the appendixes attached, if any, depends on the circumstances and requirements of the lender or investor, or the desire to enhance the loan proposal. It is recommended that the appendices be prepared for your own benefit and reference to assist your business analysis, and to be available if the information is required. The following list is a guide only. Some of the headings described may be unavailable or unnecessary.

(a) Personal net worth statement
- Includes personal property values, investments, cash, bank loans, charge accounts, mortgages, and other liabilities. This will substantiate the value of your personal guarantee if required for security.
- See Sample 8

(b) Letter of intent
- Potential orders for client commitments

(c) Description of personal and business insurance coverage
- Include insurance policies and amount of coverage

(d) Accounts receivable summary
- Include aging schedule of 30-, 60-, and 90-day periods
- See Sample 9

SAMPLE 4 — Continued

(e) Accounts payable summary
   - Include a schedule of payments and total amounts owing

(f) Legal agreements
   - Include a copy of contracts, leases, and other documents

(g) Appraisals
   - Fair market value of business property and equipment

(h) Financial statements for associated companies
   - Where appropriate, a lender may require this information

(i) Copies of your brochure

(j) Testimonial letters from clients

(k) References

(l) Sales forecast and market surveys

(m) List of investors

(n) Credit status information

(o) News articles about you and your business

SAMPLE 5
OPENING BALANCE SHEET (NEW BUSINESS)

DATE: _____ NAME OF COMPANY: _____

ASSETS

Current assets
- Cash and bank accounts .... $ _____
- Accounts receivable .... $ _____
- Inventory .... $ _____
- Prepaid rent .... $ _____
- Other current assets .... $ _____

TOTAL CURRENT ASSETS (A) $ _____

Fixed assets
- Land and buildings .... $ _____
- Furniture, fixtures, and equipment .... $ _____
- Automobiles .... $ _____
- Leasehold improvements .... $ _____
- Other assets .... $ _____

TOTAL FIXED AND OTHER ASSETS (B) $ _____

TOTAL ASSETS (A + B = C) (C) $ _____

LIABILITIES

Current liabilities (debt due within next 12 months)
- Bank loans .... $ _____
- Loans — other .... $ _____
- Accounts payable .... $ _____
- Current portion of long-term debt .... $ _____
- Other current liabilities .... $ _____

TOTAL CURRENT LIABILITIES (D) $ _____

Long-term debt

Mortgages and liens payable (attach details) $ _____

Less: current portion $ _____

Loans from partners or stockholders (owner's equity) $ _____

Other loans of long-term nature $ _____

TOTAL LONG-TERM DEBT (E) $ _____

TOTAL LIABILITIES (D + E = F) (F) $ _____

NET WORTH (C - F = G) (G) $ _____

TOTAL NET WORTH AND LIABILITIES (F + G = H) (H) $ _____

SAMPLE 6
INCOME AND EXPENSE STATEMENT FORECAST (NEW BUSINESS)

(Name of business)

For the period: _____ months ending _____ , 20 _____

PROJECTED INCOME
    SALES

    _____ $ _____

    _____ $ _____

    TOTAL SALES $ _____

    OTHER INCOME $ _____

TOTAL INCOME   (A) $ _____

PROJECTED EXPENSES
    SALES EXPENSES

      Commissions and salaries $ _____

      Travel $ _____

      Advertising $ _____

      Automotive $ _____

      Other $ _____

    TOTAL SELLING EXPENSES   (B) $ _____

    ADMINISTRATIVE AND FINANCIAL EXPENSES

      Management salaries (or proprietor/partner draws) $ _____

      Office salaries $ _____

      Professional fees $ _____

      Office expense and supplies $ _____

      Telephone $ _____

      Rent $ _____

      Interest and bank charges $ _____

      Inventory $ _____

      Bad debt $ _____

      Other $ _____

    TOTAL ADMINISTRATIVE AND FINANCIAL EXPENSES   (C) $ _____

TOTAL EXPENSES (B + C = D)   (D) $ _____

OPERATING PROFIT (LOSS) (A - D) $ _____

Add: Other income $ _____

Less: Provisions for income taxes $ _____

NET PROFIT (LOSS) $ _____

SAMPLE 7
CASH FLOW BUDGET WORKSHEET

	JANUARY		FEBRUARY		MARCH	
	Estimated	Actual	Estimated	Actual	Estimated	Actual
Cash at beginning of month:						
In bank and on hand	$	$	$	$	$	$
In investments	$	$	$	$	$	$
TOTAL CASH	$	$	$	$	$	$
Plus income during month:						
Cash sales (include credit cards)						
Credit sales payments						
Investment income						
Receivables collected						
Loans						
Personal investment						
Other cash income						
TOTAL CASH AND INCOME	$	$	$	$	$	$
Expenses during the month:						
Rent (if applicable)						
Utilities						
Phone						
Postage						
Office equipment and furniture						
Stationery and business cards						
Insurance (health, fire, liability, theft, etc.)						
Answering service						
Printing and supplies						

Typing/secretarial service			
Accounting and legal services			
Advertising and promotion			
Business licenses and permits			
Dues and subscriptions			
Books and reference materials			
Travel: in town			
Travel: out of town			
Conventions, professional meetings, trade shows			
Continuing education			
Entertainment			
Contributions			
Gifts			
Salaries			
Unemployment insurance			
Pensions			
Miscellaneous			
Loan repayment			
Other cash expenses			
TOTAL EXPENSES	$_____ $_____	$_____ $_____	$_____ $_____
Cash flow excess (deficit) at end of month	$_____	$_____	$_____
Cash flow cumulative (monthly)	$_____	$_____	$_____

SAMPLE 8
PERSONAL NET WORTH STATEMENT

Date: _____

Name: _____

Address: _____

GENERAL INFORMATION

Phone: Home _____ Business _____ Age_____ M or S

Dependents including spouse _____

Present employer _____

Position occupied _____

How long with this employer _____

Previous employer _____ How long_____

Landlord _____

Address _____

Monthly rental $_____

Salary, wages or commission per annum $ _____

Other income per annum $ _____

Source _____

Guarantees on debts of others:

Name _____ Amount _____

Name _____ Amount _____

ASSETS

Bank accounts _____

Stocks at cost (market value _____) _____

Bonds at cost (market value _____) _____

Life insurance (cash surrender value) _____

     Beneficiary _____

Automobile: year_____ make _____ _____

Home: registered

      building size_____ lot size _____ _____

Other assets _____

                            TOTAL _____

LIABILITIES

Bank loan _____

Charge accounts _____

Policy loans on life insurance _____

Other loans _____

Installment purchases _____

Mortgages: Interest rate _____

 Term_____ Payments_____ _____

Taxes _____

Other liabilities _____

     SUB TOTAL _____

NET WORTH _____

      TOTAL _____

(Name of company)

SAMPLE 9
STATEMENT OF ACCOUNTS RECEIVABLE

AS AT _____ 20 __

Date: _____

_____

(Name of company)

Names of debtors	Total	Current	31-60 Days	61-90 Days	Over 90 Days& Holdbacks	Remarks

1. Sub totals $ _____

2. Aggregate of accounts
   under $ _____ $ _____

3. Number of
   accounts _____ No. ___ No. ___ No. ___ No. ___ No. ___

4. TOTALS $_____
   Percentage   100%   %   %   %   %

CHAPTER 7
HOW TO OBTAIN FINANCING

Having completed your business plan and financial projections, you should now have a clear idea of your short-term and medium-term financial needs. You will want to be familiar with the types of financing available, the various sources, how to approach financial lending institutions, and the type of security that may be required. You should also be aware of the reasons that lending institutions or investors may turn down a request for funding. These matters and other issues are covered in this chapter.

1. TYPES OF FINANCING

There are two basic types of financing: equity and debt.

1.1 Equity

The money that you put into a company or business is equity. Initially all money must come from your own resources such as savings or personal borrowing from financial institutions, friends, relatives, or business associates. As time progresses, retained earnings in the business will increase your equity.

If you have formed a corporation, you can "buy" one or more shares and lend the rest of the money to the corporation as a "shareholder's loan." The advantages of a shareholder's loan are:

(a) Lenders consider these loans as equity as long as the money is left in the company.

(b) It is easier to repay the loan than sell shares back to the company or to other investors.

(c) Interest may be paid. For example, if you or your friends would like to earn a return on your investment, an interest rate may be established. The alternative is to pay dividends on shares when funds are available.

(d) Interest is tax deductible to the company.

1.2 Debt

A debt is a loan. It must be repaid, and the lender will charge interest on the money you have borrowed. With borrowed money, normally the principal with interest is paid back on a fixed monthly payment. You therefore have to include the principal and interest payments in a current business plan. Various forms of debt financing are discussed below.

1.2a Short-term or operating loan (demand loan)

Short-term or operating loans are used for financing inventory, accounts receivable, special purchases or promotions, and other items requiring working capital during peak periods.

The main sources of short-term loans are commercial banks or similar financial institutions. Using a short-term loan is a good way to establish credit with a bank. This type of loan can be unsecured or secured by your personal or business assets.

Short-term loans are usually negotiated for specific periods of time; for example, 30, 60, or 90 days and frequently for periods up to a year or more. They may be repayable in a lump sum at the end of the period or in periodic installments, such as monthly.

Other characteristics of a demand loan include:

- The interest rate at time of signing may be lower than for a term loan.

- There is a fluctuating interest rate.

- Repayment of the loan can be demanded at any time by the lender; this usually only occurs when the account does not perform satisfactorily or in case of serious deterioration in the affairs of the business.

- A short-term loan can often be obtained more quickly than a term loan.

1.2b Line of credit

A line of credit is an agreement between you and the lender (a bank or similar financial institution) specifying the maximum amount of credit (overdraft) the bank will allow you at any one time for general operating purposes.

Credit lines are usually established for one-year periods, subject to annual renegotiation and renewal. Other characteristics of a line of credit include:

- Loan funds increase and decrease as you use the money or make deposits. This is referred to as a revolving line of credit.

- They are available from most banks.

- There is a fluctuating interest rate.

- The interest rate at time of signing may be lower than for a term loan.

- The lender uses accounts receivable (the money owed to you by customers) and inventory as the security. For accounts receivable, the lender may lend between 50% and 75% of the value, not including amounts over 90 days. For inventory, a lender may lend up to 50%.

- A line of credit can often be obtained more quickly than a term loan.

- Repayment of the loan can be demanded at any time by the lender or the line of credit can be reduced; usually this only occurs when the account does not perform satisfactorily or in a case of serious deterioration in the affairs of the business, or reduction in the value of the security provided.

- The amount of credit granted is based on the lender's assessment of the creditworthiness of the company, its principals, and the credit requested, among other factors.

1.2c Term loans

A term loan is generally money borrowed for a term of from 1 to 15 years. A term loan is usually amortized. In other words, the regular loan payments include principal and interest and are for a fixed aggregate amount over the life or term of the loan agreement.

Term loans are commonly used to provide funds for the purchase of an existing business, to help finance expansions or capital expenditures, and to provide additional working capital for a growing business.

While the majority of term loans are secured by collateral such as fixed assets or other chattels (cars, building, land, equipment, etc.), the lender places great importance on the ability of the borrower to repay his or her indebtedness out of the business's earnings over the life of the loan.

The main characteristics of a term loan are:

- It may be repaid over a period of time generally related to the useful "life" of the assets; for example, car — three to five years; land and building — after three years.

- The lender will only give you a percentage of the value; for example, car — 80%; building — 75%. The other 20% or 25% of the cost of the asset must come from the equity you have in the company or new funds from shareholders or yourself.

- The company must be able to show the lender that future sales will generate enough cash to repay the loan.

- There are different lenders for different types of term loans. One consideration in the approval of your proposal is "leverage" or "debt to equity ratio." This is the ratio of the money you owe to the money you put in the business. Generally, the lender's assessment of this ratio is discretionary, but if you are a new business, or just building up a reputation, it is unlikely that the lender will want to go beyond 2:1 or even 1:1. Consequently, this may place an additional restriction on the amount that you can borrow.

- Interest rate at time of signing is slightly higher than for a demand loan.

- Your payments, principal plus interest, are all the same.

- Repayment period of loan is specified and agreed upon in advance.

- It could take a longer time to obtain a loan approval than a demand loan.

1.2d Trade credit or supplier financing

This is the most often used form of short-term financing. This means that a supplier will not insist on immediate payment for purchase of merchandise. Terms of payment — generally 30 to 90 days — can be arranged between both parties.

1.2e Renting or leasing

Renting or leasing assets is an alternative form of financing. Leasing companies will consider arranging a lease with an option to purchase on virtually any tangible asset. Renting premises, as opposed to buying a building, is also a financing alternative. Typewriters, office furniture, computers, automobiles, and telephone equipment are examples of assets that can be leased or rented. The advantages of leasing are:

- It frees up equity capital for investment in areas of greater return.
- It frees up borrowing power for the more critical areas of the business.
- There is no down payment requirement with leasing.
- Rates are usually fixed for a set term.
- The full payment is an allowable expense.
- Purchase options can be exercised at a later date at a predetermined price.

There are also disadvantages. You should discuss the tax and financial considerations with your accountant before you make your decision.

2. SOURCES OF FINANCING
2.1 Equity

The most common source of equity capital is personal funds from savings. In exchange for the funds provided to the company, the owner obtains all the shares of the corporation or ownership of the business.

Equity can be further increased from the savings of friends willing to invest, or even from relatives. However, many small business people have created problems by bringing in friends or relatives as investors.

Conflicts generally occur if the business is not doing as well as everyone initially imagined, or if the terms and conditions of such loans are not clearly spelled out, or if the lenders or investors insist on becoming involved in day-to-day operations.

Any agreement should be documented in writing between the parties and signed in advance to eliminate any misunderstanding. Agreement should be reached on the rate of interest to be paid, when the loans will be repaid, any options you have to pay them back early, and the procedures that all parties will follow if the loans become delinquent. Consult competent legal counsel in advance to protect your interests.

An equity investment can be in the form of stockholder loans, or common stock or shares in the company, or a combination of loans and shares. The investment structure will vary in each situation.

Generally, the advantage of money being invested as shareholder loans is that it can be paid back to lenders without tax, other than personal tax and interest you receive before the loan is paid off.

If the money is in the form of shares, it is much more difficult to withdraw since shares must be sold to someone else and may be subject to capital gains tax.

Long-term debt investors may therefore place restrictions or conditions on when and how the company can pay off shareholder loans, redeem shares, or possibly even pay dividends on shares. These restrictions or conditions are imposed to protect the long-term debt invested.

The advice of a tax accountant is recommended since your personal tax situation and that of other potential equity investors could have a bearing on whether the shareholder investment should be in the form of loans or purchase of shares.

2.2 Debt

Commercial banks are a major source of capital for new and continuing small ventures. Additional organizations that provide financing include insurance companies, pension companies, real estate investment, trust, commercial, and mortgage banks, and even trust companies and credit unions.

2.2a Small Business Administration (United States)

You may wish to consider the Small Business Administration (SBA) in the United States. The SBA was created by the federal government to assist entrepreneurs. Since 1953, the SBA has expanded to include many activities including finance and training.

The SBA is organized in ten regions and each region is subdivided, providing branch offices in many areas. SBA guidelines defining who qualifies for small business assistance vary, depending on the general classification of the enterprise. As the lender of final resort, the SBA tries not to compete with or replace the private banking system but to supplement it. There are various types of loans available from the SBA, the most common one being guaranteed loans.

Since the SBA's loan regulations do change from time to time, you should verify current conditions by contacting your nearest branch of the SBA (listed in the telephone directory under U.S. Government) or write to: Small Business Administration, Washington, DC 20416.

2.2b Business Development Bank of Canada (Canada)

In Canada, the Business Development Bank of Canada (BDC) was established by the federal government especially to help those companies that could have difficulty obtaining financing. To obtain BDC financing, the amount of your investment in the business must generally be sufficient to ensure that you are committed to it and that the business may reasonably be expected to be successful.

BDC financing is available as loans, loan guarantees, equity financing, export receivables financing, or any combination of these methods in whatever way best suits the particular needs of your business. The BDC also assists with financial packaging; for a fee, the BDC can make arrangements with other institutions or investors on your behalf. If loans are involved, the interest rates are usually at higher rates than those offered by chartered banks.

If you wish to obtain further information, contact your local branch of the BDC or write to Business Development Bank of Canada, 800 Victoria Square, Montreal, Quebec H2Z 1C8

3. COMPETITION BETWEEN LENDERS

There is considerable competition among banks and other financial institutions. Compare at least three different financial institutions to assess the most favorable loan package available.

All aspects of financial dealings are negotiable. Obtain the lending terms in writing before you sign. Have your outside advisers, such as your accountant or lawyer, review the terms. In addition, you may want to obtain the advice of your associates. Don't rush into a relationship with a financial institution without reasonably exploring all the other alternatives.

4. TIPS ON APPROACHING YOUR LENDER

When you approach a financial institution, you must sell the merits of your business proposal. As in all sales presentations, consider the needs and expectations of the other party — in this case, the loans officer. A loans officer will be interested in the following:

(a) Your familiarity with the business concept and the realities of the marketplace as reflected in your detailed business plan.

(b) Your ability to service the debt with sufficient surplus to cover contingencies, including carrying interest charges, and eventually repay the debt in full as demonstrated in your cash flow forecast and projected income statement.

(c) Your level of commitment as shown by your equity in the business or cash investment in the particular asset being purchased.

(d) Your secondary source of repayment, including security in the event of default, and other sources of income.

(e) Your track record and integrity as shown in your personal credit history, your business plan, and business results or past business experience.

(f) Your approach. During the loan interview remember you're doing business just as you do when you're with a client. Don't be subservient, overly familiar, or too aggressive. Keep in mind that a lender is in business for the same reason you are — to make a profit. Keep the profit motive in mind during the interview. Don't try to appeal to a lender's social conscience. It won't work, since loans aren't granted for their social impact.

(g) Your judgment in supplying information. Be sensible about the number of documents you provide at the outset. You do not want to overwhelm the loans officer with too much material. For example, the introductory page, summary, and financial plan sections provide a good basic loan submission if the amount requested is small. You should have all other documents prepared and available if requested.

(h) Your personal appearance. You should present yourself in a manner that projects self-confidence and success.

(i) Your mental alertness. What time during the day are you at your mental peak? This should be the time that you arrange for an interview with the loans officer.

(j) Your consideration in allowing sufficient lead time for approval. The lender needs a reasonable time to assess your proposal. Also, the loan may have to be referred to another level within the financial institution for review.

(k) Your credit rating. It's a good idea to review your credit rating periodically, as there may be errors to correct in your file. Note your positive and negative points so you can discuss them when raised by the lender.

If your request for financing is approved, find out everything you need to know about the conditions, terms, payment methods, interest rates, security requirements, and any other fees to be paid. No commitment to accept the financing should be made until all this information is provided and understood and its impact on the proposed business analyzed. Ask your accountant and lawyer to assist you in the loan application in advance and review the

bank's approval. Make certain you get the approval particulars in writing.

5. WHY LOANS ARE TURNED DOWN

If a request for financing is not approved, find out why. Use the lender's experience to your advantage. Lenders handle many requests for financing and have experience in the financial aspects of many businesses, even if they do not have direct management experience.

If there is something specifically wrong with the financing proposal, see if it can be corrected and then reapply. If not, use this knowledge when approaching other potential lenders or on future occasions when seeking funds.

A loan could be rejected for the following reasons:

(a) The business idea was considered unsound or too risky. A lender's judgment is generally based on past performance of other businesses similar to the one you are proposing.

(b) Insufficient collateral. A lender must be satisfied that there are sufficient assets pledged to meet the outstanding debt if your business does not succeed financially. If you are just starting a business, a lender generally requires you to pledge personal assets, such as your home, car, and other securities, against the loan. If you are borrowing funds under a corporate name, your personal guarantee will generally be requested and in some cases your spouse's guarantee as well, depending on the circumstances. You may therefore not have sufficient security required for the amount of loan you are requesting or for the degree of risk, in the lender's opinion, that might be involved.

(c) Lack of financial commitment on your part. A lender will be reluctant to approve loan financing for business ventures if you are not fully committed. The lender does not want to foreclose or repossess and then have to sell assets to collect your money. The lender will therefore want to know how much personal financial capital you have made available to the business venture in order to assess your commitment to repay the loan. If you have not made any financial commitment and yet have security that you wish to pledge, the security alone may not be sufficient.

(d) Lack of a business plan or a poor business plan. A lender could reject your loan application if you have not prepared a detailed business plan or do not understand its significance.

(e) The purpose of the loan is not explained or is not acceptable. It is important that the specific use of the funds being borrowed be outlined in detail. It is also important that the purpose and amount of funds being requested be reasonable and appropriate. For example, it could be considered unreasonable for you to calculate a large draw or salary from your business in the first six months. If you intend to use the loan to pay off past debts or financial obligations, it may not be approved since the funds would not be directly generating cash flow for your new business venture.

(f) Your character, personality, or stability can affect a lender's decision. It is important to appear confident, enthusiastic, well-informed, and realistic. If your personality is not consistent with the personality required for your type of business in the eyes of the lender, it could have a negative effect. If you are going through a separation or divorce proceedings or have declared personal bankruptcy or had business failures in the past, these factors could have an adverse impact on your loan application.

6. TYPES OF SECURITY A LENDER MAY REQUIRE

Lenders primarily lend money to businesses that exhibit a strong potential to repay the loan. Nevertheless, they want to be covered in case of a default. Sometimes your signature is the only security the lender needs when making a loan. The kind and amount of security depends on the lender and on the borrower's situation. The most common types of security or collateral are endorser, co-maker, guarantor, promissory note, demand loan, realty mortgage, chattel mortgage, assignment of accounts receivable, postponement of claim, pledge of stocks and bonds, and assignment of life insurance.

6.1 Endorser

Borrowers often get other people to sign a note in order to bolster their own credit. An endorser is contingently liable for the note he or she signs. If the borrower fails to pay off the loan, the lender expects the endorser to make the note good. Sometimes the endorser may be asked to pledge assets or securities as well.

6.2 Co-maker

A co-maker is a person who takes on an obligation jointly with the borrower. In such cases, the lender can collect directly from either the maker or the co-maker.

6.3 Guarantor

A guarantor is a person who guarantees the payment of a note by signing a guarantee commitment. Both private and government lenders commonly require a personal guarantor from officers of corporations as security for loans advanced to the corporation. If the corporation defaults in its financial obligations, the lender has a choice of suing the guarantor or the corporation or both for the monies outstanding. Try to negotiate a limited guarantee to cover the shortfall in the security if other securities have been pledged. Be very careful not to sign a personal guarantee for the full amount of the loan if at all possible. Recover your guarantee as soon as the business has paid off its obligation or can carry the debt on its own security. Resist having your spouse sign a personal guarantee of your debts. Your personal guarantee is often all you have left to negotiate with on another occasion.

6.4 Promissory note

A promissory note is a written promise to pay a specified sum of money to the lender, either on demand or at a specified future time.

6.5 Demand loan

A demand loan involves a written promise to pay the amount of monies outstanding to the lender upon demand.

6.6 Realty mortgage

A lender may require a mortgage against your property for the advancement of funds. It could be a first, second, or third mortgage against your property, or a collateral mortgage to a guarantee or demand note.

6.7 Chattel mortgage

A chattel mortgage is on specific property, such as a car or boat, other than land and buildings. The title of the chattel remains in the name of the borrower, but a lien against the chattel is placed in favor of the lender.

6.8 Assignment of accounts receivable

A borrower may have to assign the business receivables to the lender to secure an operating line of credit or other loan. The borrower still collects the receivables, but in a default, the lender will assume collection. The assignment is supported by submitting a list of the business receivables each month.

6.9 Postponement of claim

If there are any loans from shareholders, the lender may ask for an agreement that the company will not repay the shareholders until the lender has been repaid in full.

6.10 Pledge of stocks or bonds

The possession of stocks and bonds may be transferred to the lender, but title remains with the borrower. The security must be marketable. As a protection against market declines and possible expenses of liquidation, banks usually lend no more than 75% of the market value of "blue chip stock." On federal government or municipal bonds, they may be willing to lend 90% or more of their market value.

The lender may ask the borrower for additional security or payment whenever the market value of the stocks or bonds drops below the lender's required margin.

6.11 Assignment of life insurance

A lender may request that the borrower assign the proceeds of a life insurance policy to the lender up to the amount outstanding at the time of death of the borrower. Another form of assignment is against the cash surrender value of a life insurance policy. Banks generally lend up to the cash value of a life insurance policy.

CHAPTER 8
KEEPING RECORDS

A consultant must keep accurate and thorough financial records covering all income received and expenses incurred. Records help in producing income, controlling expenses, planning growth and cash flow, keeping tax payments to a legal minimum, and complying with the multitude of regulatory requirements. This chapter explains the basic concepts and procedures of keeping records and outlines some of the issues you will have to discuss with your accountant and bookkeeper.

1. ACCOUNTING AND BOOKKEEPING

Accounting is the process of analyzing and systematically recording, in terms of money or some other unit of measurement, operations or transactions of the business. To capture these facts and figures, a system is necessary. Such a system usually consists of

bookkeeping records which may be set up in journals, ledgers, or other records.

A professional accountant can help design a system for recording the information each consultant needs in his or her particular circumstance. Some tips on selecting an accountant are outlined in chapter 5.

Bookkeeping is the process of classifying and recording business transactions in the books of account. A bookkeeper keeps the various records, journals, and ledgers current and accurate.

Many consultants are not inclined or do not know how to maintain the books. A part-time bookkeeper can be employed to keep the books either at your home or place of business, or at the bookkeeper's office. It is highly advisable that a professional accountant establish a system for your books.

You can then hire a bookkeeper recommended by your accountant or by a business associate you trust.

Make sure the bookkeeper is competent to handle your specific type of records, as some bookkeepers specialize in certain areas. The costs of a bookkeeper are considerably lower than those for a professional accountant, and normally range between $15 to $25 per hour or more, depending on experience and whether your records are manual or on computer. Bookkeepers are not qualified to provide tax advice. Only an experienced tax accountant is able to provide you with the necessary tax planning information.

Different kinds of bookkeeping systems are discussed below.

1.1 Separate record-keeping

It is essential that your business books and records be kept separate from your personal books, records, and bank accounts. This is not only required by tax regulations, but is also sound business management. Separate records will allow you to control cash flow, budget for expenses, and draw up financial statements. A separate bank account for the business has the following advantages:

- Financial statements can be drawn and taxable income computed easily.

- When all income is deposited into the business account, the income journal is maintained by the bank in the form of complete records of all receipts.

- Applications for financing for business purposes can be prepared more accurately with business account records.

- All business expenses can be proven from one source.

- Personal draws can be budgeted carefully and completely controlled. Funds can be taken from the business account periodically and deposited into the personal account as draws or salary.

1.2 Double-entry and single-entry bookkeeping

Double-entry bookkeeping is usually the preferred method for keeping business records. Transactions are entered first in a journal, then monthly totals of the transactions are posted to the appropriate ledger accounts. The ledger accounts include five categories: income, expense, asset, liability, and net worth. Income and expense accounts are closed each year; asset, liability, and net worth accounts are maintained on a permanent and continuing basis.

Single-entry bookkeeping is not as complete as a double-entry method. This system, however, is relatively simple and records the flow of income and expense through a daily summary of cash receipts, a monthly summary of receipts, and a monthly disbursements journal, such as a checkbook.

Your accountant will advise you about the appropriate system for your needs.

1.3 One-write accounting system

"One-write" is an accounting system where all the sales you make are automatically, through carbon paper, posted to a sales journal and monthly ledger card (for sending out statements) on the receivables side, and all the checks are posted to the proper expense journal on the payables side. The one-write system is also effective for showing the "aged" balance of receivables. In other words, it shows who owes you how much for 30, 60, 90, or over 90 days.

You may use the system either for receivables or payables or both. It makes record-keeping very simple for you and your accountant, and is particularly useful if you write 50 or more checks and statements each month. If you are using the one-write system for payables, it automatically posts the checks written to a cash disbursement journal and all you need to do is summarize the sheet every 25 checks.

If you are interested in accounting systems, contact the suppliers under "Accounting Systems" in the Yellow Pages telephone directory.

1.4 Cash or accrual basis for records

Cash basis record-keeping is a method of recording transactions so that revenues and expenditures are reflected in the accounts in the period the related cash receipts or disbursements occur.

Accrual basis record-keeping is a method of recording transactions so that revenues and expenses are reflected in the accounts in the period they have been earned and incurred, whether or not such transactions have been finally settled. There are advantages and disadvantages of each system based on your circumstances. Your accountant will assist you in making the correct choice.

1.5 Computer software

There are many accounting and bookkeeping software programs available in the mar-

ketplace. Most have spreadsheets or are spreadsheet compatible. Ask your colleagues and accountant which programs they recommend and why. Comparison shop for the features and benefits that meet your current and projected needs.

2. BASIC ACCOUNTING RECORDS

As previously discussed, informal records consist of evidence of business transactions such as sales slips, invoices, checks, etc. These informal records are then gathered into a more formal structure. For accounting purposes, these formalized basic records are referred to as "books of original entries" or as "journals."

2.1 Sales journal

A sales journal is a daily register of both cash and charge sales. The sales, both cash and charge, may be recorded by numbered invoices and accounted for. The total is then entered as the day's sales in the sales journal.

2.2 Cash receipts journal

This journal often combines the function of a sales journal along with a record of all transactions resulting in money coming into the business. When combined, this journal is referred to as a "sales and cash receipts journal."

In the cash receipts journal, all cash sales, charge sales, collections on account, and total deposits to the bank are entered. This is usually done in conjunction with the cash receipts journal. Referred to as a "daily summary of sales and cash receipts," it is both a summarizing vehicle and a form of reconciliation between cash on hand, cash receipts, charge sales, and total sales.

A sales and cash receipts journal briefly describes the transaction, whether it is a cash sale or a charge sale, whether the cash receipt came from a source other than a sale, and the amount of the total deposit.

In summary, the journal will show:

(a) Cash sale

(b) Bank deposit

(c) Receipts on account from a client

(d) Other receipts

2.3 Accounts receivable ledger and control account

These records are separate. The accounts receivable ledger contains separate cards or sheets for each charge client and records the sale with the invoice number or reference, the date, and the amount of the sale. When payments are made, the amount of the payment is deducted from the balance owing and is cross-referenced to the cash receipts journal.

The control account records in total all the charge sales and all the payments by charge customers which are detailed individually in the accounts receivable ledger. At any given time, the sum of all the individual charge account balances in the subsidiary ledger will equal the total net balance in the control account. The accounts receivable aging schedule accompanies the accounts receivable ledger. This is a record of each charge customer that shows the balance owing and the age status of the charge — normally current, 30, 60, or 90 days.

In summary, each client has a ledger sheet that details name, address, telephone number, credit information, date of sale, invoice number, date of payment, receipt number, balance owing.

Periodically the individual balances are added up (usually once a month), and the totals are reconciled to the accounts receivable balance in the general ledger.

2.4 Accounts payable journal

This journal is usually a subsidiary journal to the cash disbursements journal. The accounts payable journal records invoices for purchases, the amount and date, and when the invoice has to be paid. This journal's purpose is primarily a control over the payables. It allows you to correctly determine outstanding liabilities and when these obligations must be met.

2.5 Cash disbursements journal

This journal records daily all cash outlays for purchases, expenses, payroll, cash withdrawals, and loan payments. The payee or account is referenced, the check number is given, the amount is specified, and the purpose of the disbursement, by amount, is shown under the proper heading for each day. The purpose could be payroll, inventory purchased, accounts payable falling due, tax payments, etc. Any disbursements, such as interest charges or withdrawals, are also recorded.

2.6 Payroll journal

This journal consists usually of two records. The first is the record for the individual employee; it shows the pay period, the gross amount earned, the deductions (income tax, unemployment insurance, pension plan) made at source, and the net earnings.

The second record is the "payroll summary" which, for the pay period, gives the total gross earnings, deductions, and net salaries paid to all employees. The total of the employees' salaries appears as an entry in the cash disbursements journal.

2.7 General ledger

The general ledger is the final book of entry in an accounting system. This record is required to complete even the most basic of bookkeeping systems. Every entry from the preceding journals and ledgers is listed in the general ledger. The general ledger must always be kept in balance; that is to say, all debits and credits must be equal, so that the net additions and subtractions equal zero. The general ledger is used to prepare financial statements. Because it is the book of final entry and a permanent record, none of the pages should ever be thrown away.

As it is important to understand the principles behind the bookkeeping records, it is recommended that you take one of the various bookkeeping courses that are available through the SBA (United States), BDC (Canada), community colleges, school board continuing education programs, and other educational facilities. Also see *Bookkeepers' Boot Camp: Get a Grip on Accounting Basics*, another title in the Self-Counsel Series.

2.8 Computer software for record-keeping

Most standard accounting software programs have the main bookkeeping record systems such as general ledger, accounts payable and receivable, aging of accounts, payroll, cash, and sales. Check with your local software store for products that might meet your needs.

3. NONFINANCIAL RECORDS

Administrative records can improve efficiency and profit. Nonfinancial records such as personnel records, tax records, and service records should be maintained.

3.1 Personnel records

Personnel records consist primarily of policies, benefits, and other matters pertaining to the general administration of the employees or consultants as a whole. Personnel records can also consist of individual records on each employee. These records contain all documents and correspondence relating to an employee from the time of applying for employment to termination. Individual employee records also include a summary of personal data, education and training, work history, and job and wage record.

3.2 Tax records

Tax records record details of sales taxes, income taxes, business taxes, and employee income tax deductions. Most business are regulated by a combination of federal, state/provincial, and municipal/county governments. The information for these records is obtained from different aspects of the business operations. For example, payroll deductions and service are obtained from the payroll records, and information on sales taxes collected comes from either the sales journal or the daily summary of sales and cash receipts.

Tax records detail assessments, rates, calculations, and remittances both by amount and date. Tax records also let you know when remittances must be made to avoid late filing penalties.

3.3 Service records

Service records are all the records associated with the provision of a service. Most important, these records are used to record, for each client, the cost of material, labor, and overhead. These calculations are then used to determine a price when bidding on a contract or presenting a proposal, or assessing the profitability of a particular activity or product.

Service records can also keep track of employee efficiency to control nonchargeable time and to identify activities that are not performed to expected standards.

4. OFFICE SYSTEMS

Office systems should be implemented to reduce exposure to liability and to increase business awareness and sound decision-making.

4.1 Handling new clients and projects

It is important that a form be developed to gather administrative information in a standard, consistent, and uniform manner to reduce the likelihood of an error or omission. The form should provide date and deadlines, as well as information that might give rise to potential conflicts of interest. You should have separate forms for prospective clients and new assignments. See Samples 10 and 11.

4.2 Time records

Maintenance of effective time records is critical in documenting what was done by the consultant or sub-consultant. Such records must be made as business is transacted.

Accurate time records are extremely important to ensure that clients are promptly charged and that you have accounted for all billable time expended. It is easy to forget time expended if you don't write it down immediately. Time records also reflect the expenditure of time for the benefit received, and whether or not your efficiency and profit are improving or certain activities or clients should be reconsidered. See Sample 12.

If there is a legal dispute, your time record and service documentation could make the difference between winning and losing. Keep your time records in a detailed fashion as if you had to introduce them as evidence into court. The odds are that at some point in your consulting career you will have to do so. Consider using a "daytimer" type of system for time keeping. Carry it with you at all times and transfer all notations to your daily time record docket sheet. You should get into the habit of recording all your daily activities in your daytimer, whether client related or not, so that you can graphically analyze how your time is spent. For example, make a note of hours spent each day on client entertainment, marketing, professional development, and research.

4.3 Standard form engagement letters or contracts

You should have your lawyer help you develop letters of agreement and contracts that you can modify for each particular situation. It is important that the services to be performed and fee to be rendered are clearly outlined in a written contract.

4.4 Billing, credit, and collection

Monthly or interim billing should be done whenever possible. This means bills can be sent close to the time the work was done. It also keeps your cash flow even and enables you to spot fee disputes while there is still time to remedy the problem. An effective system can include a standard credit application form, client account record, etc. This subject is covered in detail in chapter 12.

4.5 Calendars

Important dates and deadlines should be entered into an effective calendar system that will provide a double-check on entries, adequate lead time for performance of tasks, deadlines, limitation dates, secretarial administration of the system, input by associates and sub-consultants as appropriate, and follow-up to ensure that the performance has occurred.

4.6 Filing systems

An effective filing system should be developed to eliminate the possibility of misplacement of client materials. A filing reference system should be designed for speedy retrieval of client information.

4.7 Computer systems

Manual systems provide efficient office management, but you may want to consider the benefits of a computer system. All the elements of a full accounting record can be retained on a computer data base. This will save time and money. Automatic backups and off-site storage of data protect your records in case of system failure or a power surge. There are software programs available with time systems, standardized contracts, etc.

SAMPLE 10
PROSPECTIVE CLIENT SHEET

File # _____

Telephone _____

Name _____

Address _____

_____

LEAD

Date of inquiry _____

Person making inquiry _____

Source of referral _____

Nature of initial inquiry _____

Consultant contacted _____

Follow-up planned _____

Dates of:

    Phone conversations _____

    Meetings _____

    Correspondence _____

Total time expended on client prior
    to any proposal preparation _____

Status _____

PROPOSAL

Presentation date of proposal _____

Time required to complete proposal _____

Cost estimate _____

Consultant with primary

responsibility for assignment _____

Disposition of proposal _____

ASSIGNMENT

Starting date _____

Consultant(s) assigned _____

Primary client contact _____

Total billing _____

Completion date _____

SAMPLE 11
NEW CONSULTING ASSIGNMENT SHEET

File #_____ Consultant in charge _____ New client ( )

Old client ( )

Client _____ Date opened _____

Address _____ Phone _____

Contact person(s) _____

Cross index _____

Assignment _____

Type of work:

( ) Feasibility study ( ) Marketing study ( ) Research

( ) Grant acquisition ( ) Organizational study ( ) Speaking engagement

( ) Management study ( ) Personnel/labor study ( ) Training

( ) Other_____

Fees (costs additional):

Person/Class	Rate	Per	Range quoted $ to	$ _____
			Minimum quoted	$ _____
			Time value	$ _____

Other fee arrangements (method of payment) _____

Costs (projected) _____

Total fees and costs _____

Source of client contact _____

Promised completion date _____

Expected completion date _____

Opened by _____

CLOSING INFORMATION

Assignment completed on _____

Time value $_____ Total fee rec'd $_____ Variance $_____

Client available for reference: Yes ( ) No ( )

SAMPLE 12
TIME AND SERVICE RECORD

Date	Client No.	Client Name	Service	Service Code	Loc'n Code	Time		By
						Hours	Decimal Conv.	

					TOTAL TIME:		

Services codes			Local code
1 ADV Advice	7 Ent Entretain	13 REV Review	A In Town
2 AP Appear	8 INT Interview	14 SEC Secretarial	B Out of Town
3 AUD Audit	9 INV Investigate	15 TCF Phone call from	C Client's Office
4 CON Conference	10 OF Office	16 TCT Phone call to	D Other
5 DIC Dictate	11 PR Promotion	17 TVL Travel	
6 DR Draft	12 RES Research	18 TR Rain	

Decimal Conversion:

6 minutes = .1 hour	36 minutes = .6 hour
12 minutes = .2 hour	42 minutes = .7 hour
18 minutes = .3 hour	48 minutes = .8 hour
24 minutes = .4 hour	54 minutes = .9 hour
30 minutes = .5 hour	60 minutes = 1.0 hour

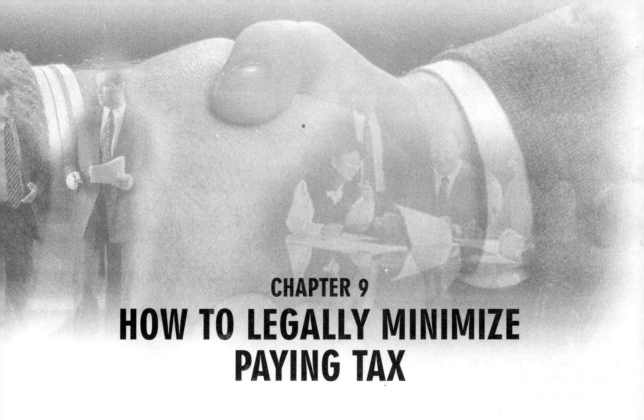

CHAPTER 9
HOW TO LEGALLY MINIMIZE PAYING TAX

It is very important to obtain professional advice on tax planning. An accountant who specializes in tax should be retained before you start your business to advise you on all the various considerations. Because tax legislation changes constantly and varies by jurisdiction, it is highly recommended that you ask an accountant to obtain current tax advice in your specific situation. It is essential that advance tax and administrative planning be done to minimize frustration and expense. If you are based in the United States but intend to provide consulting services in Canada, make sure that you obtain tax compliance advice from a Canadian accountant.

This chapter gives an overview of some of the key areas to consider when discussing your new business with your professional advisers. Your advisers will review the business plan you have prepared, your personal financial circumstances, and your anticipated profit, and then recommend the correct approach for your needs.

1. TAX AVOIDANCE AND TAX EVASION

The distinction between tax avoidance and tax evasion should be made clear. Tax avoidance is the principle by which the consultant plans his or her transactions within the law using all available tax planning benefits to minimize the liability for paying income taxes.

Tax evasion is an action that is outside the law and normally implies the receipt of monies without declaring them as income. Tax evasion is criminal in nature and can result in serious consequences including jail.

2. CASH OR ACCRUAL METHOD

Consultants have a choice about the method of accounting for financial transactions. Based on your individual situation, one method may be more attractive than the other. The cash basis of accounting is a method of recording transactions in which revenues and expenditures are entered in the accounts during the period in which the related cash receipts or disbursements occur.

The accrual basis of accounting is a method of recording transactions in which revenues and expenses are entered in the accounts during the period in which they have been earned and incurred, whether or not such transactions have been finally settled.

Tax planning is particularly difficult for cash basis consultants because expenses are generally deductible in the period paid, and income is generally taxable as it is received. For accrual basis consultants, the problem is simplified in that cash does not need to exchange hands for the recognition of income, at least not within the tax period. For either type of method, the intent is that income and expenses be matched within like periods.

An example of tax planning for the consultant who reports on a cash basis is found in the timing of bill payment. Toward the end of the year, the cash basis consultant should maximize allowable deductions by paying all bills applying to that tax year before the year closes. Accordingly, it is not wise to request advance payments from current clients before the year is closed.

3. FISCAL YEAR-END

The choice of fiscal year may depend on consideration of financial savings for accounting fees, tax deferral in the first year, and administrative convenience.

It is prudent to select a fiscal year distinct from the calendar year if you intend to retain accountants for annual audit or tax purposes. January through April is the busiest time for accountants, and you are likely to have better service and more attention paid to your financial affairs if your corporate fiscal year ends, for example, in July rather than in February.

If you experience seasonal changes in business volume, it may be wise to tailor a fiscal year-end along seasonal lines. Ask yourself if you are particularly busy at a certain time of the year. For example, if you are a consultant who specializes in education, you will likely be busiest in the winter and relatively free during the summer months. If you are a consultant to the retail business, you may be busiest during the period of time leading up to the holidays.

In these cases, you might benefit from structuring the fiscal year-end so that the highest concentration of income occurs in the beginning of the fiscal year. By doing this, you have the remainder of the year to plan for taxes, take care of business development for the next fiscal year, and regulate cash flow effectively.

4. CORPORATIONS, PROPRIETORSHIPS, OR PARTNERSHIPS

The tax implications of a proprietorship and a partnership are the same. The net income or net loss from the proprietorship or your share of the partnership are declared on your personal income tax filings. Depending on your level of taxation, you could be paying more tax than if you were incorporated.

Your particular situation will determine whether or not it is best to incorporate for tax reasons. Factors to consider include your salary draw level, value of benefits a corporation would absorb, tax bracket, and projected growth patterns. The immediate and long-range tax liability of the individual is a governing factor.

Remember, in the United States an exception to the normal corporation exists which allows the consultant to have the advantages of a proprietorship and a corporation. The features of an S corporation are briefly discussed in chapter 4. Your accountant can better advise you in detail.

5. MAXIMIZING DEDUCTIBLE EXPENSES

It is very important for consultants to have a record-keeping system that keeps track of all expenses relating to the consultant's overhead as well as expenses that are directly payable by the client. For a specific project, you may have given a fixed price contract incorporating the expenses that otherwise would be passed on to the client for separate payment.

Expenses are allowed if they are related to the operation of the business, are reasonable, are "ordinary" and "necessary," and if they are for items to be used within a period of one year. Your accountant can advise you regarding your situation.

If you are going to incur expenses on items that would be useful for more than one year, generally that expense cannot be fully deducted within the year the money is spent. The depreciation formula for expenses such as computers, desks, autos, etc., may be claimed for the useful life of the asset.

To ensure that you account for all expenses, keep all payment stubs, receipts, and vouchers, and maintain a record of entertainment and automobile expenses. The tax department can disallow claims for expenses if there is no verification that the expense was indeed incurred and that it was related to your business and the generation of income.

Some of the areas you should discuss with your accountant to obtain advice and guidelines are discussed below. The examples given are general guidelines only. It is critical that you receive expert tax advice in advance on these and other expense deductions related to your consulting practice. As mentioned earlier, tax regulations and interpretations are constantly changing and tax court decisions alter the law on an ongoing basis. Only a tax accountant can properly advise you on the appropriate deductions in your individual situation.

5.1 Home office

It is quite common for consultants to operate out of their homes to keep overhead costs down. An office in the home is deductible, but the guidelines are very strict.

(a) The office must be necessary to the conduct of the business.

(b) A room or area must be used 100% of the time exclusively for the business.

(c) Deductions are allowed on a square foot percentage or other reasonable basis.

(d) Any deductions that are being claimed for an office in the home must be disclosed on the consultant's tax return.

It is important to keep an accurate account of home office expenses, as the potential for abuse in this area is well known. Deductible expenses are made on a percentage basis. For example, if 15% of the home's living space is used exclusively for the conduct of business, 15% of the following expenses are deductible:

(a) Interest paid on home mortgage

(b) Rent of home or apartment

(c) Home owner's or tenant's fire insurance

(d) Property taxes

(e) Reasonable expenses such as maintenance

(f) A portion of the telephone charges might also be deductible. Expenses related to the telephone should be itemized as applicable to business use rather than estimated as a percentage of the total. An alternative is for the consultant to install a corporate business telephone in the home office.

Your tax consultant can advise you about home office expense deductibility. It is necessary to maintain careful documentation of home office expenses to support deductions claimed on an income tax return.

5.2 Automobile

This is a potential problem area if one car is being used for both business and pleasure.

A full deduction for business use is difficult to claim if you are using it personally at any time. A ledger record of business usage is essential.

A complete log should be kept of all mileage pertaining to business with a description of the purpose of each trip. In addition, a record of all tolls and parking expenses, repairs, purchases, and insurance payments should be kept. In some cases an estimate of business use for a jointly used car may be allowable if it seems reasonable in the circumstances. Because an estimation may be disallowed, good management requires accurate record-keeping.

If you have two cars, one for business use and one for personal use, it is easier to establish a case for full deduction of all expenses related to one car.

5.3 Entertainment

It is difficult to claim a deduction for entertainment unless an accurate record is kept showing the date, amount, location of entertainment, who attended, connection to business, and the purpose of the meeting. As this area is one of potential abuse, it is looked at very carefully on an audit and may be disallowed. It is important, therefore, to mark on the back of the receipt the necessary information immediately after the entertainment function and before you forget.

5.4 Travel

This is another area in which potential abuse occurs, and it is therefore scrutinized very carefully. Travel that is strictly for business is deductible. This normally includes the cost of transportation; lodging of a reasonable nature; meals; transportation while away such as taxis, rental cars, and buses; personal services such as laundry; and telephone costs.

A personal trip cannot be written off as a business expense. Some consultants believe that a personal trip may be "converted" into a business trip if business is conducted while away from home. The key criterion is whether or not the trip was primarily personal in nature. If it was, any business expenses may not be deductible.

A careful distinction must be maintained where business expenses and personal expenses are combined. For example, a spouse may accompany a consultant on a business trip. The consultant is only able to deduct the portion of the expenses that relate directly to business. The primary purpose of the trip must be for business, not pleasure. All expenses pertaining to the spouse's share of travel, lodging, or meals would not be deductible.

There are limits on the number of business conferences and conventions outside the country that can be attended and deducted each year. You must obtain specific advice on these points.

5.5 Bad debts

Income is recognized only as the cash is collected. Therefore, cash basis taxpayers cannot deduct bad debts for uncollected fees. However, the consultant can deduct returned checks as bad debts. If you are an accrual basis taxpayer and want to deduct bad debts, two important tests are required to determine if the debt can be declared "uncollectible." The criteria are the record of your attempt to collect the debt and the length of time the debt has been outstanding.

5.6 Insurance

Insurance premiums for all business-related insurance policies are fully deductible. If coverage extends to both personal and business protection, only the business portion can be deducted.

5.7 Education and professional development

All expenses related to professional development are deductible if they are directly related to your business and generating income and if they are reasonable. Again, detailed documentation is required to support the deduction. Keep receipts for all expenses for conventions, conferences, seminars, books, magazines, periodicals, newspapers, newsletters, etc.

5.8 Salaries

You many wish to use the services of your spouse, children, or others to assist you in your business. Bookkeeping, record-keeping, word processing, desktop publishing, research, marketing, and administration are just some of the areas that can be delegated to staff. All these expenses should be deductible. Make sure you receive professional tax planning advice in advance. You may wish to structure the terms of employment so that any staff are self-employed rather than employees of your company.

5.9 Equipment

All your equipment costs can be depreciated over time, depending on the percentage permitted each year for the particular equipment. Your computer, printer, software, fax machine, photocopier, modem, cellular phone, etc. may all be depreciable. If you already personally own some or all of the above before starting your consulting business, you can have your business buy them from you to make the equipment an asset of your business.

5.10 Furnishings

You will require various office furnishings such as desk, chairs, storage areas, filing cabinets, etc. These are all legitimate office expenses. They have to be depreciated over time however. If you already own furnishings for your business, you can have your business buy them from you so that they become an asset of your business.

CHAPTER 10
INSURANCE

Proper risk management means planning for potential problems and attempting to insure against them. You should be familiar with the numerous types of insurance available, the method of obtaining the insurance, the best way to reduce premiums, and the pitfalls to avoid.

1. OBTAINING INSURANCE

Insurance companies market their services chiefly through the methods discussed below.

1.1 Agencies

These are the small, individualized operations that place home, car, or other common types of insurance with several insurance companies to which they are contracted. In some cases, small agencies, to earn their commission, are under an obligation to place a certain volume of insurance with each company they deal with. Therefore, it is possible that you might be sold policies offered by companies that may not suit your needs and may not necessarily be priced competitively.

1.2 Insurance brokers

Insurance brokers claim to have complete independence from any insurance company and more flexibility than the common agencies. In comparison with agencies in general, brokers from the larger companies are more knowledgeable about and flexible in the types of coverage and policies they offer, and they specialize in certain areas. Also, a broker should have no vested interest in placing insurance with any particular company and will therefore attempt to get you the best price and the best coverage to meet your needs. You should make specific inquiries to satisfy yourself.

As in all matters of obtaining professional advice or assistance, you should have a minimum of three competitive quotes and an opportunity to evaluate the relative strengths and weaknesses of each. If the brokers are using the same insurance base for the best coverage and premiums, then all three brokers should recommend to you, in theory, the same insurance companies for the different forms of coverage you are requesting.

1.3 Clubs and associations

Ask your local Better Business Bureau and chamber of commerce about their group rates for insurance. These two organizations frequently have various types of insurance coverage available at a reduced group rate.

2. PLANNING YOUR INSURANCE PROGRAM

It is important to consider all criteria to determine the best type of insurance for you and your business. Your major goal should be adequate coverage, avoiding both over- and under-insurance. This is done by periodically reviewing risk and keeping your agent informed of any changes in your business that could potentially affect your coverage.

The following principles will help in planning an insurance program:

(a) Identify the risk to which your business is exposed.

(b) Cover your largest risk first.

(c) Determine the magnitude of loss the business can bear without financial difficulty, and use your premium dollar where the protection need is greatest.

(d) Decide what kind of protection will work best for each risk:

- Absorbing risks
- Minimizing risks
- Insuring against risks with commercial insurance

(e) Insure the correct risk.

(f) Use every means possible to reduce costs of insurance:

- Negotiate for lower premiums if loss experience is low
- Use deductibles where applicable
- Shop around for comparable rates and analyze insurance terms and provisions offered by different insurance companies

(g) Risk exposure changes, so a periodic review will save you from insuring matters that are no longer exposed to the same degree of risk. Conversely, you may need to increase limits of liability. Review can help avoid overlaps and gaps in coverage, and thereby keep your risk and premiums lower.

(h) If you are pleased with a particular broker who can handle your various forms of insurance, it is preferable to be selective and have just one broker company. An advantage of the larger broker firms is that they have a pool of insurance professionals, expert in various areas, who you can call on as resource people.

(i) Attempt to keep your losses down in every way. Although your business may have adequate coverage, losses could be uninsurable, exempt from coverage, or have a large deductible. Problems with insurance coverage could seriously affect the survival of your business.

3. TYPES OF BUSINESS AND PERSONAL INSURANCE

The types of insurance you might need will vary widely according to the type of consulting practice you have. The following overview of insurance policies is provided to make you aware of what exists and of what might be appropriate in your situation. As mentioned earlier, these types of insurance are not necessarily recommended. Only you can make that decision after an objective assessment of your needs following comparative research in a competitive insurance market.

3.1 General liability

Most liability insurance policies encompass losses such as:

(a) Money you must legally pay because of bodily injury or damage to the property of others.

(b) All emergency, medical, and surgical expenses incurred from the accident.

(c) Expenses for investigation, your defense, settlements, and a trial.

A general liability policy covers negligence causing injury to clients, employees, and the general public. The policy is normally written up as a comprehensive liability policy.

3.2 Products or completed operations liability

This policy offers protection against a lawsuit by a customer or client who used your product or service and, as a result, sustained bodily injury or property damage from it.

3.3 Errors and omissions liability

This coverage protects you and other professionals against litigation arising from losses incurred by your clients as a result of an error or omission in your advice to them.

3.4 Malpractice liability

This insurance protects you from claims arising from any losses incurred by your clients as a result of negligence or failure on your part to exercise an acceptable degree of professional skill.

3.5 Automobile liability

This coverage includes other people's property, other automobiles, persons in other vehicles, and persons in the insured automobile.

If you are using your car for business purposes, exclusively or occasionally, it is important that you have your premium cover business use. It is possible that your current motor vehicle insurance policy has a premium based on personal use only. Problems could occur if there were an accident and it was discovered that your car was indeed used for business purposes.

3.6 Fire and theft liability

You probably already have fire and theft insurance if you are working out of your home as a consultant. If you are working in an office or an apartment, it is important to make sure that you have satisfactory coverage.

3.7 Business interruption insurance

The indirect loss from a fire or theft can be greater than the loss itself. If your premises or files are destroyed, you can lose revenue. Certain expenses must still be met. Such a situation could put a severe strain on working capital and seriously affect the survival of the business.

Business interruption insurance is designed to cover the period between the time of the loss and the return to normal operating conditions. The insurance policy could also include the costs of temporarily renting other premises.

3.8 Overhead expense insurance

Consultants whose business income would cease if they were temporarily disabled by illness or accident may take out insurance to cover the cost to them of their fixed business expenses or overhead which have to be met even when they are unable to earn income.

3.9 Personal disability insurance

You could possibly be disabled for a short or long period of time. This insurance pays you a certain monthly amount if you are permanently disabled, or a portion of that amount if you are partially disabled but capable of generating some income.

3.10 Key person insurance

The death of a key person could seriously affect the earning power of your consulting practice. For example, if you have an associate, partner, or sub-consultant who is critical to a particularly large project or your business as a whole, life insurance should be considered.

If the key person dies, the loss may result in a decrease of confidence by your existing or potential clients, leading to a loss of future contracts, competitive position, and revenue, and the expense of finding and/or training a replacement. The amount and type of insurance will depend on many factors, as designing an evaluation formula for a key person is difficult.

Proceeds of the key person policy are not subject to income tax generally, but premiums are not a deductible business expense.

3.11 Shareholders' or partners' insurance

If it is your intention to have a partner in your consulting practice or a shareholder in your corporation, you may wish to consider shareholder or partnership insurance. Normally this type of insurance is part of a buy-sell agreement which allows for a deceased shareholder's or partner's interest to be purchased by the surviving partners or shareholders of the corporation.

In the absence of a buy-sell agreement funded by life insurance, the death of a partner could cause the immediate dissolution of the partnership in law. Unless there is an express agreement to the contrary, the surviving partner's duty is to liquidate the business, collect all outstanding accounts, pay off all debts, and account as trustee to the personal representative of the deceased partner for the value of the deceased's interest in the business.

In the case of a corporation, the deceased shareholder's interest would be considered an asset and would go to the beneficiary outlined in the will, if a will existed. Naturally, the introduction of a new shareholder who owns an interest in the company, especially a majority interest, could have a very traumatic effect on the shareholders and the company's continued operation.

In summary, the procedure is that each partner shareholder applies for a life insurance policy on the life of the other. The applicant is the beneficiary and pays the premiums on his or her partner's life insurance policy. When a partner dies, the funds from the insurance are received tax free by the beneficiary (the partner). These funds are then used to purchase the deceased partner's share of the business. The surviving partner retains control of the business, and the heirs of the deceased get cash for their interest.

3.12 Business loan insurance

In many cases your lender will be able to provide you with insurance coverage for the outstanding amount of your loan and will then incorporate the premium payments into the loan. In the event of your death, the outstanding balance of the loan is paid off.

3.13 Term life insurance

This type of insurance insures a person for a specific period of time and then terminates. The most common period is five years. If the insured dies within the term of the policy, the insurance company pays the full face amount to the heirs. The costs of premiums are based on life expectancy for the person's age during the five-year period. Term life does not have a cash or loan value.

Because term life insurance can be written for various time periods, and because of inexpensive premiums, it is valuable to the business person. Such term policies are often used to provide collateral security for loans to the firm or for personal obligations.

It is wise to have term insurance in the amount of at least your personal and business financial obligations for which you have a direct or contingent liability. This area is frequently overlooked.

3.14 Medical insurance

It is important to take out sufficient medical coverage for your needs. If you are doing any consulting assignments outside the country, you should have extended coverage that pays for medical bills that may be incurred by injury or illness.

3.15 Group insurance

You may be eligible for group insurance rates if you have four or more employees. The policies of insurance companies vary, but medical and dental plans are available for small groups.

3.16 Workers' compensation insurance

If you have a number of employees, you should make certain that you are covered by workers' compensation insurance if you are eligible. With this coverage, the insurer pays all costs that the employer is required to pay for any injury to the employee. The insurer also covers the employees for all benefits and compensations required by the appropriate laws.

If you have failed to pay your employer's portion of the insurance coverage, or have failed to meet your responsibilities

adequately to your employees in terms of safety, it is possible that you as the employer could be held liable for any injury to the employee as determined by the common law as well as under workers' compensation laws. Employee coverage and the extent of the employer's liability vary considerably.

CHAPTER 11
PROFESSIONAL LIABILITY

Consultants have the same degree of potential for lawsuits against them as do other professionals such as physicians, accountants, and lawyers. Claims could be made that the consultant was responsible for a wrongful act or omission or professional misjudgment. Professional liability claims may be brought by the client or by third parties such as investors, creditors, or lenders.

If the consultant is doing business as a proprietorship or partnership, liability extends to the consultant personally. It may also extend to the consultant's estate after death. Liability can also extend to persons who were the consultant's partners long after the error or omission occurred. The statute of limitations in many jurisdictions will not begin until the claimant discovers or should have discovered, or knows or has reason to know of your alleged mistake.

As a consultant, you must weigh the degree of risk involved in your specific area of practice. Obtain expert legal and insurance advice about the proper methods of protecting yourself.

1. CONTRACT AND TORT LIABILITY

It is not uncommon for a consultant to be sued for both breach of contract and tort liability.

1.1 Contract liability

A claim made against a consultant by a client could be based on the allegation that the consultant failed to perform the services described in the contract in a reasonable and prudent manner. This liability involves only those who are parties to the contract, and it applies whether there is a verbal, implied, or written contract.

For the client to succeed in the claim against the consultant, all of the following elements must be proven:

- There was a valid contract between the client and the consultant. This contract, as mentioned earlier, could be verbal or written.

- The consultant materially failed to perform his or her obligations under the contract.

- The client suffered damages as a result of the consultant's breach of obligation.

In actions brought under a breach of contract, it is irrelevant in most jurisdictions whether the consultant's breach was innocent, negligent, or willful. The client need only prove that a material breach of contract occurred and that damages resulted. There are, of course, numerous defenses a consultant can raise depending on the particular circumstances. The amount of monies assessed against the consultant would be an attempt to restore the client to the position held if the contract had not been breached.

A consultant can be sued for breach of contract, for example, if the precise duties and responsibilities or services required under the contract were not met exactly as detailed in the contract. This is a good reason to make certain that a contract is written, not verbal. In a verbal contract it is difficult to establish exactly what the terms of the agreement were.

Another example is a consultant who signed a fixed price contract for a service to be provided by a certain date. If the consultant miscalculated the fixed price and abandoned the project before it was completed, he or she could be sued. This is not uncommon among new consultants unfamiliar with the skill required in preparing a fixed price proposal.

1.2 Tort liability

Tort liability is a violation of civil law rather than a breach of contract. Liability in tort is incurred toward the public at large. Any third party who has suffered through the direct or indirect actions of the consultant can make a claim against the consultant even if no contract existed with the consultant and the claimant had never met the consultant. For example, if a consultant submits a report with recommendations to a client and the client follows the recommendations, expends a large sum of money, and subsequently loses the money, the client suffered (damages) due to negligent advice of the consultant. It would have to be shown that the consultant knew or reasonably should have known that others would be seeing the report with recommendations, and they would be relying on that report before investing or lending money.

For the claimant to succeed in a claim against the consultant, all the following elements must be proven:

- The consultant owed the claimant a duty of care.

- The duty or standard of care was breached.

- Measurable damages resulted from the breach.

- There was a direct connection between the breach of duty and the damages that occurred.

In a suit based on tort, evidence introduced into court must establish that the consultant departed from the local custom and standard of practice. If a consultant is found to be negligent, the court will attempt to compensate the claimant for the damages incurred.

2. REASONS FOR CLAIMS

2.1 Counterclaims

In many instances when a consultant sues a client to collect overdue fees, the client will counterclaim. The client may have a valid reason for not paying the fee, but very often the countersuit is intended to create delay and act as a leverage mechanism for settlement.

2.2 Conflict of interest

A consultant could be liable if it can be shown that the consultant had a vested interest in the outcome of the recommendations. For example, a client requests a computer consultant to review existing hardware and make recommendations for replacement. The consultant recommends replacement equipment. At some later point the client learns that the consultant received a large kick-back from the distributor of the product line for recommending a very large order. The client could sue the consultant for the undisclosed profit; if it could be shown that the recommended hardware system was not the appropriate system in the circumstances, there could be additional liability on the consultant's part.

2.3 Conflicting interest of clients

A consultant could be working for two clients who are in competition with each other. If it can be shown that confidential information was disclosed or the benefits of assistance to one client were at the expense of the other client, then possible liability of the consultant could be present.

2.4 Delegation of part of contract to employee or sub-consultant

The primary consultant is responsible for the work of employees or agents under the primary consultant's control. If the client maintains that the consulting work was not done, or not done properly by the employee or sub-consultant, legal action can be taken against the primary consultant.

2.5 Third party damages

If a third party such as a creditor, investor, or lender suffers damages as a consequence of the recommendations of the consultant to a second party, a third party can sue in tort.

2.6 Unclear expectations by client

It is possible that a client has unclear or unrealistic expectations of the work to be performed by the consultant and of the benefit to the client. This lack of clarity can be a basis for dispute if the performance was not perceived to be related to expectations.

3. HOW TO AVOID PROFESSIONAL LIABILITY AND PREVENT LOSSES

Although the possibility of being exposed to legal liability cannot be totally prevented, it can be substantially minimized by implementing effective administrative systems and procedures.

Many professionals concentrate on the technical aspects of their profession. Good management is equally important. Consideration must be given to proper staffing, training, credit and collection, and office procedures such as keeping diaries, checklists, and properly written records of every aspect and phase of the consulting business. As well, it is important to stay within the limits of your training, experience, and expertise. Do not take on work that is beyond your capability. Some good management techniques that can help keep you out of trouble are discussed here.

3.1 Client control

Clients who habitually try to avoid paying fees by claiming that errors have been made, or clients who frequently resort to litigation can be costly for your business. Make sure that you have control over the areas for which you are responsible. In other words, do not assume responsibility for matters that your clients control.

You should implement a prescreening process to select clients. Ways of prescreening are covered in chapter 16.

3.2 Cost estimates

Avoid giving firm cost estimates for activities arising from your services if possible. Depending on the type of consulting practice you have, you could be locked into a situation where a fixed cost has been given and the project suffers an overrun. Architects and engineers especially should avoid giving firm billing cost estimates.

3.3 Carefully drafted contracts

It is most important that a consultant operate with written contracts with clients. The contracts should be drafted carefully and based on competent legal advice. Contract ambiguities and misunderstandings are a major source of professional liability claims.

Letters of understanding or contracts should be sent out to the client for acknowledgment and signature and returned by the client.

3.4 Free opinions

Be careful not to provide free opinions without knowing all the facts. You could be put in a position of being liable, even though you were not officially retained and had not received any fees. If it can be shown that someone relied on your advice and subsequently suffered because of your advice, you could be held liable.

3.5 Law

Make sure you understand the law pertaining to your specific work in the jurisdiction where the law would be interpreted. For example, if you are performing consulting assignments outside your home jurisdiction, different laws may apply that could create problems for you.

3.6 Sub-consultants

Sub-consultants should be carefully selected. Check to see that they carry adequate professional liability insurance. Make sure your insurance covers any work performed by a sub-consultant.

3.7 Records, systems, and procedures

Effective systems for your files, records, billing, and office procedures are essential for any business. See chapter 8 for specific ideas on how to keep your records straight.

3.8 Continuing education

It is important that the consultant develop more expertise and training on an ongoing basis through various professional development and continuing education courses. This shows a professional attitude and desire for knowledge and current information.

3.9 Quality control

The consultant should set up some system for monitoring the activities and performance of employees or sub-consultants. If a system is in place, this will show that you have developed a high standard of care in the operation of your business.

3.10 Communication

Effective communication helps eliminate many client problems. This topic is covered in chapter 16.

4. PROFESSIONAL LIABILITY INSURANCE

The procedures outlined in the previous section, if implemented, should substantially reduce the risk of professional liability. However, professional liability insurance is necessary since the risk cannot be completely removed. Professional liability coverage should indemnify the consultant for losses and costs involved in the defense of claims.

The liability insurance coverage is limited to claims "arising out of the performance of professional services" including errors, omissions, and negligent acts. If you provide a service outside the specified designation for your specialty, the insurance coverage could be voided.

There are two types of professional liability insurance coverage: claims made and occurrence. A claims made policy insures only against claims made during the policy period. Occurrence coverage provides protection against claims occurring during the policy period, even if the claims arise long after the occurrence and the policy period.

There are many provisions in the policy that should be thoroughly explained, and if you are not completely satisfied, alternative coverage should be considered. The seven most important factors that have to be reviewed in selecting or analyzing a professional liability insurance coverage are:

(a) Declarations

(b) Exclusions

(c) Insuring agreements

(d) Definitions

(e) Limits of liability

(f) Deductibles

(g) Policy conditions

Your premiums can be reduced in a variety of ways, some of which are discussed here.

4.1 Increase deductibles

The greater the deductible, the less expensive the policy premium should be. Check to see if the policy deductible applies to each separate claim or just once a year.

4.2 Comparing prices

There is competition in the marketplace for professional liability coverage. Make certain that the reduced premium presented to you does not reflect less attractive provisions in the policy that you may not understand. Again, you should obtain professional advice from independent sources to satisfy yourself as to the nature of the coverage that you are getting. It is a prudent investment to have a lawyer who specializes in insurance law review the proposed insurance terms and conditions.

4.3 Changing the type of coverage

Claims made policies are generally less costly than occurrence policies. The reason, as discussed earlier, is because the claims made policy covers just claims made during the policy term. The risk, therefore, to the insurance company is reduced compared to occurrence coverage.

In occurrence coverage, the insurance company's risk is considerable as a claim can be made against the insurance company many years after the negligence occurred and after your policy expired. The cost of settling a claim long after the event could be much higher than a settlement today. It is this risk and uncertainty on the part of the insurance company that is passed on to you in the form of higher premiums for occurrence coverage.

5. PRACTICING WITHOUT INSURANCE

Some consultants choose to conduct their business without any professional liability insurance. If the degree of exposure and risk is very low, this might be a viable alternative. If the consultant has very few personal assets and is effectively judgment proof, then personal bankruptcy may be an alternative in the most extreme circumstances if a claim is made.

Incorporating a company and conducting the consulting practice through the company should add some protection in a lawsuit if the company lacks any assets. The danger of operating a consulting business that has a risk element but no professional liability insurance is the uncertainty if problems occur. A client or third party could sue the consultant personally as well as the corporation and, until the trial, you would not know what the outcome would be. In the meantime, you would have to incur the costs and pressure of the process. In other words, conducting a business through a corporation is not an automatic guarantee of personal protection. The other uncertainty is the nature and amount of damages that your advice caused your client or third parties. It may be very difficult to project at the time you are conducting a consulting assignment what the financial damages could be if your advice is in error.

If you do intend to practice without professional liability insurance, it is most important that you receive expert legal advice to maximize your protection in advance.

CHAPTER 12
CREDIT, BILLING, AND COLLECTION

Many consultants starting out in businesses are more interested in performing their skilled service than developing a clear credit, billing, and collection policy. In many cases a consultant has had no previous business experience and does not realize the pitfalls that can occur.

A system rigidly followed is essential to your survival. It does not take many bad debts to completely eliminate the profit of the business for the whole year. In more serious cases, you could go out of business if a substantial debt owing by a client is not paid.

A number of common mistakes occur with beginning consultants. First, the consultant, wanting to build a clientele and reputation as quickly as possible, takes on many clients, performs the service, and incurs expenses, but allows the client to defer payment. Second, the new consultant may

be too busy or too inexperienced to monitor receivables carefully. Third, unpaid bills are not followed up quickly with appropriate steps to collect funds. The effect of this sloppy approach can be disastrous.

This chapter outlines the pitfalls to be aware of and the procedures to adopt when reviewing your collection policy. If you develop the correct system for your needs, it will enhance your cash flow and profit and minimize stress, client problems, and bad debts.

1. DISADVANTAGES OF EXTENDING CREDIT

When you extend credit, the understanding is that the client intends to pay, is capable of paying, and that nothing will occur to prevent the client from paying. You assume that most clients are honest and acting with goodwill and in good faith. Many of these assumptions may not be accurate.

There are a number of potential disadvantages to extending credit.

Extending credit may take a great deal of your time, and the administrative paperwork — checking references, monitoring and following up on slow paying clients — may be tedious.

The expense of credit checking and collection could be more than you wish or are able to pay. Expenses could consist of credit reporting agency fees and memberships, collection costs, legal fees, and time lost that you could otherwise spend generating revenue.

You will need to increase your working capital requirements to keep your business in operation because receivables from your clients may or may not be paid when you expect or need them. You will be paying interest on additional working capital that you may have to borrow to offset your decreased working capital.

2. ASSESSING THE CLIENT

It is important to be very careful about extending credit. Apply the following general guidelines to your business:

(a) Develop a clear credit policy for your business after consultation with your accountant and lawyer. Experienced professional advice is essential before you extend credit.

(b) Develop a credit application information sheet that has all the necessary information for your files.

(c) Consider joining a credit bureau as well as a credit reporting agency

such as Dun and Bradstreet. Check into the past debt payment profile of your potential client in advance.

(d) Check references from your client if appropriate. Ask about the client's length of time in business.

(e) Ask the client if consultants have been used before and, if so, what method of payment was negotiated.

(f) Consider carefully the amount of credit being extended. The greater the amount of money unpaid, the greater the risk for you.

(g) If the work you do is highly specialized and you have very little competition, you have a lot of leverage in the nature of credit that you would be extending.

(h) If the client is a large institution or government, ask about the customary length of time for accounts rendered to be paid. Specify in your contract the exact terms of payment; government payments in particular can be delayed by bureaucracy for two or three months or longer.

(i) If the client requests deferred fees, you run the risk of default or other problems. Sometimes clients request a deferment of fees or payment because it is a large project, the client is suffering cash flow difficulties, or other considerations. If you are faced with a decision about deferral of fees, you should consider charging interest on the total amount, charging higher fees, requesting a sizable retainer fee before you start the project, or obtaining collateral to protect yourself if your total fees are substantial.

(j) Consider the future benefit of a relationship with the prospective client. If there is a possibility of future contracts or contacts with other prospective clients, you may wish to weigh the benefits against the risks.

3. AVOIDING CLIENT MISUNDERSTANDINGS ON FEES

Communication is vital to minimize client misunderstandings about fees. Many consultants feel uncomfortable discussing money matters during the first interview with the client. Or sometimes consultants become so involved in the client's problem that the fee is not discussed. It is important that the amount of money you expect is understood and agreed upon by the client before you commence work.

Three ways to eliminate misunderstanding on the issue of services performed for fees are through communication, written contract, and invoice.

3.1 Communication

Communication is a critical element to a satisfactory client relationship. It is important that the subject of fees is discussed openly at the time of the initial interview and resolved so that the client feels satisfied with the final bargain. Ask potential clients if they have hired consultants in the past; if they have, find out the nature of the contract relationship that existed.

The interview should be followed by a letter of confirmation outlining the essence of the discussion about fees, among other matters. Progress reports should be sent to the client from time to time if the circumstances warrant it; copies of correspondence concerning the client should be sent to the client. If appropriate, try to involve the client with the project in some way so he or she feels a bonding to you and sees and appreciates the work you are doing on an ongoing basis. This should minimize the risk of a client disputing your fees for services.

3.2 Written contract

A written contract must be signed before work is commenced. The contract can take various forms as outlined later in chapter 18. Basically, a letter of agreement or formal contract explains the nature of fees involved and the method of payment whether it is payment upon receipt, net ten days, or net 30 days.

Be very wary about financing a client; if at all possible, have payment upon receipt. This should assist your cash flow and minimize risk of late payments. The contract should also state the interest that will be added to the outstanding debt if it is not paid within the terms of the contract. The contract should spell out in detail the exact services that you will be performing for the fee.

In certain circumstances a stop work clause could be inserted in the agreement to the effect that if payment is not made within the terms of the contract, at the option of the consultant all work will stop.

Finally, the contract must be signed by the client's decision-maker in authority. It is preferable that this individual be the same person with whom you negotiated the contract.

3.3 Invoice

To minimize misunderstanding on invoiced amounts, it is advisable to provide a detailed breakdown of the charges for services and expenses for the particular phase of the contract. If appropriate, reference should be made on the invoice to the contract agreement on fee structure and method of payment.

4. MINIMIZING RISK OF BAD DEBTS

There are several effective techniques to minimize the risk of bad debts. As discussed previously, most consultants cannot afford to have one or two nonpaying clients without seriously affecting the viability of the business. The following general guidelines may not all be appropriate in a given client situation. Your judgment in each individual situation must dictate the appropriate approach.

4.1 Advance retainer

A client can be asked to pay a retainer or deposit of 10% to 25% or more of the total contract amount prior to the work being performed. This can be justified on the basis that you are very busy and if you are going to schedule in a commitment to that client, it is your policy to require an advance commitment retainer.

This is an effective technique for a potentially high-risk client who has a reputation for nonpayment or late payment, or who constantly argues about bills. This approach can also be considered when dealing with a new client who has not used consultants before.

4.2 Prepaid disbursements

Depending on the length of the job and the type of client, you may wish to request prepaid disbursements if they are going to be sizable. You do not want to carry the client for out-of-pocket expenses at the risk of your own cash flow. You also do not want to run the risk of a nonpayment or dispute of the overall account. As mentioned earlier, it is one thing to lose your time; it is another thing to also be out-of-pocket your own funds.

4.3 Progress payments

It is common for consultants to request funds by means of invoicing at specific points in the project. The stages at which progress payments are to be paid would be outlined in the contract.

4.4 Regular billing

Statements can be sent out on a weekly or monthly basis, depending on the circumstances. It is important to outline in the contract, if appropriate, your policy on the timing of billings. That way the client will not be taken by surprise. This also provides you with the advantage of knowing at an early stage in the consulting project if the client is going to dispute your fees, and at this point you can either resolve the problem or discontinue your services. It can be very risky to allow substantial work to be performed, or to wait until the end of the project, before rendering an account.

4.5 Billing on time

Generally a client's appreciation for the value of your services diminishes over time. This is a common problem. It is important, therefore, to send your bill while the client can see the benefit of the service you have provided. Present your final bill at the completion of the project.

4.6 Accelerated billing

If you sense that the client may have problems paying the bill, or if other factors cause you concern, accelerate your normal billing pattern. You want to receive payment on your account before difficulties can appear.

The risk of rendering an account that states "net 30 days" is that the client is not legally overdue in payment to you until after 30 days. If you become aware of client financial problems, it is difficult to commence legal action or garnishee before the 30-day period has expired.

4.7 Withholding vital information

If you have documents, records, reports, and other material related to the client and the project, you may feel it appropriate, if circumstances warrant, to withhold returning all the necessary material to the client until your account has been paid or other appropriate arrangements made.

4.8 Holding up completion of important stage of project

If client problems occur, you may wish to stop providing your services and resources at a critical stage until the matter has been resolved to your satisfaction.

4.9 Personal guarantee of principals of a corporation

Depending on the project and client, you may want to have the principals behind a corporation sign a formal contract as personal guarantors. Another variation is to have the contract in the name of the corporation and its principals as co-covenantors of the contract.

4.10 Monitor payment trends of clients

Record and monitor the payment patterns of clients so you can watch for trends that may place your fees at risk.

4.11 Follow-up of late payments

If you see an invoice is more than a week or ten days overdue, begin the various steps of your collection system immediately.

4.12 Involving client in assignment

As mentioned previously, try to involve the client in some fashion during each step of the project. By making your client aware of your services, benefits, time, and skill, you should minimize problems that could occur because of an unbonded or remote relationship.

5. BILLING FOR SERVICES

Billing requires a system that is carefully designed and effective. It is important to have a third party review your billing procedures before you open your business. Examine your billing procedures on an ongoing basis, especially during the first year, to make sure they are effective. This also gives you an opportunity to review your fee arrangements to make sure you are bringing in the appropriate cash flow for the time you are spending. As mentioned previously, it is important to monitor each client's file to see general trends in your client billing patterns.

Proper records must be maintained that detail the time and expenses incurred so that the bill can be prepared at the appropriate time. You should have an established procedure for regular billing so outstanding accounts are rendered on a regular basis, thereby minimizing collection disputes or bad debts.

When rendering a bill, make sure you send the account either directly to the appropriate person who has the authority to pay your account, or deliver the bill personally to the client. Your style, the client, and the circumstances will determine the most appropriate approach.

You may choose to send a general bill to your client outlining briefly the services performed, the number of hours, the expenses, and the total fee. A note on the bill might say, "detailed particulars are available upon request." See Sample 13 for a general bill and Sample 14 for a detailed bill.

Your bill should be rendered on your consulting firm's stationery showing your name, address, and telephone number. Always use stationery, not a blank piece of paper with your name typed on it. Prepare three copies of the bill. Send the original and a copy to your client and keep a copy for your files.

The wording on your bill should include the following:

(a) The date the bill was mailed

(b) The name and address of the person being billed

(c) The phase of the project that has been completed

(d) A detailed outline of the services performed

(e) The consultants or other resource personnel who performed the services

(f) The date services were performed, and the total hours worked

(g) Total charges for services

(h) Expense column separated and listed underneath the services column and then totalled

(i) Total of fees and direct expenses payable by client

(j) The date charges are due and payable (if appropriate, make reference to "as per letter of agreement (or contract) dated (month/year)"

(k) Use "thank you" or some other positive and appreciative closing remark

(l) Your signature and title

6. WHY CLIENTS PAY LATE

If you have established appropriate precautionary measures and a credit and billing policy, you should have very few overdue accounts. However, overdue accounts will occur in any practice, and understanding your options should minimize your problems in this area.

There are several common reasons why a client might be late in paying for consulting services. The client could be indifferent to your deadlines. Some clients have a sloppy attitude about paying accounts due and are accustomed to being pressured or reminded frequently before they finally meet their obligations.

Institutional or government payment procedures sometimes involve a two- or three-month wait for accounts to be paid. This type of information is easily available by asking the right questions before you

SAMPLE 13
GENERAL INVOICE

John Smith & Associates
CONSULTANTS
123 Main Street
Anytown, Anywhere
(000) 555-4567

Date: August 1, 20--
File reference: XYZ 123
Invoice number: 123456
Terms: Net cash

To: Superior Conglomerate Ltd.
789 Jones Street
Anytown, Anywhere

RE: South Branch Computing System Analysis

PROJECT CONSULTANT: John Smith

For professional services provided between July 15 and July 30, 20--:

Review, analysis, and recommendations
pertaining to computing system:

26 hours @ $100 $2,600.00

Direct Expenses:

Photocopies, long distance telephone calls,
and automobile mileage   157.50

TOTAL FEES AND DIRECT EXPENSES ARE DUE UPON RECEIPT $2,757.50

Detailed particulars supplied upon request.

Thank you.

Yours truly,

John Smith & Associates

SAMPLE 14
DETAILED INVOICE

John Smith & Associates
CONSULTANTS
123 Main Street
Anytown, Anywhere
(000) 555-4567

To: Paul Roberts, President
Superior Conglomerate Ltd.
789 Jones Street
Anytown, Anywhere

Date: August 1, 20-
File reference: XYZ 123
Invoice number: 123457
Terms: Net cash

RE: South Branch Computing System Analysis
PROJECT CONSULTANT: John Smith

Professional Services:

July 15	Attendance at South Branch site to review operations (4 hours)	$ 400.00
July 17	Meeting with Mr. Roberts to discuss findings (3 hours)	300.00
July 19	Attendance at South Branch site to analyze operations (5 hours)	500.00
July 22	Preparation of report and recommendations (8 hours)	800.00
July 26	Meeting with Mr. Roberts to review recommendations (3 hours)	300.00
July 30	Prepare final report of recommendations (5 hours)	500.00

Total professional services (28 hours @ $100) $2,800.00

Direct Expenses:

Photocopies of five progress reports (400 pages @ 20¢)	80.0
Long distance telephone call on July 20 to Mr. Roberts	17.50
Automobile mileage (200 miles @ 30¢)	60.00

Total Direct Expenses $ 157.50

TOTAL FEES AND EXPENSES DUE AND PAYABLE UPON RECEIPT $2,957.50

Thank you.

Yours truly,

John Smith & Associates

begin. Your account may be lost in the maze and require personal attention.

A client may deliberately delay payment in order to save money at your expense. You save the client interest on working capital if he or she can use your money for free. This is why you should have an interest factor for overdue accounts built into your initial contract as well as showing on the statement. If the overdue interest is high enough, that should act as an incentive for the client to pay on time. If this is in the contract, the client cannot argue that there was no agreement on overdue interest. Rendering a statement with the interest factor noted on it is not in itself evidence of an agreement between the parties on the amount of interest on overdue accounts.

A client may prefer to give priority to other creditors, where pressure to pay is greater.

The client may not have the money. This does not necessarily mean that the client is going out of business, but is cash poor at the moment. The technique to handle this problem is discussed in the next section.

7. COLLECTING LATE PAYMENTS WITHOUT LEGAL ACTION

Because of the expense, time wasted, stress, and uncertainty of legal action, it is preferable to collect as much as you can from clients yourself. Some steps that you may wish to consider are:

(a) Send out a reminder invoice with a courteous comment that the invoice is "overdue and that perhaps it was an oversight or the check is already in the mail."

(b) The alternative to the above is to telephone the accounts payable department or the client directly to ask when the payment can be expected. Courteously ask if there was possibly a misunderstanding, or if they need further information or clarification on any matter. Make sure that you note in the client file the date and time, the person you spoke to at the client's office, a summary of the conversation, and when payment can be expected.

(c) If you have not received payment within a week of the preceding step, send a letter stating that the account is in arrears and that it is to be paid on the terms of the contract. The alternative is to again telephone the client and ask about the reason for the delay.

(d) Another technique is to ask when the check will be ready. Say that you will be around to pick up the check or will arrange for a courier service to pick it up as soon as they telephone your office to advise that it is ready.

(e) If the client has still not paid, stopping work on the project is another option.

(f) If the client refuses to pay, legal steps may be required immediately depending on the size of the bill, the importance of the client, the reasons for nonpayment, and the cost of legal action. Alternatively, you may decide to compromise with a client and settle for a reduced payment.

(g) If the client is unable to pay because of cash flow problems or other financial difficulties, you have to assess your options. If the client is not disputing the bill and wishes to have credit, there are basically three options:

(i) Installment payment plan: the client would agree on definite dates for payment and would send you the amounts owing upon receipt of statements from you.

(ii) Post-dated checks: you would receive post-dated checks from the client for the agreed period and amount.

(iii) Promissory note: the client would sign a promissory note agreeing to the total amount of the debt and the date on which the debt would be paid. The note should be signed by the principals if the client is a corporation. Interest on the full amount of the debt should be built into the promissory note. It is negotiable whether or not interest is added onto the other two payment plans.

8. LEGAL STEPS IF ACCOUNT REMAINS UNPAID

If it is apparent that the client has no intention of paying you, is objecting to your bill, or is unable to pay you, then legal action must be considered. It is critical that legal action be commenced as quickly as possible after it becomes apparent that you will not be paid by other arrangements. At this stage you are not interested in keeping the client for present or potential future business. You just want to salvage the best of a bad situation. There are basically three legal options available.

8.1 Collection agency

You may wish to assign the debt to a collection agency for which you will be charged between 25% and 50% of the amount collected. This is better than writing the account off as a total loss. Different agencies have different styles of collection, and one agency may achieve better results with your bad debts than another. If your client pays you directly during the period of the contract with the collection agency, you are obliged to pay the commission to the collection agency. Collection agencies are listed in the Yellow Pages telephone directory.

8.2 Small claims court

Small claims court is a relatively quick, informal, and inexpensive method of taking your client to court. If you are successful and obtain a judgment against your client, that does not necessarily mean you are going to collect on the judgment. There are additional steps you will have to take, such as garnisheeing the client or filing a judgment against the title of any properties owned by your client. Your client could turn out to be judgment proof.

8.3 Lawyers

Lawyers can be very effective in the collection of debts if you act promptly and select a lawyer who is experienced in the law and tactics of collecting. Lawyers generally bill on an hourly basis, and the more time expended on attempting to collect a debt, the more money it will cost you without any assurance that you will be successful at trial. If you are successful and do obtain a judgment, your client could be bankrupt or judgment proof in terms of assets. As mentioned previously, the litigation process can be very protracted, uncertain, stressful, and expensive.

9. BAD DEBTS AND TAXES

Keep accurate record of any bad debt accounts and the procedures you went through to attempt to collect. Generally you will be allowed to deduct bad debts from your other income, but this is a matter that should be discussed with your accountant as the laws and circumstances can vary.

CHAPTER 13
SETTING FEES

There are many ways to set fees: by the hour, by the day, by the month, or by the project. The most common fee arrangements (approximately 85% of them) are daily rate (per diem), fixed price, and fixed price plus expenses.

This chapter discusses in detail how to determine the fee structure most appropriate for your situation and how to give an accurate quote to a prospective client.

1. DAILY BILLING RATE (PER DIEM)

The daily billing rate has three components: labor, overhead, and profit.

1.1 Labor

The labor daily rate is obtained by taking the average of your most recent annual salary, your current annual salary, a recent job offer annual salary or the prevailing annual salaries in the marketplace for your type of work, and dividing the number by 261, which is the number of days in the year excluding weekends. For example, if your annual salary is $46,800, the daily labor rate is $180 ($46,800 ÷ 261).

1.2 Overhead

Before calculating your daily overhead rate, it is important to understand a number of concepts pertaining to overhead and daily billing.

1.2a Fixed and variable expenses

Fixed expenses are those expenses for overhead that are constant and do not change based on your volume of workload. Variable expenses are expenses that can change based on volume of workload; they include extra secretarial time to administer various aspects of your office operation, additional postage for promotional or marketing purposes, additional phone calls for promotional or marketing purposes, etc.

1.2b Indirect and direct expenses

Indirect expenses are those you incur as overhead and the cost of doing business and are not directly attributable to a specific client. Direct expenses are those incurred on behalf of a specific client and are charged directly to that particular client. These expenses can vary considerably from one consulting project to another. Some examples of direct expenses frequently encountered in consulting are the following:

- Computer time
- Printing and photocopying
- Postage
- Other consultant's time
- Long distance telephone calls
- Out-of-town living expenses such as meals, lodging, tips, etc.
- Air travel
- Car rental
- Parking and tolls

When quoting a daily rate, it is common practice to state "plus expenses" after the daily rate. This includes all the direct expenses that have been outlined, plus any other direct expenses you might incur. If you are quoting your fee on a fixed price basis, direct expenses are incorporated within your estimate cost sheet.

1.2c Calculation of overhead

Sample 2 in chapter 3 gave a checklist for determining your monthly overhead. Multiply that figure by 12 to get your annual overhead for the purpose of these calculations. Divide the figure by 168 to get your daily overhead. The number 168 represents the average number of billable days per year you have available. Although there are approximately 21 days a month of potential billable days, the norm is that one-third of that time is used for nonbillable functions such as vacation, sick leave, professional development, administration of the practice, and marketing. Studies have shown that approximately 15% to 20% of an experienced consultant's time is spent on developing and implementing various marketing plans.

The overhead rate is expressed as a percent of your labor rate by dividing your daily rate for labor by your daily rate for overhead. For example, if $180 is your daily labor rate and your daily overhead rate is $130, the overhead rate is 72.2%, rounded out to 72%. This percent is a guide to the efficiency of your practice as well as a factor you would use for the overhead estimate in a fixed price contract.

1.3 Profit

Profit is the reason you are in business. It is your reward for taking business risks and the responsibility and pressures of ownership. It is above and beyond your salary for labor. Profit for consultants generally ranges from 10% to 30% of your salary, plus benefits, plus overhead. The amount of profit you decide to build in will depend on many factors, including your expertise, the demand for your services, and the competition in the marketplace.

To calculate your daily billing rate (or per diem), the formula is as follows:

Daily labor rate	$180.00
Daily overhead rate	130.00
Total daily cost	310.00
Profit (15% of $310)	46.50
Total daily billing rate	$356.50
(Rounded out to next highest $25)	$375.00

It is usual for consultants to calculate their daily or hourly billing rate rounded out to the next highest $25 amount. Recent studies have shown that the daily billing rates for all types of consultants range between $300 and $1,200 per day with an average of approximately $700 per day. There are many factors that will determine your rate, such as the economy, competition, experience, repeat business possibilities, and your financial needs.

In the example above, the daily billing rate would be quoted as $375.

When calculating per diem time, normally all time spent on the client project is billed out, including the time recorded for phone calls and travel. Your client should be advised in advance in writing that these charges will be passed on as direct costs. Many consultants prefer to charge the client directly for the time expended on travel on an hourly or per diem basis. Other consultants prefer not to charge directly for travel time. They may work on a client's project while traveling and charge out their work to the client as if working in the office.

Another approach is to charge a higher billing rate for work that requires travel. For example, if your normal billing rate is $50 per hour, you may charge $65 per hour for work that requires travel, in addition to a minimum rate of a half-day or a full day for travel regardless of how much time is spent. You have to develop guidelines that meet your client's needs as well as your own.

2. HOURLY RATE

The hourly rate is calculated by dividing the daily rate by eight hours. Some consultants divide by seven hours or nine hours, depending on their style of operation, but the average is eight hours. For example, a daily billing rate of $375 divided by eight is $46.80 or, rounded out to the next highest $25 amount, $50. You quote your fee as $50 per hour.

Most consultants have a minimum charge (such as four hours) for any work contracted on an hourly basis. In addition to a minimum number of hours, some consultants prefer to add an extra factor of 10% to 20% onto the billing rate to compensate for the inefficiency of this type of fee arrangement. For example, at 20% extra, the hourly billing rate of $50 plus $10 equals $60 per hour. You should also charge travel time in addition to your hourly rate or minimum charge, depending on the circumstances.

3. CALCULATING A FIXED PRICE QUOTATION

3.1 Determining a fixed price estimate

Another method of quoting fees is to calculate a flat rate for the entire project. To calculate a fixed fee, a number of factors are determined, such as direct labor (that is, the cost of any consultants or secretarial or clerical staff), overhead (which is the percent you have previously calculated of the total direct labor cost), and all direct expenses related to that specific consulting project.

The last factor in the formula of calculating a fixed rate estimate is the profit factor. In each situation you determine what you believe to be a fair profit for the risk, the time involved, the skill, the competition, your need for the job, and the ongoing work that might arise from this project. The profit is a percent of the total of the preceding expenses; that is, direct labor, overhead, and the direct expenses. You then have calculated the total fixed price to quote to your client. Normally, only the total price, not your costing sheet, is shown to the client. An example of a fixed price costing sheet is shown in Sample 15.

A fixed fee arrangement is often preferred by a client, as the total cost of the project can be budgeted and planned. The risk is the consultant's. If you have a budget overrun, you could lose a lot of money or go out of business. If you are very efficient and accurate in your costing of the fixed price and the management of the project, you could obtain the reward of an underrun which means a higher profit margin.

A fixed fee should only be used when you have effective cost control of the project and are able to estimate your time and costs with a high degree of accuracy. It is very risky to propose a fixed price contract for projects with which you have little experience, especially if the assignment is unique or complex.

If you are very experienced in a certain area, you would probably prefer a fixed price contract due to the efficiency of your mode of operation. In other words, because of your expertise and efficiency, you might not make as much on an hourly per diem basis as you could make by negotiating a fixed price.

3.2 Tips on preparing fixed price estimates

Because of the risk involved in a fixed price contract, many consultants avoid that type of fee arrangement. In many cases, though, a client requires a fixed price because that is the style of operation. To minimize the risk of an overrun (i.e., costs exceeding your revenue) and to increase your confidence in the preparation of estimates, the following guidelines are provided:

(a) A precise and specific definition of the project must be obtained. This is either obtained from the client, as in government projects where considerable detail is provided for costing purposes, or the consultant must obtain as much information from the client as required to produce a detailed reconstruction of the entire project requirement. This involves having a checklist of questions that you ask the client to ensure you have not forgotten any of the key components of the contract.

(b) It is helpful to draw a functional flow diagram (FFD) showing the interconnecting parts and stages of the project. This could be the same functional flow diagram you include in your proposal, or a less detailed one.

SAMPLE 15
FIXED PRICE COSTING SHEET

DIRECT LABOR

Senior consultant (15 days at $300)	$4,500	
Senior consultant: B. Smith ($525 per day) 3 x $525	1,575	
Junior consultant (7 days at $150)	1,050	
Secretarial (12 days at $60)	720	
TOTAL DIRECT LABOR		$7,845

DIRECT EXPENSES

Air fares (5 x $191) (3 x $30) (1 x $61)	$1,106	
Automobile mileage (550 x .22)	121	
Entertainment	375	
Postage	190	
Printing and photocopying	550	
Rental cars	430	
Telephone	210	
Miscellaneous	470	
TOTAL DIRECT EXPENSES		3,452
SUBTOTAL		11,297
PROFIT (15%)		1,695
TOTAL FIXED PRICE		$12,992

(c) Once you have determined the various activities you will need to do for the project, list them all in order of priority. Then do a breakdown of the stages within each of those areas. If you need more detail to assess the amount of time and direct expense, continue breaking down each of the sub-components into the various parts.

(d) Use a bid sheet when pricing a project. Each function of the project should be outlined and the direct labor and direct expense costs allocated.

(e) The advantage of the detailed costing, apart from a higher degree of accuracy, is the ability to be more flexible with your client. For example, if your client rejects your first fixed price proposal as being outside the budget allotted, you could reduce your estimate by reviewing your costing sheet in areas that still allow you to perform the overall project. You maintain your credibility with your client by not discounting your prices because of pressure from the client or your financial need. You are adjusting the price downward as a direct outcome of reducing the expense and time you will be putting into the project.

(f) Before you submit your bid to a client, make sure you have a person with bidding experience in the area you are working review your detailed costing sheet to find any areas you may have missed or that could be improved.

4. FIXED PRICE PLUS EXPENSES

A fixed price plus expense fee arrangement is quite common; it is used when a fixed price is desired by both parties but expenses cannot be calculated with certainty. For example, you may have an estimate for the number of trips required, but there could be factors outside your control which could affect that financial outlay and, therefore, your costing. You should estimate the direct expenses for the benefit of your client, but the contract would clearly state that the client is responsible for all direct expenses.

5. CONTINGENCY FEE

In a contingency fee arrangement you do not receive any income unless you perform the objective successfully. The normal procedure is that you obtain a percentage of the final benefit that the client receives. For example, if you are skilled at appealing property reassessment taxes for your clients, and you save your client considerable money, then you receive a portion of the saving.

The advantage to the client of this arrangement is the lack of risk — if taxes are not reduced, no fee is paid to the consultant. It is, therefore, an effective marketing device for clients who would otherwise not want to commit themselves to a consultant. From a consultant's viewpoint, considerable money can be made, much greater than the profit earned under the traditional consulting fee arrangements.

Many professional associations consider contingency fees unethical because of the risk of conflict of interest for the consultant. For example, if a consultant is retained to find a key executive for a client and performs an executive search, the final recommendation could be biased to obtain the commission payment.

6. PERCENTAGE FEE

A percentage fee is a common arrangement for engineers and architects on construction projects. Normally a uniform percentage is applied to the cost of the project. Percentage fees are not dependent on a successful result of the performance of a service, which makes them different from contingent fees.

7. PROJECT VALUE FEES

There are times when a consultant has unique and effective skills in a given situation, and thereby saves the client considerable money. The client is usually charged a substantially higher fee than a normal hourly rate. It is not uncommon for lawyers to apply this method. For example, a lawyer, through skill and experience and tactical negotiating techniques, might purchase a business at a considerable savings to the client. The lawyer may have spent only 15 hours at $150 per hour on the file, but saved the client $2 million. Because of the "value" obtained by the client, the lawyer charges a substantially higher fee — possibly five or ten times more than the actual time spent.

8. RETAINER FEES

A retainer relationship involves a consultant being "on call" either for continual services or to ensure that he or she is available when needed. The retainer is normally a fixed amount of money paid to the consultant every month. The consultant keeps track of the time spent, a running balance of the account, and bills for any excess. An account is rendered every month for extra time spent over and above the monthly retainer.

Another type of arrangement might involve not submitting additional accounts until the end of the retainer period, at which time any overage would be made up. A third variation could be that you are committed in your retainer arrangement to providing a certain amount of service every month. If you underestimated the amount of monthly time involved, you would be then paid the extra time per month.

If you have an "on call" arrangement with the client and are therefore unable to commit yourself to other projects, the client would pay the fixed amount every month for the privilege of having you on call, whether or not your services were used. This could be whatever you negotiated; for example, 25% to 50% of your average monthly billable time. In addition to the on call retainer, when you perform services for the client you would bill out at your hourly or daily rate, depending on the nature of your arrangement.

9. EQUITY FEES

If a client is having difficulty in a business venture and you have skills in obtaining financing or business management, a fee could be negotiated in the form of equity or a percentage of the shares in the company. This is normally negotiated when the client lacks the financial resources to pay for your time. The risk for the consultant and the business is high, so the equity arrangement would have to be very attractive to justify the risk, depending on the situation.

The problem with an equity fee arrangement is that it changes your role from a consultant to a part owner. You could lose your ability to be an objective consultant due to your vested interest in the outcome of your advice. It would be prudent, due to potential conflict of interest, to remove yourself from the situation by either selling out your interest once you have received it, or resigning as a consultant.

10. UTILIZATION RATE

The utilization rate tells you how efficient you are; that is, the cost/benefit factor. It tells you the percentage of your total working hours that you bill to clients. To determine the utilization rate, divide the number of billable hours by the number of total working hours available. For example, if you assume a 40-hour work week and allow two weeks' vacation, you would have approximately 2,000 total work hours available each year. If you divide 1,000 hours of billing to clients each year by 2,000, you have 50% utilization rate. If you consult part-time at 12 hours per week and you bill for four hours each week, then your utilization rate is 33.3%.

Your utilization rate quickly informs you how much of your time clients are directly paying for and how much you must absorb as overhead. The fewer hours you bill, the more you must charge per hour or reduce your overhead; the more hours you bill, the less you need to charge to maintain your profit level. You can see how important it is to keep an accurate record of how all your time is spent when operating a consulting practice, so that you can accurately and graphically see how efficiently (or inefficiently) you are operating.

11. VARYING YOUR FEES

The fees you quote a client can vary depending on various factors. As mentioned earlier, you should consider your experience, the ability of the client to pay, the future benefit of ongoing work the client might provide, your need for cash flow, and the different regional areas for which you are submitting a consulting proposal.

If you are submitting a proposal outside your region, you should check out the cost of doing business in that area. Is it more or less expensive than your own region? Check on your competitors and their rates within the region you are considering. If local rates are higher, consider raising your rates to meet local schedules. If the rates are lower, consider reducing your rates, but only with a very clear analysis of the benefit and profit. The rates might be too low to be attractive. It is important that you go through these steps, as a prospective client will be able to detect inadequate preparation if your costing does not reflect local variances and customs.

12. INCREASING FEES

From time to time you will want to increase your fees. This could be based on your regular monthly, quarterly, or other review of your cash flow statements, profit and loss statements, or projected needs. Your utilization rate, as described earlier, is also a factor.

If you are considering increasing fees, it is a good idea to do it at a fixed time every year, such as January 1. You should also attempt to notify your clients at least three months in advance, in writing, of your intention to increase your fees. Include a brief explanation about the reasons, such as an increase in costs, if appropriate. Invite the client to contact you if there are any questions. It is important, for obvious reasons, to keep the increase competitive.

13. INCREASING PROFITS WITHOUT INCREASING FEES

There are many ways you can increase your profits apart from raising fees. Naturally, clients are not always going to appreciate your reasons for increasing your fees so other effective methods can be used to increase your profits. Some methods you may wish to consider are as follows:

- Keep your overall fixed overhead down. Review all the ways of saving costs on space, telephone, and personnel discussed earlier.

- Use company cars, space, and supplies wherever possible.

- Obtain the client's agreement to supply necessary support services such as secretarial and clerical, mail rooms, postage, delivery service, and other support services and personnel. This will keep your administration costs down.

- Obtain approval to charge authorized purchases pertaining to the project to the client.

- Keep an accurate record of all out-of-pocket expenses incurred pertaining to the client's project, document them, and bill for them properly.

- Arrange with the client to pay you in advance for entertainment or travel expenses you anticipate. That way you can use the client's money and

provide an accounting for any extra funds.

- If you are consulting on an hourly basis, attempt to arrange to be at your client's office or project for a full day if possible, rather than a portion of the day.

- Transportation costs and time of travel are not always accurately reflected in the adjustments with the client. Make sure that you have realistically calculated your commuting time.

- Determine a minimum fee requirement. The time and costs of a proposal, and the administrative work required by a project will dictate a minimum fee and profit before you make a proposal.

- Avoid giving away free consulting. There are techniques to avoid giving away your time, which is worth money. This will increase your effective utilization rate and therefore increase profits. The various ways of avoiding free consulting are covered in chapter 17.

- Increase your rates for work requested outside of regular business hours. A premium fee should be charged for work performed on the weekends or evenings or part of a day. In the latter case, you should have a minimum charge (e.g., you will be paid for four hours whether you work four hours or less time). This suggestion also applies when clients ask that their project be given priority over other projects.

- Consider obtaining advance payment on account for projected initial or total disbursements if they are considerable. The deposit can be collecting interest for your benefit. As discussed previously, you should consider negotiating in advance for a sizable deposit if your services are in demand and you are expending time for the client at the expense of other client work you could do.

- Review your credit policy regularly. If you extend credit, make sure your receivables are promptly collected; otherwise you will be paying more interest to the bank on your operating line of credit loan.

- Attempt to minimize bad debts by adopting the various procedures suggested in chapter 12, with modifications for your own situation. Ask for your lawyer's advice on this. Eliminating bad debts is a very effective way of increasing your profits.

- Consider negotiating a bonus with a client for meeting contract needs. For example, if you complete a project for less than the amount allocated in the budget, you could negotiate a percentage of the saving. If your client has deadline schedules, you could agree to give the project priority, which would involve considerable overtime and other disruptions for you, and negotiate a bonus for the number of days you are ahead of the deadline.

- Consider negotiating a "value of the project" fee or a contingency fee arrangement if the circumstances and the nature of your consulting practice make this approach feasible. You could therefore increase your profit without spending additional time by receiving a higher return due to your skill, knowledge of the industry, or tactical or negotiating abilities.

CHAPTER 14
DETERMINING MARKET OPPORTUNITIES

Before determining market opportunities and identifying clients with accuracy and success, various matters have to be considered.

You have to be very certain in your own mind of your area or areas of specialization. It is impossible to target your market without this basic information. Review the exercises in chapter 2 to determine your specific skills, talents, and attributes, and attempt to visualize the market that is suited to your abilities. It is important to avoid the tendency to be too restrictive in your view of the market for your services. Look for a wide spectrum of opportunities to apply your services in vertical and horizontal markets and in both the public and private sector. Identify common themes and processes. Know why there is a demand for consulting services so you can aim your marketing at those concerns when targeting prospective clients.

Thorough research is required to educate yourself and stimulate your mind on the wide range of possibilities. Read selected newspapers, magazines, and trade journals on a regular basis, and look for consulting opportunities created by political, economic, and social changes affecting your area of expertise and interest.

The next chapter discusses marketing techniques in more detail. This chapter is intended to provide a brief overview of the private and public sector and the possibility of market opportunities.

1. PRIVATE SECTOR

There are numerous opportunities in the private sector. By being aware of the issues and problems and solutions in your service area, it will be easier for you to identify and think of opportunities every time you are exposed to information through personal communication, television, radio, newspapers, magazines, trade journals, or books. The habit of training yourself to be aware of marketing opportunities at all times is essential.

It is important to understand the motivating factors that will cause a potential client to want your services. You might be very aware of the needs of your service within your specialty area, but a client who does not recognize that your service is needed will not be receptive to your offer of assistance.

There are many reasons that motivate a client to retain a consultant, but three of the basic reasons are to obtain information, to save time, and to save money. If you can visualize the ways you can save a client time and money, and provide the most current and accurate information in the client's area of interest and need, market opportunities in the private sector will be considerable.

1.1 Individuals

Individuals buy the services of consultants in a wide variety of fields. A walk through the Yellow Pages should provide a good example. Advice on how to save money or how to make money is fairly common. In this instance, the target market is anyone in the higher earning bracket, including executives and professionals. Some examples of consultants in this area are tax consultants, financial consultants, investment consultants, and real estate consultants. Other consulting areas include interior design and fashion.

1.2 Small businesses

Small businesses provide an excellent client base for a new consultant. The failure rate of small businesses is very high. The small business owner/operator's lack of knowledge in important areas of small business management is often a factor. If your skills include small business management and making or saving money in a small business, you can find a market. There are numerous books available on small business management that will provide ideas for you. Some are listed in the Bibliography.

Various techniques can be used to attract small business clients. You can offer a fee based on percentage of savings or profits that occur as a result of your advice. Naturally, you would have to have a measurable basis for showing the positive benefits that your advice has created. A percentage fee is a good marketing device. It shows confidence in yourself and it is a difficult offer to refuse as your payment is based on performance.

Small businesses also need to raise funds, either through the venture capital market, commercial banks, or government grants and loans. Most small businesses go through growing pains. Wherever business growth occurs, problems occur, and wherever problems occur, a need exists for solutions.

1.3 Medium-size businesses

There is a high demand for consultants in medium-size businesses. Companies often hire experts as required instead of hiring staff. Hiring staff involves the related costs of training, benefit packages, and long-term commitments for possibly short-term needs. Businesses are vulnerable to economic changes, and their survival is based on keeping overheads low and making a profit. Any areas of need you can identify to increase efficiency and productivity and sales and to decrease overhead and losses will create a demand for your services.

Medium-size businesses, as well, are constantly going through various stages of growth with all the predictable problems involved.

The advantage of dealing with a medium-size business is that projects tend to be more lucrative. There is also a greater chance of repeat business. Another advantage is that the decision-makers are generally more sophisticated than small business owners, better able to see the need for a consultant more readily, more accustomed to dealing with consultants, and able to respond more quickly on proposals.

1.4 Large companies

It is more difficult to obtain contracts from larger companies. Many large companies prefer dealing with large consulting firms or well-known consultants with considerable experience and contacts.

Because of the money available in larger businesses, consulting opportunities do exist, particularly in the area of temporary technical assistance. It is common for consultants to large companies to have developed their experience and confidence with smaller and medium-size companies before marketing to the larger companies.

2. PUBLIC SECTOR

Government is a major user of consulting services. Marketing opportunities are available in various forms in the public sector. You can submit a solicited or unsolicited proposal and attempt to get the contract directly. You can indirectly benefit from government by subcontracting with other companies who have been awarded the main contract. An additional way of making money through government is as a grants consultant assisting organizations or businesses to obtain grants or subsidies.

If you are considering government as a source of business, you should be aware of the various ways of obtaining contacts or information to assist you. You should also understand the way the government approval system operates.

2.1 Making contacts and obtaining information

There are various steps you can take to obtain the necessary information and make the necessary contacts to assist you in your government dealings.

(a) Read government advertisements and publications pertaining to your areas of interest.

(b) Place your name on the government mailing list. There are numerous government departments and you can request that your name be placed on each list to receive all relevant information, including proposed procurements and contracts awarded relating to your field.

(c) Attempt to have your name placed on the government sourcing list as a consultant in various specialty areas. When the government is looking, your name should come to their attention. There are various computerized sourcing lists throughout the departments of government; make sure that your name is on all the ones that relate to your areas of interest.

(d) Contact government contract officers. Most government contracts are awarded at the department or agency level where the specific needs are best known and money has been allocated. The phone book has listings for various branches of government. The public library has updated lists of all the key government departments, individuals, their titles, and phone numbers. Once you have obtained the correct department, ask to speak to the contract officer who can provide you with further background.

(e) Visit government departments and agencies. After you have submitted your resume to various government departments, you may wish to introduce yourself to the person in charge of approving contracts. This may or may not be appropriate or possible, depending on your geographic location and government policy. Maintaining contact with the key person who could award a contract shows your interest in keeping your name current. It also demonstrates initiative and confidence. On the other hand, it could cause irritation or you could discover you have a personality conflict. (In which case you may decide that you don't want to pursue contracts with this person.)

(f) Contact large consulting firms that are the recipients of government contracts and might require additional consulting assistance for those contracts.

(g) Contact other companies that have recently received a government contract. You can discover the names of these companies by obtaining copies of government award publications or viewing them in the public library. These are published weekly and announce all the contracts that have been awarded, who received the contract, and the amount and nature of the services to be performed. With this information, you can determine what subcontracting opportunities might be available in your area of specialty and immediately contact the companies concerned.

(h) If you have friends or acquaintances who work in government, tell them you are looking for consulting assignments in your specialty. You should also provide them with your resume and brochure if possible. They might be in a position to inform you if they hear of an agency in need of your services. You might therefore hear of a need before the department has advertised for services or selected a consultant. You can then submit an unsolicited proposal.

2.2 Understanding the government approval system

The government approval system is very formal and bureaucratic in its operation.

Most government contracts are awarded only after a call for proposals, whereas in the private sector, submitting an unsolicited proposal is the most common method for obtaining work. The general procedure for government approval is given below. The procedure is the same for any level of government (i.e., municipal, state/provincial, federal).

(a) A government department head or agency requiring consulting service assigns personnel to an internal search to see if the service can be performed in-house.

(b) If no civil service employee is available to perform the work, a request for proposal is advertised, proposals are received, and the consultant is eventually selected. It is quite common that consultants are "preselected" before the closing date of the advertisement. This is because the consultant may already be on the source list and be known as best suited for the project. The advertisement is a required government formality.

(c) The government department drafts a contract and submits it to the consultant for review and signature.

(d) The signed contract is reviewed and approved again by the government's legal department.

(e) A contract is forwarded to the chief administrative officer of the division for approval.

(f) The contract and specifications are forwarded to the government purchaser for approval.

(g) The contract and fee schedule are forwarded to the government controller to verify that funds are available and have been set aside to honor the payment commitment.

(h) Notification of formal approval is sent to the consultant to begin the consulting services within the terms of the contract.

(i) Work begins and is completed.

(j) Payment is received at the end of the project or throughout the project, depending on the terms of the contract. Many government departments are slow to pay because of the bureaucratic nature and requirements within the system for approval before payment. As this may cause cash flow difficulties for you, you should make arrangements for progress payments if at all possible. If necessary you can get a bank loan for your cash flow needs based on the strength of a government contract.

3. GRANT CONSULTING

A grants consultant attempts to obtain grants, loans, or subsidies for a client. The federal government and its various agencies award large sums of money to eligible applicants. The process followed by grants consultants is as follows:

(a) The consultant learns as much as possible about the sources of funding, the amount of funding, the procedures required, and the key contact people. The consultant contacts the approval officer and obtains information on the appropriate or desired detail and format for successful applications.

(b) The consultant determines the potential target market and the names of the firms and individuals who could be future contacts.

(c) A personal letter with brochures is sent to the key people, followed by a telephone call and meeting if possible.

(d) The consultant identifies the specific needs of the organization or company in the interview process. The interview process is similar to that described in chapter 16.

(e) The consultant advises the organization of the availability of government funds and the consultant's expertise in obtaining them. Most organizations and businesses do not have people who realize that money is available or know how to effectively submit an application to obtain it. The consultant performs the analysis, collects all the necessary detail for documentation, and prepares the application for signature by an authorized representative of the organization or company.

(f) The consultant normally takes an administration fee which is a negotiated percentage of the amount awarded. The client therefore has an incentive to deal with the consultant, because the consultant's fee is based on performance only and paid from the funds received.

(g) The consultant could also be responsible for coordinating the implementation of the program on which the funding was based, if applicable.

(h) Once a grants consultant has succeeded with one group, marketing to all other organizations similar to that group can be effectively performed.

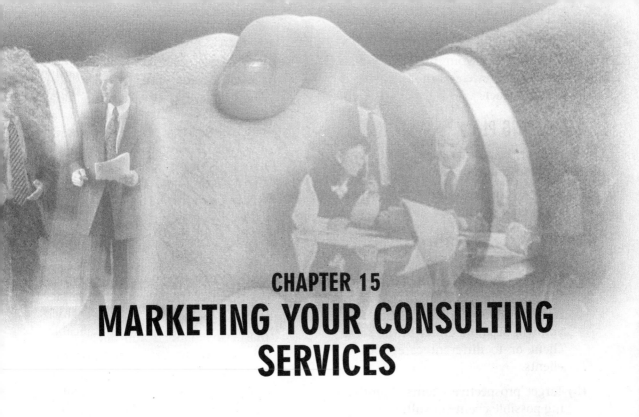

CHAPTER 15
MARKETING YOUR CONSULTING SERVICES

1. WHAT YOU NEED TO MARKET YOUR SERVICE

Marketing, the stimulus that creates an awareness of and demand for your services, is essential for success in the consulting business. This process involves a wide spectrum of activities, ultimately directed at convincing prospective clients that their needs can be met and their problems can be solved by your specific services. Selling is one part of the marketing program that is intended to result in a consulting assignment by means of personal interaction begun at the initial interview and maintained during and after the assignment.

The dynamics of the marketing/selling stages have to be clearly understood and cultivated by the consultant. For example, when you are marketing yourself, you have to calculate the image that you want to project when you are packaging your product that is, yourself and your services. You and your marketing efforts must project authority, confidence, friendliness, candor, expertise, competence, and leadership.

Many consultants fail, or maintain a marginal income, because of poor marketing. Consultants frequently do not appreciate the necessity of marketing, do not know how to market, do not like to market, do not want to market, or do not take the time to market.

This chapter will help you understand the various techniques required to build your image as an expert or authority, thereby creating a demand for your services. The next chapter covers some of the personal selling techniques involved in the first interview. Once your marketing plan has stimulated the interest, the next step is to close the contract.

2. MARKETING PLAN

A summary of the factors that go into your marketing plan follows:

(a) Define your skills and services. This is covered in chapter 2. You should have a clear idea now of the nature of services you will be offering potential clients. You may have decided on just one particular area of interest and specialty, or you may have decided on several areas that you will promote either to the same client or to different categories of clients.

(b) Target prospective clients. Identifying possible client consulting opportunities is the next step in the marketing plan. This was covered in the last chapter.

(c) Make potential clients and the general public aware of your services, and create a demand. The various techniques required for this step are covered in the next section.

(d) Respond to inquiries with direct client meetings. Naturally, once interest has been shown by a prospective client due to your effective marketing, your next step is to follow up on the lead quickly, personally see the client if that is possible, attempt to ascertain the client's precise needs, and determine how to remedy the problem.

(e) Prepare a proposal. This step follows the preceding one, confirms the client meeting, and outlines what you intend to do, how, for how much, and when. You can only write a convincing proposal after you have had an opportunity to ascertain the client's needs and the benefits that you can provide.

(f) Perform the project. This is the purpose of the whole marketing exercise — to end up with the client so you can provide your service, generate revenue, and make a profit.

(g) Follow-up is the final step in the marketing plan. If you did not obtain a contract after your previous attempts to market, you should maintain some follow-up procedure in case the client needs your services in the future. Possibly there were budget restraints the first time.

If you were able to obtain a contract and provide a service, you should have a follow-up routine in place to encourage repeat business with that client. Open communication with the client is important to ensure goodwill and possible referral business.

3. MARKETING TECHNIQUES

The following suggestions describe traditional as well as unusual ways of marketing consulting services. Many of the techniques cost little or nothing except for your time. Whether you use just a few of the techniques or all of them depends on your style, your priorities, the nature of your service, and your type of clientele.

3.1 Newspaper

Most consultants do not use newspapers as a source of advertising for their services. It is looked upon as unprofessional by many. Most clients select a consultant by reputation. But it depends on the nature of your consulting business. For example, if you specialize in small business cash flow problems, and if there are small businesses with problems in your region, you might put a tasteful, professional advertisement in the display ads in the business section or in the classified section to stimulate interest.

3.2 Advertising in trade or professional journals

The advantage of advertising in these publications is the very specialized market you reach — the readers could all be potential prospects. Therefore, the cost/benefit feature of this form of advertising can be low. You should attempt to get all the trade and professional journals related to your area of skill and services and familiarize yourself with the format and the nature of the journal ads.

3.3 Directories

There are many excellent reference guides listing technical, professional, and trade organizations and associations. Your public library might have the *Encyclopedia of Associations* and *The National Trade and Professional Associations of the United States*. Many of the organizations listed in the directories publish annual directories of their memberships.

Of the organizations that have directories, approximately half of them will include your name in their directory free of charge as a consultant in that area of interest. Most of the other organizations have paid advertising available, which could be of benefit if the directory is read by a prime segment of your market.

For additional sources of information on directories in the United States and Canada, refer to Appendix 1.

3.4 Brochures

Brochures are a very important part of marketing your practice. There are many ways to use a brochure.

(a) Leave the brochure with a prospective client after a face-to-face meeting.

(b) Mail the brochure after a written or formal request for further information.

(c) Send the brochure in a direct mail campaign targeted to prospective clients.

(d) Distribute the brochure at a seminar or presentation you are giving.

(e) The day after a seminar or presentation, send the brochure out to those attending as a form of follow-up communication.

Keep in mind that your brochure is probably the first contact a prospective client has with you and the services you offer. The reaction to the brochure may be positive or negative, depending on its format, content, and quality. Following are some tips on preparing a brochure.

(a) As first impressions are critical, it is important that the layout, graphics, and paper be of top quality. You want to stimulate a desire in the recipient to retain you as a consultant, or at least to inquire further.

(b) Use an 8" x 11" size of paper that will have two folds and six panels. Obtain advice from typesetters and graphic artists and printers before you finish your draft. Seek out comparative opinions and quotes until you are satisfied with the quality and cost offered. The design of the brochure should be consistent with your stationery and business cards.

(c) The phrasing of the text should reflect a confident, positive, dynamic yet professional tone. Have the spelling, grammar, syntax, and style of your text reviewed by someone with skills in that area.

(d) The text should be concise, clear, and brief. Text in point form can be easily read. Refrain from using large or complicated words. Keep the words simple and direct. Focus on the benefits that a prospective client will receive from your services. Draft the text from the viewpoint of the client's needs.

(e) Provide information on the history of your business, the nature of your business, your clientele, and the type of services you perform. Explain why a particular service might be required. Explain or list the benefits that you can give to provide the service and meet the need or resolve the problem. Think of previous clients who benefited from your advice and assistance.

(f) List your academic and professional achievements and experiences.

(g) Do not list your associates unless you have a long-standing relationship or know that they will be staying with you for an extended time. Refer instead to the resource base of talent your firm offers. You may wish to itemize the skills that are provided by key associates.

(h) If appropriate, a number of testimonials from clients, or a list of important clients, could be included in the brochure.

(i) Many consultants prefer not to have their photograph in the brochure as a matter of personal choice and style. The reaction of a potential client to your photograph could be negative or positive based on your picture alone.

(j) Before you have the brochure printed, have a number of your friends, relatives, and business associates look at the draft copy of the brochure and obtain their candid feedback.

3.5 Direct mail

Direct mail can be a very effective means of making potential clients aware of and interested in your services. There are several advantages to direct mail: the cost is flexible, the sales message can be personalized to the needs of that particular target group, and with a word processing program, letters can be individually addressed to specific persons. An important cost/benefit aspect is the controlled circulation to a very select audience.

An integral part of direct mail marketing is the development or rental of a mailing list. There are many sources of rental lists. The major ones are Standard Rates and Data Service and Dun and Bradstreet. Both these companies have extensive mailing lists available for the United States and Canada. The lists include names, addresses, and postal/zip codes broken down into specific categories and regions. For further information, look under "Direct Mail" in the Yellow Pages.

The various directories of organizations related to your specialty may also rent or sell mailing lists. The advantage of this type of mailing list is that prospective clients may be members of the organization that publishes the directory. You would therefore be targeting your services to your specific trade or interest market.

There are brokers who represent all the major direct mail marketing companies. For a fee, they will determine the best mix of mailing lists for your purposes, depending on the amount of money you are prepared to budget. The broker will obtain the best rates for you and charge you a fee.

Mailing lists are generally rented for one-time use, and are "seeded" with the names of fictitious companies or individuals to ensure you do not use the list more than once. However, if someone responds to your mailing, for information or with an assignment, you can add that name to your mailing list.

It is difficult to estimate with certainty, but approximately 1% to 4% of direct mail marketing ultimately results in consulting assignments. Many factors will determine your response rate, for example, the type of consulting service you provide, the economic climate at the time, the cyclical or seasonal demand for your type of service, and the techniques and format you use in the direct mail approach. It is important to keep a record of all contacts you make and record the names and particulars. All clients should be added to your mailing list.

There are various stages involved in direct mailing, all of which are equally important to obtain the desired objective. The basic steps are as follows:

(a) Your first mailing should be within the regional area you can realistically service. It is also an opportunity to test market and analyze the effectiveness of your mailings without spending a large sum of money.

(b) Your mailing should consist of a personalized cover letter (printed on a word processor if available) addressed directly to the key decision-maker. Use quality letterhead stationery to create a professional impression. You might also enclose your business card. Enclose a copy of your brochure with your letter. Outline briefly the services you offer and the benefits that will be obtained by the prospective client. State that you will contact the client in ten calendar (or business) days to answer any questions and discuss the matter further at that time.

(c) Keep an accurate filing system of all prospective clients you intend to follow-up on. List all pertinent information on the card so you can review it and familiarize yourself with it before you contact the client. Note the date you will contact the prospective client in your daily calendar.

(d) Follow-up with a telephone call ten days after you mail the letter. This will give the client a positive impression of your administration and professionalism. Follow the telephone call with a visit to the prospective client if circumstances allow. The next chapter outlines other procedures and techniques to follow before, during, and after the first meeting with the prospective client.

(e) If the response to your mailing is poor, thoroughly review all your techniques and format. This includes the direct mail target group, cover letter, brochure, telephone techniques, and meetings.

(f) Constantly revise, refine, and upgrade your mailing list with new prospects.

(g) Send out mailings on a quarterly basis (or more often) as your finances, marketing plan, and other circumstances dictate. This will remind people of your services and expertise, and the repetition ultimately does have an effect. When sending out repetitive mailings, consider enclosing a newsletter, which you could easily prepare, and copies of any articles or other papers pertaining to the industry that is your target base. You may want to have a tear-off coupon in the newsletter that readers can send back if they want to be put on your newsletter mailing list. This way you should be able to track the response. Over time, a large portion of qualified prospects should respond to regular and consistent promotional efforts.

3.6 Contact network

You need to develop a contact network to develop future prospects and a mailing list. It is a very effective way to acquire clients by referral. Studies have shown that a high percentage of a consultant's clientele comes from referrals through a contact network or from satisfied clients. A contact network is a collection of relatives, associates, and acquaintances who will give you an introduction to, or pave the way to your acceptance by an organization or individual who needs your services.

You already have a network, and you can cultivate many more contacts. A partial list includes past and present clients, employees, professional colleagues, business associates, bankers, lawyers, accountants, friends, neighbors, and relatives. Also included are contacts you develop in associations and religious, professional, trade, business, or other organizations. If you sit down and list everyone who comes to mind as a potential contact, the list will be longer than you think.

Developing the contact network is the most effective and inexpensive way of increasing your exposure and credibility. Continually update your network by adding leads and other contacts to your mailing list.

3.7 Membership in professional, trade, or business associations

Joining a group and then actively participating in meetings and other functions is an effective means of developing leads. Attempt to attend meetings regularly and get involved in discussions. Evaluate a group or association on the basis of potential consulting prospects who are active in the association. You want to look for members who are likely to give you consulting opportunities. Because of the time commitment involved to develop your reputation within an organization, you must be very selective in your membership. Limit your memberships to one or two. You may wish to consider civic or trade organizations or associations such as the Chamber of Commerce, Rotarians, Kiwanis, or associations directly related to your service area. Obtain a list of all the members of the organization and review the list thoroughly. Most lists provide the name, position and company, type of business or profession of the member, and address.

3.8 Donating your services

You may wish to donate some consulting time and commitment to a worthwhile nonprofit organization as a gesture of goodwill. Naturally, you have to be very cautious about the time involved relative to the potential benefit, but your services without charge can enhance your image and result directly or indirectly in referrals.

3.9 Attending public and professional meetings

Consider attending meetings covering a subject directly related to your field of expertise. You want to see and be seen. Plan to contribute your opinion, if appropriate, in a well-planned, concise, and intelligent fashion. Prospective clients could be attending the meeting. Attempt to identify and talk to people you believe are worthwhile contacts. There are many meetings held on an ongoing basis, such as city council meetings, federal commissions, public hearings on specific areas of concern, and appeal board meetings.

3.10 Lectures

Many organizations or associations need speakers for breakfast, luncheon, or dinner meetings, conferences, or conventions. Look in the Yellow Pages under "Associations" to obtain appropriate names. Also, review directories of associations available at your local library. Two publications worth checking are *National Trade and Professional Associations of the United States* and *Associations Canada: Directory of Associations in Canada*. See Appendix 1 for other useful directories.

When you contact the program chairperson, offer your services for free and advise him or her that you have a number of prepared talks you believe would be of particular interest to the membership. Mention that your subject areas are topical and interesting, and your talk can be between 10 and 30 minutes long. This is the normal range of time required for a speaker. Ask about the mix of membership and the number of members who normally attend meetings. Attempt to get in advance a list of members to review so that you can direct your comments more accurately toward your group.

It is helpful to have ready two or three 10- to 20-minute presentations with supporting material. You will then be available on short notice for any presentation.

The object of the presentation is not to make money, but to obtain contacts and increase your credibility and exposure for future consulting opportunities. Those who attend the presentation will probably tell their friends or acquaintances about you if your presentation is interesting. Make sure you tell the audience that you are a consultant. During your presentation you can give a number of examples or anecdotes based on your experiences. This will reinforce your image as an expert. People will remember you better by the examples or stories that you relate.

You may also wish to consider Dale Carnegie courses, Toastmaster membership, or public speaking workshops to enhance your communication ability. For more tips about presenting your ideas in front of an audience, check with your public library for public speaking books and tapes.

3.11 Teaching

There are many opportunities to offer your services as a teacher for school board adult education classes or university or community college continuing education courses. You generally get paid for your time, but ideally the students who attend the course will be potential clients or will recommend you to friends or associates. Make sure that you teach adults only to maximize the potential benefit. You are primarily looking for credibility, exposure, and contacts. The preparation required to teach a course also keeps you current on your subject area.

3.12 Seminars and workshops

You may wish to consider offering your own seminar or workshop. You can offer the seminar for free or for a nominal charge. The people who attend are excellent potential clients. You should try to select a subject that allows you to provide a practical overview of important tips and ideas within your specialty area. You can promote your seminar through your direct mail list. Allow four to eight weeks lead time to ensure that people can schedule in your seminar.

Other items to consider are the length of the seminar; the location; the time, whether day or evening; when refreshments would be served, if any; and the number of people you can accommodate. Make sure your announcement states that space is limited and available by advance registration only. In your announcement you can request that registration be made by telephone one week in advance of the seminar. This will give you some idea as to the response and assist you in the preparation of your material. (If your registration deadline is one week before the seminar and not enough people appear to be interested, you can try to negotiate a cancellation arrangement with the hotel facility by paying a portion of the room rent, or possibly nothing at all, if the hotel is able to re-book the facility.)

You may also wish to consider the free advertising possibilities in the local newspaper and other monthly or weekly publications. If you allow yourself enough lead time, you should be able to conduct the seminar at a cost of $100 to $500. Depending on the number of people and the amount you are charging, you could break even on the seminar.

Make sure you distribute your brochures, newsletters, and any other appropriate material at the seminar. Develop a seminar evaluation form where participants can give their opinions of you and your seminar topic through rating scales and space for additional comments. Also include questions that will provide you with biographical information on the participants. Attach a coupon to the seminar evaluation form for participants to complete if they wish to be kept on your mailing list for newsletters. Also have a space on the form to ask what particular areas of interest or concern a participant might have. This should assist you in developing other seminars or improving the existing one.

When a person phones in to register prior to the seminar, and on the day of the seminar, make sure that you get the full company name, address, phone number, and name and position of the person attending. You will want this information for your mailing list.

For further information on conducting seminars and workshops, visit your local public library for books regarding these topics.

3.13 Free media exposure

There are many ways to obtain free media exposure. Exposure provides you with credibility and develops public awareness of you as an expert or authority in one or more areas. If a seminar or presentation is offered, either through your own company or through some other organization, consider preparing a news release. Send it in advance to the appropriate radio, television, newspaper, or magazine contact person. Determine who the contact person is and call

in advance so he or she will be expecting your letter or news release. This also gives you an opportunity to introduce yourself and to make sure that the approach you are adopting will obtain the desired free exposure.

Ask the contact person what format is preferred for the information required. Spell out in your letter, and in your conversation, why you feel the topic of the presentation is of interest to the readers, viewers, or listeners. The subject matter may be topical or controversial.

3.14 Radio and television talk shows

You might also appear in person on a radio or television talk show. The same approach applies as in free media announcements. Locate the appropriate contact person and sell him or her on the benefits to the listeners or viewers of your being interviewed on the program. If possible, try to be on the program a week before your seminar or presentation in order to stimulate attendance. If the talk program is too distant from the seminar date, the listener may forget about it.

For more information about writing press releases and handling the media, see *Getting Publicity*, another title in the Self-Counsel Series.

3.15 Letters to the editor

It is easy to get published in the "letters to the editor" section of a magazine or newspaper. Write a letter that is topical and relevant and reflects a controversial or divergent opinion. Refer to an earlier article if you are reacting to something previously published. Mention in the letter that you are a professional consultant in the field and have expertise in the subject area.

3.16 Writing articles

Writing is an effective way of developing exposure, credibility, and contacts. Once you have developed the format, style, and discipline, you should be able to write three or more articles a year for various publications. All publications are looking for articles; many do not pay very much, if anything, for unsolicited articles — but they will publish your work.

To locate magazines that reach your target audience, look at *Business Publications Rates and Data*, a publication from Standard Rates and Data Service. You should be able to find this publication in your library or university, or through a local advertising agency.

Write an article about your area of expertise that you believe would be of particular interest to the readership of the publication. Use examples and stories in your article. The subject matter could be new trends, the effect of pending legislation, technical information, or any other angle that will enhance your image as an expert.

Contact the publishers of your targeted magazines or journals and obtain free copies so you can review them and familiarize yourself with their style and length. If your article is accepted for publication, request a byline and a brief biographical comment at the end of the article. Say that you are a consultant in your area of expertise, and invite questions or comments about the article. (Not all publications will permit this.)

There are numerous books on writing style. Have your article reviewed by at least one, if not two, friends or relatives who will candidly comment. Submit a good quality 5" x 7" glossy photograph of yourself and a biography with the article. Submit the article to one trade or business magazine at a time. Keep a list of editors at several trade journals and business magazines whose readership constitutes your potential target base. If one does not publish your article, send it on to the next editor on your list. When it is published, obtain extra copies of the publication to distribute in your next direct mailing or presentation.

Additional benefits to writing articles are the contacts you can make and the credibility you can develop as you go through the research process. For example, you could select 20 or 30 people to interview for background information for the article. These people could include key potential clients. Have a script ready before you phone them, ask open-ended questions, listen carefully and note their answers. Ask follow-up questions to their responses. This should show that you are knowledgeable and an intelligent communicator. When you contact prospective clients to interview them over the telephone, introduce yourself as a consultant writing an article. You can ask their opinion on matters such as the effect of pending legislation, unique problems they encounter in their field of interest, and major opportunities or trends they perceive.

The telephone conversation can be followed by a letter thanking people for their cooperation and assistance. Depending on the responses to your questions, you may see that many consulting opportunities exist with the people contacted. They may have mentioned some of their problems. At a comfortable time in the future, you may wish to contact these sources and follow up with a personal letter and brochure. You might feel it appropriate to say you will contact them ten days later to ask whether you may be of service. Subtlety is essential.

3.17 Writing a book

Having a book published is another marketing technique to establish yourself as an expert in your field. There are a number of limitations though. You have to find a publisher for your book or publish it yourself, which can be quite expensive. Your book could be obsolete by the time it is published, as a lead time of approximately one to one-and-a-half years is required before publication. The time you would have to spend on the book might not be justified in terms of the cost/benefit due to loss of income or potential income. It could be far more beneficial to spend the time writing articles rather than a book. Regularly publishing articles also keeps your name in front of the public and reinforces your image as a specialist.

3.18 Have articles written about you

Every field of consulting has news value. By carefully cultivating relationships with editors and reporters, you could be looked on as an expert in your area. They might invite your opinion and quote you in an article on the topic. You could also have articles written about you if you can demonstrate a newsworthy feature, topical benefit, or uniqueness. Attempt to look for news angles that could have a direct or indirect effect on the public at large or your target group in particular. Look at economic, political, or legislative factors. Over time you could build up a reputation as an authority that will generate inquiries from prospective clients.

3.19 Announcement columns

Many professional, trade, or university alumni publications have sections devoted to announcements of interest about their members. Make a point of regularly updating information provided to these publications whenever you can find an excuse to justify it, if your style allows. If you give a presentation, expand the services that you provide, or announce new associates or distinctions, you can get your name inserted. If you are giving a seminar or workshop, give yourself enough lead time for an announcement to be inserted, if possible, in these publications. Many daily or weekly publications have a free announcement section available.

3.20 Newsletters

Newsletters are a very common way for consultants to promote themselves. They offer a subtle form of advertising that can give you credibility, as well as providing advice to readers. Most newsletters are distributed free since they are used as a marketing device. Once you establish a reputation and a large mailing list, economics and demand may justify charging a fee for a subscription.

The important features of a newsletter are effective use of color and layout, a professional appearance, and well-written articles on interesting subjects. Most potential clients who will receive your newsletter are very busy; unless the newsletter captures their attention and is easily readable, it will not serve the purpose that you intend. The newsletter should have tips, news, ideas, and possibly a question and answer column. It should be two to six pages long, on 8" x 11" size paper, and published on a regular basis, such as monthly, bimonthly, quarterly, or semi-annually. The frequency of your publication will depend on your finances and time.

A newsletter is distributed in the same manner outlined earlier for brochures. When sending out brochures with covering letters in response to an inquiry, you should also include a recent copy of your newsletter. As in the case of direct mail marketing and brochures, you should address the newsletter to the key people in target organizations.

3.21 Web site

As discussed in Chapter 3, you may want to seriously consider the many marketing benefits of having your own Web site. Look in the Yellow Pages of the phone book for similar or competing consultant's Web sites, by finding out the Web site address. Also check out the listing of consultants practicing in the same field, by looking at consultant directories in your specified field, or generic consulting directories. All these directories should be available in your public library, from your professional association, or on the Internet. Then research the Web sites of other consultants in your field, to determine how you can develop a better professional Web site that meets your needs and goals.

CHAPTER 16
THE CLIENT INTERVIEW AND CLIENT RELATIONS

Your efforts at marketing have now been successful. The prospective client is aware of your services and a meeting has been arranged, requested by you or the prospective client. The initial interview is a critical step before preparing a proposal and obtaining a contract. There are many important techniques that you will have to understand and adapt for your particular needs. This chapter covers the matters you should consider before, during, and after the client interview.

1. PURPOSE OF INTERVIEW

The purpose of the interview is primarily fact finding, followed by an analysis of the client needs and problem identification. After these steps, you will be able to prepare a proposal. The meeting, of course, has other purposes, such as assessing the prospective client's personality, ability to pay, and expectations. It also provides an opportunity for an interchange of ideas and mutual assessment.

2. BEFORE THE MEETING

If the client contacted you, you know a need exists and the client has some confidence in you. You should not have an interview over the telephone if at all possible. You want to have a face-to-face talk. Do not quote your rates over the phone, as they could be misinterpreted and the prospective client may not wish to continue to the next stage of the interview. If you are asked about your rates, attempt to defer an answer until the time of your meeting by stating that your rates vary depending on various factors such as estimated time involved, the type of work required, and whether the client is a profit or nonprofit organization. None of these factors can be ascertained accurately before an interview. In addition, there are different forms of fee structure that can be negotiated. This response should satisfy any inquiry.

The initial interview is normally free as a goodwill and marketing technique. Once a specific date and time have been set for the interview, confirm them in writing beforehand so no misunderstanding occurs. If the consultation is to be without charge, state that. Send your brochure with the letter. Your brochure should describe your background, past experiences, and nature of service and references, if you think that is appropriate.

There are specific steps to take to prepare for the interview.

Review the client's circumstances so you are familiar with them before the interview. Find out everything you can about the company, industry, and problems affecting the industry. Learn the client's jargon and way of doing business. You can obtain considerable information from business publications, annual reports, trade journals, newspapers, and other clients in similar industries.

Try to find out about the client's likes and dislikes, hobbies, memberships, sports, recreation, and travel. Look for clues of personal interest or accomplishment when you are in the client's office. If you can find common links, a basis for friendship can be quickly established.

Prepare specific questions to ask during the interview. Concentrate on client needs and problems. Some of the basic questions to ask include:

(a) Has the client used a consultant before? How long ago? What was the experience like? What was the purpose?

If the client has not used a consultant before, you may need more time to convince the client, and there may be more problems to be aware of in working with him or her. If the client has used a consultant before and the relationship was a positive one, you should find out what particular aspects were considered favorable. If a previous consultant relationship was not satisfactory, you should find out the reasons for that from the viewpoint of the client.

(b) Has the project been attempted previously? If so, who attempted it and why was it abandoned? The assignment might be impractical or impossible to complete to the client's satisfaction.

(c) If a client had a past relationship with a consultant, what type of financial fee arrangement was negotiated? It is not necessary for you to know the dollar amount, just the type of contract. You can then ask if that type of arrangement was satisfactory. That will provide you with guidelines on the type of fee arrangement to present in your proposal. Naturally, you want to offer the kind of fee arrangement a client feels comfortable with. If you prefer a different type of fee arrangement, you will have to discuss the benefits of that with the client during the interview, if possible.

(d) What specific measurable results and benefits must be obtained for the client to feel satisfied? The nature of the change, what form it will take, and how long it will take must be clarified. It is essential that the expectations of the client be specific, measurable, attainable, and realistic.

(e) Has a time period for the proposed project been discussed, and is that possible within your time schedule and other commitments? Has the subject of the cost of the project in general terms been discussed? What was the client's tentative reaction? If the type of payment has been discussed, what are the terms?

(f) Has a discussion taken place about the client's responsibilities in matters such as availability of the client's personnel, equipment, and work area, etc.? Does the consultant report to a committee or to one person? Access to information resources is required in order to complete the project. Can that access be obtained and how? Has the client been effectively convinced of the consultant's role as an agent of change? Does the client demonstrate appreciation and respect for the consultant?

(g) Is travel involved?

(h) Do you feel confident that you are qualified and able to help the client?

(i) Do you feel comfortable that a clear understanding exists of the client's problem or need?

Try to understand and anticipate client fears or concerns in advance and deal with them. A client may have underlying biases about you as a consultant that could affect the interview and its outcome. By knowing in advance the fears that might exist, you can counter them directly during the interview and proposal stages. Studies have shown that the following anxieties often exist. They are listed generally in order of priority.

- A consultant may be incompetent.
- The client may be continually dependent upon the consultant once the first relationship begins.
- The consultant might assume or interfere with managerial control during the project.
- The consultant's fees are excessive relative to the services provided.
- The consultant may not be able to complete the project in time.
- The need for a consultant is an admission of failure on the part of management.
- The consultant might disclose confidential internal information.
- The consultant might have inaccurately analyzed the needs and therefore will give an improper diagnosis.
- The consultant will lack impartiality.

Normally, a consultant will meet a client in the client's office. The client feels comfortable in familiar surroundings and is therefore more relaxed. The advantage to the consultant is he or she has the opportunity to view the client's offices and operations, and can leave diplomatically if the meeting is unproductive or continues too long.

Try not to have a meeting just before lunch, as the client could have a lunch commitment, be distracted by the time, or feel hungry.

Attempt to arrange an appointment for the time that you are at your peak of mental clarity so that you will create the most productive impression.

Make sure you arrive on time. Being late automatically creates a negative impression and can destroy the client's desire to deal with you. A small matter such as being late for an important appointment might represent an attitude and management style, which could cause conflict during the consulting project.

3. DURING THE INTERVIEW

The day has now arrived. You made certain you were at the client's office 10 to 15 minutes prior to the appointment so you had time to relax and compose yourself. You are feeling self-confident and positive about the meeting because you have thoroughly prepared yourself and worked through a mental role-play of events that are soon to occur.

Arriving early gives you an opportunity to observe the dynamics of the office and personnel and the general tone of the company. If you are going to have a relationship with a client, these simple factors are important to know beforehand.

When the meeting starts, it is important to shake hands with a firm grasp. A less than firm grasp will betray an insecure personality or lack of confidence in your abilities, and that impression alone could lose the project. It is important to consciously project a confident personality, positive attitude, firm method of speaking, and an attentive and relaxed stance. Exhibit a sense of control and leadership. A client wants to associate with a person who projects himself or herself well.

During the interview, you should spend almost all the time asking questions and little time answering them. After the initial social pleasantries and after you have briefly exchanged background information, control the meeting by asking your prepared questions. It is helpful to advise the client that you will be taking notes as this is a fact-finding interview. Having a prepared checklist is evidence of efficient administration. It also ensures that no questions will be overlooked, so interview consistency can be maintained.

Ask for examples to illustrate general statements. Ask open-ended, specific questions, and let the client do the talking. If a pause occurs, be prepared with the next question or other appropriate reaction. Listen intently to what the client says and how the client perceives the problem. If you want the client to continue elaborating on a situation, use questions starting with how, why, who, what, or where, or state, "That's interesting, can you tell me more about that?"

Be aware of nonverbal communication in body posture, mannerisms, voice patterns, and behavior. When forming an impression of a client's situation or opinion, restate it back to the client for confirmation.

If a client attempts to ask you a lot of questions, try to deflect the line of questioning back to the client. If the client asks specific questions about how you think the problem can be dealt with, or the various stages that should be considered, don't answer the questions directly. Your first interview is a fact-finding stage and you should not get involved in speculation or offering advice. Tell the client that you will certainly give an opinion later, after you have had an opportunity to review and analyze the facts and determine the options. Say that it would be premature and unprofessional for you to provide an opinion at the early stage. You don't want to give away free consulting, especially based on incomplete information.

At the end of the interview, ask the client if he or she would like to see a proposal and whether it should be a simple or detailed one.

Throughout the interview, be aware of the fears and concerns that might be present. Try to make sure you have dealt with all of them to the client's satisfaction.

4. AFTER THE INTERVIEW

Once the interview is over, you should review the data while it is still fresh in your mind. Identify the problems as you see them, and analyze the needs. Then outline the possible solutions and draft a proposal. The proposal steps are outlined in the next chapter.

The normal steps that follow include writing a thank-you letter to the client as soon as possible after the meeting and saying a proposal will follow as soon as it is complete.

5. WHY YOU SHOULD TURN DOWN BUSINESS

After your interview and assessment of the client, the project, and other factors involved, you may decide that it would be wise not to accept the project. That decision takes insight and foresight, and many consultants find it a difficult one to make. Consultants may be influenced by factors such as the need for cash flow; the challenge offered by the project; the potential marketing opportunities; the urge to do something

when there are no other projects on the go; or the desire help a client is in need. Some of the reasons you should consider turning down business follow:

(a) A client looks as though he or she is on the verge of business failure. (Studies have shown that there are various reasons for business failure, including management incompetence, imbalanced experience, lack of management experience, or lack of experience in the product or service line. Some of the danger signals may include lack of a business plan, high overhead costs, low morale, lack of cash flow, lack of understanding of financial information, indecisiveness, backlog of commitments, inefficiency, poor communication, and general chaos. You do not want to be burdened with the stress of a client failure or the risk of not collecting your fee.)

(b) A client has a reputation to pay late or not pay at all.

(c) The client has a bad reputation for other reasons, and you do not want to be associated with that client.

(d) You do not like the client personally.

(e) A proposed project is illegal or unpleasant.

(f) You are overcommitted with other projects and unable to accept the work and perform satisfactorily and on time.

(g) The potential job is too small for your time, priorities, or cash flow.

(h) The potential job is too large for your ability or desire to administer it.

(i) You lack the expertise to perform the job to the standard that would be required.

(j) You do not offer consulting services in that client's industry area.

(k) The client does not want to pay you the fee that you have requested, but wants to pay you less than you feel is fair to complete the project.

(l) The project would force you to compromise what you consider to be your professional and ethical standards.

(m) The client does not appear to fully appreciate your skills and abilities.

(n) The client does not have any money.

6. HOW TO TURN DOWN UNWANTED BUSINESS

Once you have decided that you do not want the business at all, or not in the form that it is available, there are various tactics and techniques to turn down the project in a way that maintains goodwill and does not hurt the client's feelings.

If the proposed project is simply unsuitable for you, you may wish to turn it down completely. There are different ways of rejecting projects directly:

(a) Tell the client that your present workload is very heavy and unfortunately you are unable to accept the job. This option makes you appear more attractive and desirable to the client for possible future projects.

(b) Tell the client you are unable to comply with the job specifications. This typically occurs with government agencies. If you are expected to take a government job because of previous projects, and you want to be considered favorably in the future, you could propose an approach that you feel the client will reject because it is outside the stated or unstated guidelines.

(c) Tell the client that you do not perform the particular type of service being requested, either because you do not have the capacity or it isn't your current field. If you normally perform that type of consulting, state that at the present time you are directing your talents and priorities in a slightly different direction.

(d) Bid the job too high. You can quote a fee much higher than you think the job is worth or that other competitors might bid. The risk here, of course, is that your bid might be accepted.

There may be occasions when you would accept a job if it was changed to meet your needs. Some of the techniques you could consider include:

(a) Accept only part of the proposed project. You could encourage other consultants to accept parts of the project you do not wish to handle.

(b) Redefine the project to meet your needs, and offer to conduct the assignment on your own terms. This approach works only if the client's goals, objectives, and expectations can be met without additional costs.

(c) Accept the job but act as project manager and employ other consultants to assist you in completing the work.

CHAPTER 17
CONSULTING PROPOSALS

Most initial interviews result in a request for a proposal. The proposal plays a significant role in your ability to obtain consulting assignments. Because of the vital nature of writing and presenting successful proposals, you may wish to refer to the Bibliography for further references. This chapter covers some of the basic concepts and tactics required to produce successful proposals.

1. WHAT IS A PROPOSAL?

A proposal is a letter or document that you prepare for a client describing your understanding of the client's needs. This is very important because your client, in order to have confidence in you, must be satisfied that you understand the problem as well as he or she does.

The proposal states what you intend to do for the client and indicates in specific terms the anticipated results and potential benefits to the client.

A proposal is a selling document. It is intended to be informative and appealing and to convince the client to contract for your services.

2. PRIVATE VERSUS PUBLIC SECTOR PROPOSALS

Public sector proposals tend to be more formal than private sector proposals. When a client requests a proposal, the request is made on the assumption that anyone offering goods or services is properly qualified and equipped to do so. The government requires that you demonstrate your own competence and prove that your facilities, experience, resources, and whatever else are adequate to handle the requirements.

The client is evaluating not only the merits of the program you propose versus the merits of competitive programs, but also your credentials versus the credentials of your competitors. It is common for government agencies to require that you outline your personal qualifications. One reason government agencies request such information is that they are required by procurement regulations to make an objective evaluation of each proposal. Your qualifications provide one specific comparison.

Government agencies have various evaluation factors. An example of the criteria a government agency might use is shown in Appendix 3.

Private sector proposals are far more flexible in their selection requirements because they are not governed by legislation. Therefore, pragmatism and subjective factors have more of an influence on the final decision.

3. SOLICITED VERSUS UNSOLICITED PROPOSALS

Solicited proposals are proposals requested by a prospective client from the public or private sector. An organization requesting a proposal has already identified some needs. Your proposal will be judged on its quality, timeliness, reliability, and effectiveness.

An unsolicited proposal is designed by a consultant who perceives a need and is confident that it can be met through the use of the consultant's services.

Solicited proposals generally involve a competition between large numbers of consultants who bid on the project. In an unsolicited proposal situation, you may be the only person being considered.

4. SIMPLE AND FORMAL PROPOSALS

4.1 Simple proposal

The simple proposal is a written statement, typed on the consultant's stationery, that includes the following items:

(a) A description of the work to be done

(b) The name of the consultant performing the work

(c) The services or personnel to be provided by the client

(d) The date work will begin and the length of time required to complete the assignment

(e) An outline of anticipated categories of costs to be paid by the client

(f) The fees to be paid for services rendered and the terms arranged

The proposal is signed by the consultant and normally sent by mail or delivered in person to the client. If the proposal is agreed upon, the client should sign a copy of the proposal or letter. The letter of proposal and agreement constitutes a legal contract and is similar to a letter of agreement.

4.2 Formal proposal

A formal proposal is considerably more detailed in that all aspects of the project are spelled out in full. It is similar to a formal contract and offers protections to both the consultant and the client.

The proposal does not become a legally binding contract until the client agrees to and signs the proposal document, until a covering letter referring to the proposal as a binding contract is signed, or until a formal contract is drafted reflecting the contents of the proposal and signed by both parties. A sample format for the formal proposal is described in the next section.

5. GUIDELINES AND FORMAT FOR A SUCCESSFUL PROPOSAL

The basis for your written contract will be the matters that you discuss at the proposal stage. Make sure you expand on the need, outcome, benefits, and results. Do not expand on the process or methods. This protects you from a client who might reject the proposal and perform the project in-house using your proposal as a guide or from a client who submits your proposal to other consultants for estimates and then hires someone else who uses the process you detailed.

Also keep in mind when you are preparing the proposal that your client might have some of the concerns and fears outlined in the preceding chapter. Attempt to minimize any concerns in the content of your proposal.

You should consider having a number of standardized proposals if there is similarity in the type of services you offer. If the standardized documents are on a word processor, they can easily be adapted to include or exclude paragraphs and to make the document an original. It is also very easy to revise a document on a word processor. The standardized proposal contains all the basics of any proposal, leaving open those items that are specific to each project. Another advantage of standardized proposals is your ability to deliver the completed proposal to the client within a short time after your initial meeting.

The sample proposal format (see Sample 16) is rather formal and detailed. It may include clauses that are not applicable or appropriate in all situations, as each project is unique. Delete the clauses that you do not need in your proposal — and be sure to renumber the clauses that remain!

6. PRESENTING YOUR PROPOSAL

How you package your proposal is nearly as important as how it is stated. If possible, your proposal should be prepared on a word processor as that reflects professionalism and quality secretarial resources. Your signature and the date should appear at the end of the proposal.

A covering letter accompanying your proposal should thank your client for his or her time and cooperation during the meeting and for the opportunity to submit a proposal. Highlight the topics discussed and state that you can help because you have had experience with this type of problem and would like to have the opportunity to be of service. You may want to flatter the client in some way by referring to his or her contribution in the meeting. Offer to answer any questions either by phone or at an arranged meeting. State that you will call within ten business days to discuss the proposal further. Put that date on your calendar. If you have not heard from the client within that period, make sure that you contact the client on the tenth day.

You may wish to suggest in your covering letter, if you didn't mention it in the proposal, that references are available upon request. You may wish to suggest that the client contact some of your other clients to discuss work you have performed. This should demonstrate your self-confidence and increase the client's trust and confidence in you.

SAMPLE 16
PROPOSAL FORMAT

1. TABLE OF CONTENTS: This should include headings and page numbers.

2. INTRODUCTION: It is important to persuade the client that you understand the project and the underlying factors that influence it. Briefly outline and analyze the factors that demonstrate the need. State that the matter is important and warrants professional outside assistance. Emphasize that you want to help and that you are the most appropriate source of help.

3. PROJECT PURPOSE: The purpose and goals of the engagement are outlined here in clear and accurate fashion. State the purpose and goals in the client's own words so that the client can identify with the proposal. During your initial interview you should have tried to find out what the client perceived as the needs or problems and the means to resolve them. Detail the goals in such a way that you can refer to them as specific and measurable outcomes so you have a reference point for measuring the progress of the project and satisfying the client.

4. PROJECT BENEFITS: Highlight the anticipated benefits the client will receive. Do not promise results you cannot guarantee, but keep in mind the client has to be given some realistic hope of success. This is a particularly important section as the client has to clearly understand and recognize the benefits in order to justify the financial and administrative commitment. Your client may have to account to other directors or shareholders. You assist your client to assist you by providing more detail.

5. APPROACH, SCOPE, AND PLAN: Compare and contrast several possible approaches to the project, if appropriate. Explain how you will proceed in general terms. Define the scope and limits of the proposed consulting service. Divide the tasks into smaller segments that provide clear stages in the project as reference points for you and your client. As mentioned earlier, provide sufficient information to demonstrate your competence, but not enough about the process and techniques to provide a formula for the client to perform the project without you.

6. PROJECT SCHEDULE: Determine the schedule and list the specific tasks required to attain the objectives. State the timing sequence of tasks according to the various stages. A functional flow diagram might help to graphically assist the client's understanding and provide a reference point for progress.

7. **PROGRESS REPORTS:** It is important to maintain continual communication with the client. As explained in earlier chapters, the more information you provide your client, the more confidence the client will have in you and the less risk there is of problems occurring. Progress reports are frequently made at specific stages, when interim bills are sent. A client is more disposed to pay if tangible benefits can be seen and specific problems have been resolved. The frequency and format of periodic progress reports should be specified.

8. **COSTING SUMMARY:** Explain your fees, types of fee arrangement, billing procedures, and timing of bills. Detail the expected expenses that will be passed on directly to the client. Your client should understand that your estimate for time and costs is an estimate only. Provide sufficient detail about your fees so that your client appreciates the correlation between the amount of time expended and the cost of your services. Outline any other terms and conditions or variables that could affect the final cost.

9. **PERSONNEL AND QUALIFICATIONS:** Provide a brief background history of your firm and the personnel who will be consulting on the project. If you have had experience solving problems similar to the client's, make reference to that. Select only those aspects of your background experience that relate directly to the client and the proposal.

10. **SUBCONTRACTS:** If you are subcontracting or collaborating with other consultants, it is important to specify who they are and what duties they will perform. To avoid any future problems, specify whether you or the client is responsible for their technical performance.

11. **USE OF CLIENT PERSONNEL:** It is important that the client understand what commitments and obligations will be his or her responsibility. If you are to delegate responsibilities or otherwise receive assistance from the client's staff or executives, you should make it clear that your fee estimate is based on the use of client personnel. Specify personnel duties and time required if possible.

12. **SENIOR MANAGEMENT SUPPORT:** Make the executives aware that their support is vital to the success of the project. It is important that support for the project be communicated throughout the organization to gain cooperation and compliance. If regular meetings are going to be held with senior executives, specify the purpose and frequency of such meetings.

13. STEERING COMMITTEE FUNCTION, IF APPLICABLE: A steering committee reviews, coordinates, assists, and implements the consultant's work. It provides momentum, organizational credibility, and decision-making functions for the project. Detail the purposes, composition, and responsibilities of this committee.

14. OUTPUT MATERIAL INCLUDED: Describe any reports, surveys, instructional material, or other products that are part of the proposal.

15. MANAGEMENT PLAN: Describe your approach to managing the overall project. Who will be the client contact person, and what will his or her management role and authority be pertaining to the project?

16. DISCLAIMERS: If you have used disclaimers regarding the project, make sure that the reason is outlined. Your role is strictly that of adviser, not decision-maker, and any benefits achieved are based on both your recommendations and the client's actions and decisions. If your client does not fulfill his or her obligations and support, your responsibility and choices should be outlined. Indicate who has ownership and control over any proprietary information that could develop from your services for example, instructional material.

17. REFERENCES: If requested, or if it is your style and wish to provide client references, make sure that you obtain written permission in advance from the clients. Contact references occasionally to make sure they still think highly of you.

18. SUMMARY AND CLOSING OF PROPOSAL: This should be a short restatement of your belief in the importance of the engagement. Mention your availability to answer questions. If you are prepared to begin the project within a short time after the client's acceptance, state that clearly. You want to stimulate the client's need and persuade the client that you can fulfill the need.

7. PROPOSAL FOLLOW-UP

Your client may be slow in responding to your proposal. You do not want to appear to be pressuring the client, but you may have to take certain steps to clarify the situation or obtain a contract.

You stated in your covering letter that you would contact the client within ten business days. It is appropriate, then, that you do contact the client on the tenth day to answer any questions. You may receive further questions at that point, or obtain a positive or negative response to your proposal.

If the reason for the delay appears inexplicable, you may wish to wait for a further five business days and then drop in to see the client in person to ask if a decision has been made. This approach may or may not be appropriate in a given situation.

If a client is waiting for a committee decision, determine when the committee will meet to discuss the proposal and follow-up by phone to the client the day after the committee meets. You may also wish to consider giving an acceptance time limit in your proposal to encourage prompt consideration. In a given situation you might adopt the attitude that you would like to know one way or the other within a certain time. The client could construe the acceptance time limit in a positive fashion, as it could imply that you are in demand and may commit to other projects if the client does not book you in the allowed time.

8. WHAT TO DO IF YOUR PROPOSAL IS NOT ACCEPTED

It is helpful if you can determine why you received a rejection. Budget restraints, other priorities, or lack of consensus could be reasons. Possibly another consultant was awarded the contract. If possible, find out who obtained the assignment and why that proposal was selected over your own. Rejected proposals can provide a good learning experience. However, it may not be appropriate, practical, or possible for you to obtain the answer from client.

Regardless of the circumstances, write a thank-you letter to the client expressing your appreciation for his or her time, interest, and cooperation, and mention that you would be pleased to submit a proposal for consideration in any future projects.

9. HOW TO AVOID GIVING AWAY FREE CONSULTING

At this stage you should know whether your proposal was rejected or accepted. If it was rejected, you may have provided too much information in your proposal to your client, The client, in turn, may have used the information for his or her benefit. In other words, you gave away free consulting. If your proposal was accepted and you now have a contract or a contract is being prepared, you should be aware of the various ways that clients can innocently or intentionally obtain your advice for free.

Occasionally, you may decide to share your knowledge and ideas in an attempt to build goodwill with the client or prospective client. That is a judgment you will have to make at the time. But you are running a business, which requires income and profit. You cannot carelessly give away the only product you have, which is time and skill.

9.1 Potential client interview or discussion

A potential client may contact you and wish to discuss ideas and problems with you on the telephone, over lunch, or at the client's office or your office. The potential client wants to "pick your brains." You willingly cooperate due to your desire to obtain a consulting assignment.

The strategic solution is to confirm that you do provide service in the area concerned and you are available to the client on a professional basis and would be pleased to establish a relationship. Answer any concerns raised by the client by asking questions aimed at drawing out information. Do not offer solutions but imply that there are solutions to the problems discussed.

If answers are specifically requested, respond that you require far more information before providing an answer. State that it would be unprofessional for you to provide an opinion without sufficient information on which to base that opinion. Again, restate that you would be pleased to discuss the matter further on a professional basis if the client so wishes.

These deflective techniques are the same ones outlined in the preceding chapter relating to the initial interview. Ask the client directly if he or she is interested in retaining a consultant to provide assistance in the specific area of concern. Clarify if the client would like you to submit a proposal to resolve the problem. Decide if the client is a serious enough prospect to spend the time on a proposal.

Make it clear throughout the discussion that you are paid for professional services and that you are capable of assisting the client on a fee for service basis.

9.2 Analysis of client's need

A client might perceive that a problem exists, but does not understand the precise nature of the problem. The client implies that if you analyze the need and make recommendations for resolution, an attractive contract could immediately result. This teaser can entice unsophisticated or new consultants to provide a thorough diagnosis without fee.

A naive consultant can be easily exploited by a person using this technique. The risk, of course, is that no subsequent contracts materialize or some other consultant is retained. One way of resolving this problem is to recommend that the client enter into a contract with a first stage that is a diagnostic stage. After the diagnosis is made, with recommendations, then the consultant could proceed to the next stage of the contract and implement the recommendations. In this way the consultant is protected by contract and the sincerity of the client is assured.

An option can be inserted in the contract stating that if the client elects not to proceed with the recommendation, then the consultant is assured of payment of an agreed sum in consideration for the time and energies spent during the diagnosis.

9.3 Free detailed advice in the written proposal

In your proposal you may write a complete, detailed formula with all the necessary instructions together with an outline of the methods and steps required to attain the objective. The client now has the prescription for resolving the problem and can give it to other consultants to submit an estimate or can implement the detailed proposal with in-house personnel.

You can avoid this problem by writing a proposal that highlights in detail the need that exists, the objectives that must be achieved to resolve the client's problem, and the measurable, specific outcomes and benefits that will be attained at specific stages of the assignment. A functional flow diagram graphically illustrating the steps is an effective marketing tool. De-emphasize or omit information on the processes or methods to be used.

9.4 Potential future benefit

A client may try to convince you that some future benefit, such as goodwill or contacts, could occur if you perform the service, on the condition that you provide the service for free or a reduced amount as the price to pay for future opportunities.

This technique is normally exercised by larger or more influential clients who take advantage of a consultant's impressionable, desperate, or opportunistic nature. The client may attempt to blame the lack of financial recompense on budget allocations having been spent, internal financial restraints being imposed, or a general hold on all project commitments. From a consultant's viewpoint, the mere association with an influential or prestigious client could be an inducement.

As long as you are aware of the business and psychological dynamics at work, you can make a responsible, pragmatic decision.

The decision might be to accede to the client's overtures, resist them, or attempt to negotiate a more realistic package.

9.5 Additions to the original fixed price contract

It is not uncommon for a client to request additional work outside the original contract terms, as all needs cannot be foreseen in advance or changing circumstances can change the needs. Once you are aware that the request is outside the fixed price contract terms, you should contact the client, draw this fact to the client's attention in a polite fashion, and suggest that a modified contract or addendum be negotiated to incorporate the additional work.

This situation reinforces the importance of being specific in the fixed price contract as to the services that are to be performed. Ambiguity in terms could lead to a difference of opinion, an impasse, legal problems, and loss of goodwill as well as loss of a client.

Depending on the circumstances, a formal contract amendment may not be required; a confirmation letter outlining the amendments and signed by both parties may be enough. The method is a matter of style, nature of client, and other circumstances.

9.6 Free consulting in a follow-up situation

You can run into problems when you have performed your services as outlined in your contract, but the client continues to need your services for operating the project. For example, suppose you recommended a type of computer hardware that was subsequently installed in the client's premises, and the client's personnel had difficulty learning the new equipment. You might feel an obligation to assist the client by explaining the necessary matters to the personnel. You may then be continually phoned by the client who requests you to return to explain various features to the personnel. Unless you are aware this process is occurring, you could be providing considerable free consulting.

The obvious solution is to anticipate the situation and incorporate provisions for follow-up consultation fees into the original contract. The contract can specify the method and terms of payment. One option is a time retainer contract, which means that you perform a specified service regularly (e.g., several specified hours or days per month). Another option is an availability retainer contract. This means you are "on call" for a fixed monthly fee as outlined in the terms of the agreement.

9.7 Relatives, associates, and friends

Relatives and friends may frequently come to you for advice. You must develop ways to maintain the relationship while clarifying your role as a professional who provides service for a fee.

You can develop various subtle but effective approaches. One technique is to say that you have a policy of not advising family or friends because of possible conflict of interest or bias. Because you value the relationship and operate by professional standards, you feel it would not be appropriate or responsible, and you would prefer not to provide professional advice that they might rely on.

Another approach is to say you are unable to provide advice because of incomplete information, and it would be irresponsible, unprofessional, and unfair on your part to give an opinion based on incomplete facts.

You have choices. You can either decline to provide advice, provide advice for free, or establish your relationship in the context as a business one and negotiate a fee for service. It is also helpful to keep in mind that you can be exposed to professional liability and negligence claims if your advice is followed and problems occur, even though you did not charge or get paid for your advice.

CHAPTER 18
CONTRACTS

As a consultant, you will quickly become aware of the necessity for written contracts in all your business and client relationships. A contract is the framework within which your obligations, rights, remedies, and remunerations are clarified. There are oral, written, and implied contracts. You want to make sure that your consulting business assumes no commitments or financial outlay without the security of an agreement in writing. Many consultants and other small business people commence their business with the trusting attitude that a verbal agreement is sufficient. It only takes one bad experience to demonstrate the folly of relying on a verbal agreement. This chapter explores some of the important aspects of contracts.

1. ESSENTIALS OF A VALID CONTRACT

A contract is an agreement between two parties to perform mutual obligations. The most common forms of contract are the oral contract and the written contract. The problem with an oral contract is that if the parties disagree, unless there are reliable witnesses or part performance of the agreement, it is difficult to reconstruct what the original bargain was. A written contract simply records in a formal or informal manner the nature of the bargain. For example, if you send a letter to a client confirming your agreement, and if the five essential elements of a contract are present, you have a simple informal contract.

The five elements of a contract are as follows:

1.1 Offer

If you submit a proposal or a contract to a client, it constitutes your offer to the client to accept your proposal. Your offer, naturally, will be in writing and will spell out the particulars in some detail.

1.2 Acceptance

Acceptance of your proposal must be clearly demonstrated. Normally this takes the form of your prospective client confirming in writing his or her acceptance of your proposal letter or document or contract, and acknowledging the terms you have outlined.

In certain situations an acceptance can be assumed and the contract made valid by part performance. In other words, it could be argued that your offer was accepted if your client permitted you to perform in part or in full the terms of your written proposal, even though a written acceptance had not been received. Naturally, this is a high risk manner of doing business. Never begin a project without first protecting yourself in writing.

1.3 Consideration

Consideration is something of value being promised to you or given to you in exchange for your services. Valuable consideration normally refers to money or some other valuable assets, but a promise to pay money or provide some other benefit can be deemed to be consideration.

1.4 Competency

An agreement will not be considered binding if signed by persons lacking competence to understand the "nature and quality of their actions." This includes minors, the mentally infirm, or a person who was intoxicated at the time the agreement was accepted or signed. The age at which a person ceases to become a minor varies depending on the jurisdiction. In some circumstances a contract signed by a minor is considered to be binding.

1.5 Legality

A contract created to perform an illegal act is void. For example, if a number of businesses signed an agreement to fix prices in their area of product sales, and one of the parties failed to follow the agreement, the other parties to the agreement would not be able to sue for breach of contract as the subject matter of the agreement was illegal.

2. WHY A WRITTEN CONTRACT IS NEEDED

There are many reasons why a written contract is essential. Some of the reasons are listed below:

- *Project professional image:* A written contract enhances your image as a responsible professional and businessperson.

- *Avoid misunderstandings:* It is difficult to remember complex details without having them in writing. Subsequent events and distractions can cloud your recall of earlier conversations. Both parties can have differing assumptions and interpretations of what was agreed on critical points of issue. It only makes sense to prevent this problem by the simple act of writing down the agreement.

- *Untruthful client:* It is not uncommon with verbal agreements for one party to reconstruct the agreement in a self-serving fashion at some later point. This could be to negotiate a more favorable contract or to get out of the contract obligations altogether. If it is just one person's word against another's, it is difficult if not impossible for a court to reconstruct with certainty the original bargain. The time, delay, and expense of attempting to assert your rights eliminates the profit and possibly your business as well.

- *Death of either party:* If either party to an unwritten contract dies, the estate of the deceased would have difficulty determining the actual bargain. This could give rise to lawsuits against the estate of the deceased consultant if the client claimed damages had been suffered due to breach of contract because of the death. The estate of the deceased would be in a difficult position to defend any action, not knowing the exact terms and obligations of both parties.

- *Terms of payment outlined:* If you do not have specific terms of payment (i.e., payment each month or at specific stages in the project) in writing, the client could attempt to wait until the end of the job to pay, claiming there was no other agreement to the contrary. You want to avoid this problem by having a written agreement before you expend your time, energy, and resources.

- *Fee for service confirmed:* You want to make clear that you are being paid for your time and that your efforts are not being supplied free as a marketing device or preliminary assessment.

- *Avoiding and limiting liability:* You want to protect your interests in writing by having provisions in the agreement to protect yourself from liability. For example, you may want to have a contingency clause to the effect that if events occur outside your control, you are not to be held responsible. You might also consider a limited liability clause which sets a fixed amount of money that you would be responsible for if you are held liable. For example, you might have a clause stating that your liability is limited to $15,000 or the balance of the contract, whichever is less.

- *Preventing litigation:* If you do not have an agreement in writing, a client could claim that you acted improperly or that the work was not completely done. Unless an agreement in writing spelled out the nature of the services that you were going to provide, it would be difficult for you or your client to show exactly what you agreed upon. Because of this impasse on the terms and obligations of the agreement, litigation might be difficult to avoid.

- *Collateral for financing:* A written contract outlining benefits that you will receive for performing services is as good as money. You can pledge the contract at a bank as security for loan advances. This ability to lever your legal documents for working capital or cash flow purposes is just 'good business sense. No banker will lend money on the strength of your verbal assurance that you have a consulting agreement with a client.

- *Potential for increase of revenue:* If you have a contract that details the exact services and supplies you are providing, any variation will allow you to negotiate an addendum to the agreement. With an oral agreement, there could be a dispute over the exact point at which your services and supplies are not included in the bargain.

- *Independent contractor status confirmed:* Without a written agreement specifying your independent status of operating, within the terms of the agreement, without direction or control, you could be considered to be an employee by the tax authorities. Make clear in the written agreement the nature of the roles of the parties. Also, the client might set down his or her own specifications, or question you in detail on an ongoing basis about what you are doing, thereby reducing some of your independence. To prevent this, take the initiative to specify the detail, nature, and form of the services you are going to provide.

- *Encourages contract acceptance:* Many prospective clients feel nervous about agreeing to have you perform a project unless they know the exact detail and terms of the relationship in writing. The person with whom you might be negotiating frequently has to explain the particulars to colleagues or superiors. Without a written contract in writing, you might not win the assignment.

- *Communication:* As mentioned previously, good communication is an essential ingredient for client satisfaction and goodwill. A well-written contract helps build client confidence.

3. STRUCTURE OF FORMAL CONTRACT

A consulting contract can vary widely in its complexity depending on the nature and value of the project being performed and the clients being served. Sample 17 describes the format for a formal contract and discusses clauses that are frequently included. Not all the clauses are necessarily appropriate or applicable in each case. A simple contract or letter of understanding does not need the same detail.

If a proposal letter or document exists, it can be referred to in the contract as part of the agreement and attached as an appendix.

4. TYPES OF CONTRACTS

There are several types of contracts frequently used in the consulting business. It is important to understand the options that are available to you as they involve various tactical and legal considerations. Following is a brief summary of the most common types of contracts.

4.1 Letter of agreement

This simple contract is in the form of a letter stating a summary of the agreement between the parties. This includes the nature of services to be performed, the method and time of payment, the starting date and duration of the contract, the resource materials and personnel to be supplied by the client, if applicable, and the consultants who will be involved on the project, if applicable.

SAMPLE 17
CONTRACT FORMAT

1. PARTIES INVOLVED: Name all parties involved in the contract and state the date the contract is signed.

2. TERM OF CONTRACT: The starting and completion dates of the contract are written here, or a reference is made to an appendix in which the dates and hours are described. The contract may state either the beginning and ending dates of an assignment, or both, or a maximum of hours within a fixed time period. The time period can either be closed or open. An open contract simply states that a specific job is to be performed, without giving a deadline for completion. Or a contract might simply state that an ongoing relationship is commencing, the length of which shall be at the pleasure of both parties.

3. DUTIES OF THE CONSULTANT: Outline your proposed consulting in detail, by specific task and scope. In previous meetings during the proposal stage you have probably clarified services to be offered, and the proposal letter or document spells out what you are offering. If this is included in the contract for practical, tactical, or legal reasons, or choice of style, the following areas might be covered:

   - Services that you, as consultant, will provide
   - The timing of the submission of various documents pertaining to the project
   - The nature of reports to be furnished, if any, and the approximate dates when they will be completed
   - Any special materials to be prepared, such as brochures, etc.
   - The timing and nature of any consultant/client meetings, either on fixed dates or at specific stages in the project or upon mutual request
   - Travel that might be required, the nature of compensation, when that is to be paid, and what is required to obtain payment
   - Your authority to use client resources, office equipment, computer, files and records, and access to client's customers
   - Your right to use third party information; for example, ledgers and journals and other financial information in the possession of the client

- A provision restricting you from performing services for the client's competitors (Be careful of this provision, especially if you intend to develop a clientele base within a certain industry.)

4. **DUTIES OF THE CLIENT:** Wherever a consultant requires access to information or to employees, customers, or advisers of the client, it should be specified clearly in the agreement that the client agrees and will have the responsibility of facilitating and performing in those specified areas. For example, if you require information from a third party, you should try to have the client responsible for obtaining the information for you. If the client does not or cannot cooperate and therefore impedes the project, how will you be compensated?

5. **PAYMENT FOR SERVICES:** This is an important section and should state the basis on which your fees will be paid; i.e., per diem, fixed rate, fixed price plus expenses, or another form. Various types of fee structures are discussed in chapter 13. When and how the invoices will be rendered should be spelled out clearly; for example, invoices could be rendered at specific identifiable stages throughout the project. If the client is being billed on an hourly or daily rate, that rate should be specified in the contract. If a down payment (retainer) is required, that should also be specified.

6. **EXPENSES:** Any job-related expenses to be paid by the client are described here. In the case of a fixed price contract, your expenses are incorporated in the fixed price agreed upon. Most other forms of fee structure involve expenses to be paid by the client. Outline what is required for payment.

7. **LATE PAYMENT:** The contract should specify when a payment should take place — either at specified periods, upon receipt of invoice, 30 days after invoice, or whatever arrangement is agreed upon. A clause can be inserted in the agreement stating that if the invoice is not paid within the agreed upon billing period, interest on the overdue account will be added. The interest rate is normally slightly higher than the prevailing bank rate, which acts as an incentive to pay.

8. **STOP WORK CLAUSE:** This clause allows the consultant to cease providing services on the project until the outstanding fees and interest have

been paid. Generally this clause is not applied until a certain period has elapsed and all other attempts at getting payment through goodwill have been unsuccessful. Stopping work is a last resort. It is important that the basis on which you can discontinue your services be stated in the contract.

9. INDEPENDENT CONTRACTOR: State that you are an independent contractor and therefore not eligible to participate in any benefit programs or tax withholding obligations on the part of the client. This clause makes it clear that you are not an employee.

10. WORK DELEGATION: Outline the basis on which you are permitted to hire assistants and delegate work. Depending upon the nature of services you are providing, your personal service and expertise is probably desired by the client. If you plan to subcontract out to other people, protect yourself by clarifying that in the contract.

11. ADDITIONAL WORK: This clause allows a client to request a modification to the contract and add a provision for additional services. Any modification to the contract should be confirmed in writing with particulars and signed by both parties before any additional service work commences.

12. CONFIDENTIALITY: State that any information disclosed to you pertaining to the project or any information that you become aware of during the period of the project will be kept strictly confidential.

13. OWNERSHIP: This clause covers ownership of materials or ideas resulting from your services. Many rejected ideas and plans could be useful for another project. Naturally, it is not in your best interests to have the client own this information. You should require that rejected plans or ideas are to remain your property.

14. LIMITED LIABILITY OF THE CONSULTANT: You may wish to insert a clause saying any liability that is the result of your mistakes or breach of contract is limited to the amount of the contract price, assuming that there is a fixed contract price, or the amount of loss, whichever is lower. If there is no fixed contract price, set a specific maximum to the loss. However, such a clause is difficult if not impossible to enforce. You

should also take out professional liability insurance and errors and omissions insurance as a protection (see chapter 11).

15. CONTINGENCIES: This clause states that you have complete control of all services rendered, with the exception of events beyond the control of you or the client such as accidents, delays, strikes, or supplier problems. This clause attempts to protect both parties if the contract can not be completed.

16. ADVERTISING: This clause restricts the use of the client's name for media release without the written approval of the client.

17. ARBITRATION: Outline the procedures to be followed in the event of disagreement by either party about the terms or interpretation of the terms of the contract. Normally, provision is made for a dispute to be settled by an independent arbitrator, with details about the basis on which the arbitrator will be paid and by whom, and the criteria for selecting the arbitrator.

18. GOVERNING LAWS: This clause simply states that the contract shall be governed by the laws of the jurisdiction in which it is written.

19. TERMINATION: Either party is allowed to terminate services upon written notification a set number of days in advance. Outline the details and the reasons under which termination can take place.

20. AGREEMENT BINDING: State that the written agreement is the total agreement between the parties and shall take the place of any previous contracts or verbal or written agreements. This clause normally states that any modification to the agreement must be in writing and agreed between the parties to be enforceable.

21. SIGNATURES: The parties to the contract sign the agreement. It is very important that the client representative who signs has the authority to do so and that his or her position is written on the contract. In some cases, corporate seals are required if corporations are involved.

The letter of agreement is normally prepared by the consultant and forwarded to the client for signature and approval. An example of a letter of agreement prepared by a consultant is shown in Sample 18.

Sample 19 shows a letter of agreement prepared by the client. Note the differences in tone and format between the two. The one prepared by the client has the appearance of a short formal contract.

4.2 Letter of agreement with general terms and conditions appended

Another option is to have a letter of agreement accompanied by a statement of standard terms and conditions (see Sample 20). The statement is a standardized form that you can use often for similar type of agreements. It covers matters such as fee structure, reimbursable expenses, subcontracts, invoices and payments, warranty, and limitation of professional liability. Other clauses can be included in this form based on your own needs and precautions. If you prefer this format, the letter of agreement attached to the terms and conditions need not be detailed. It can outline the specific, not general, terms of the agreement.

The letter of agreement and/or general terms and conditions form are frequently used if the client does not want a more formal contract. From a tactical viewpoint, you might use these if you feel that a client would be intimidated by a formally structured contract. Another factor might be your personal style of consulting practice. If the contract is not complex and the fee is low, you might favor the simpler contract format.

4.3 Formal contract

A formal contract is preferred if the financial cost of the project is high, the project is complex, substantial financial commitment to suppliers or sub-consultants is involved, or it is the style of the client to require such a detailed contract.

Normally when government contracts are involved, the government prepares the formal contract.

Other situations where you might consider using a formal contract are when you have a new client, a client who has never used consulting services before, or a client who has a reputation for being difficult in general or complaining about fees in particular. Naturally, in this last case, if you have advance notice it would be very wise to reconsider any involvement with that client.

Sample 21 illustrates a formal contract. Table 4 is a checklist of provisions frequently covered in contracts with government or industry.

4.4 Sub-consulting agreement

This is an agreement between you and any sub-consultants you employ to undertake a part or all of a consulting project you have arranged.

It is quite common for consultants to subcontract work out to other consultants. You may use sub-consultants to keep overhead low, or if you are unable to perform the task yourself because you lack expertise in the area, or because a large project requires a large number of support resource personnel.

SAMPLE 18
LETTER OF AGREEMENT
(Prepared by consultant)

(Consultant's Letterhead)

_____ , 20 ___

Mary Roberts, President
ABC Corporation
7890 Front Street
Anytown, Anywhere

Dear Ms. Roberts:

RE: CONSULTING AGREEMENT

This letter will confirm our understanding concerning the terms of retainer and nature of services to be performed for ABC Corporation. These terms are as follows:

1. TERM. This agreement will be for a period of_____ commencing on _____ Either of us may terminate this agreement with thirty (30) days' written notice to the other party. In the event of termination, I will be compensated for services rendered through the date of termination.

2. DUTIES. My duties will include:

    a. Review of, analysis of, and recommendations for changes in the systems and organizational structure of the research division.

    b. Preparation of weekly reports on the progress of the project.

    c. Preparation of a final report and oral presentation for the management of the company, with recommendations for implementing system and organizational improvements and related costing.

3. COMPENSATION. The compensation for my services shall be at the rate of $450 per day, payable on receipt as billed. Other out-of-pocket costs, such as travel expenses and secretarial services, will be billed separately.

Enclosed is a copy of this agreement for your records. Please sign the original and return it to this office in the enclosed envelope. If you have any questions, please contact me.

Sincerely,

David Jones
Consultant

Accepted and agreed to:

_____   _____

Mary Roberts, President   Date

ABC Corporation

SAMPLE 19
LETTER OF AGREEMENT
(Prepared by client)

ABC Corporation
7890 Front Street
Anytown, Anywhere

Smith Jones & Associates
Consultants
1234 Main Street
Anytown, Anywhere

Dear _____:

_____20_____

RE: CONSULTING PROJECT

I am pleased to announce that your proposal to ABC Corporation has been accepted. The conditions of our acceptance are as outlined below:

1. TERM. Your appointment as a consultant to ABC Corporation (hereinafter called "the Corporation") is confirmed for the period _____ to_____.

2. SERVICES. You shall perform such work or services as are set forth in Exhibit A, attached hereto and specifically made a part of this Agreement. The work or services to be performed by you may be changed by the Corporation from time to time by letter requests sent to you. You shall keep the Corporation informed on the progress of any work being performed under this Agreement.

3. COMPENSATION AND EXPENSES.

(a) The Corporation will pay you a total fee of $_____ for all work performed hereunder on satisfactory completion of the work.

(b) Your compensation will be at the rate of $_____ per month for all work performed hereunder. You will be paid at the same time you are reimbursed for a proved expenses under paragraph 3(c) below.

(c) You will receive reimbursement for the actual cost of reasonable expenses arising out of the work performed under this Agreement (not to exceed $_____), subject to the approval of the Corporation. You shall deliver an itemized statement to the Corporation on a monthly basis that shows fully the work being performed under this Agreement and all related expense. The Corporation will pay you the amount of any authorized expenses within thirty (30) days of the receipt of the itemized statement of all expenses, submitted together with receipts for all hotel, car rental, air fare, and other transportation expenses, for all other expenses of $25 or more.

4. WORKING FACILITIES. You will be furnished with such facilities and services as shall be suitable for your position and adequate for the performance of your duties under this Agreement.

5. REPORTS. Any and all reports, manuscripts, and any other work products, whether completed or not, that are prepared or developed by you as a part of the work under this Agreement shall be the property of the Corporation and shall be turned over to the Corporation promptly at the Corporation's request or at the termination of this Agreement, whichever is earlier.

6. INDEPENDENT CONTRACTOR. You shall exercise control over the means and manner in which you perform any work requested hereunder, and in all respects your relationship to the Corporation shall be that of an independent contractor serving as a consultant and not as an employee.

7. TERMINATION. This Agreement may be terminated upon thirty (30) days' written notice by either party.

8. CONFIDENTIAL INFORMATION. You agree that for the term of your appointment hereunder and for two (2) years thereafter, that you will not disclose to any person, firm, or corporation any confidential information regarding the Corporation, its business, directors, officers, and employees.

9. NONASSIGNABLE. This Agreement is personal in nature and is not assignable by you or by the Corporation.

10. ARBITRATION. Any controversy or claim arising out of the interpretation of this Agreement shall allow either party to submit the disputed clause to Arbitration under the Arbitration Act of (name of jurisdiction). The costs of such arbitration to be borne equally by both parties.

11. ENTIRE AGREEMENT. This letter, including Exhibit A, contains the entire agreement of the parties. It may not be changed orally but only by an agreement signed by the party against whom enforcement of any waiver, change, modification, extension, or discharge is sought.

I trust that the terms of this appointment meet with your approval. If so, please indicate this by signing a copy of this letter and returning it to the Corporation. An additional copy of this letter is enclosed for your records.

Very truly yours,

_____

Client Signature

Accepted and agreed to this_____ day of _____, 20___ .

_____

Consultant signature

STATEMENT OF GENERAL TERMS AND CONDITIONS

1. **FEE STRUCTURE**

   All the time, including travel hours, spent on the project by professional technical and clerical personnel will be billed. The following approximate ranges of hourly rates for various categories of personnel are currently in effect:

Category	Hourly Rate
Principal	$70
Consultant	50
Analyst	40
Technician	30
Typist	15

   Hourly rates will be adjusted semi-annually to reflect changes in the cost of living index as published by (state name of appropriate government department). If overtime for nonprofessional staff is required, the premium differential figured at time and one-half of their regular hourly rate is charged at direct cost to the project. Unless otherwise stated, any cost estimate presented in a proposal is for budgetary purposes only, and is not a fixed price. The client will be notified when 75% of any budget figure is reached, and the budget figure will not be exceeded without prior authorization from the client.

2. **REIMBURSABLE EXPENSES**

   The following expenses will be billed at direct cost plus 15%.

   (a) Travel expenses necessary for the execution of the project, including air fares, rental vehicles, and highway mileage in company or personal vehicles, which will be charged at _____ cents per mile. Air travel will be by tourist class, except when tourist class service is not regularly available.

   (b) Telephone charges

   (c) Postage

   (d) Printing and reproduction

   (e) Computer services, including word processing

   (f) Other expenses directly attributable to the project

   Subcontracts will be billable at cost plus 15%.

3. INVOICES AND PAYMENTS

Invoices will be submitted monthly and payment is due on receipt of invoice. A 2% per month service charge will be added to all delinquent accounts. In the event Consultant shall be successful in prosecuting any suit for damages for breach of this agreement, including suits for nonpayment of invoices, to enforce this agreement, or to enjoin the other party from violating this agreement, Consultant shall be entitled to recover as part of its damages its reasonable legal costs and expenses for bringing and maintaining any such action.

Rates for foreign contracts are negotiable and the above rates do not apply.

4. WARRANTY

Our professional services will be performed, our findings obtained, and our recommendations prepared, in accordance with generally and currently accepted management consulting principles and practices. The warranty is in lieu of all other warranties either expressed or implied.

5. LIMITATION OF PROFESSIONAL LIABILITY

The Client agrees to limit any and all liability or claim for damage, for cost of defense, or for any expenses to be levied against Consultant to a sum not to exceed $15,000, or the amount of our fee, whichever is less, when such claim arises from any error, omission, or professional negligence on the part of the Consultant.

6. OTHER DOCUMENTS

(e.g., Proposal letter dated _____) is hereby made a part of this document.

7. ACCEPTANCE BY CLIENT

Client, by signing below, hereby agrees to these general terms and conditions of Client except as noted below:

CLIENT (typed name of client)

BY: _____

(Signature)
(Name and Designation)

SAMPLE 21
FORMAL CONSULTING CONTRACT

ABC Trainers Inc. (hereinafter called "the Company") desires to utilize the expert assistance of _____ (hereinafter called "the Consultant") in the field or fields in which the Consultant has professional qualifications.

1. PARTIES AND RELATIONSHIPS

The Company is a corporation engaged in the business of consulting and the provision of technical assistance and training to small business through the use of skilled independent contractors. The Consultant is a person who by education, training and experience is skilled in the provision of the service required.

2. CHARACTER AND EXTENT OF SERVICES

(a) It is the mutual intent of the parties that the Consultant shall act strictly in a professional consulting capacity as an independent contractor for all purposes and in all situations and shall not be considered an employee of the Company.

(b) The Consultant reserves full control of his activities as to the manner and selection of methods with respect to rendering his professional consulting services to the Company.

(c) The Consultant agrees to perform his activities in accordance with the highest and best state of the art of the profession.

3. PERIOD OF SERVICE AND TERMINATION

(a) The period of service by the Consultant under this agreement shall be from _____ through _____ and may be renewed upon the mutual agreement of the parties hereto.

(b) Either the Company or the Consultant may terminate this agreement by giving the other party 30 days' written notice of intention of such action.

(c) The Company reserves the right to halt or terminate the conduct of a seminar-workshop by the Consultant without prior notice or claim for additional compensation should, in the opinion of the Company, such conduct not be in the best interests of the Company.

4. COMPENSATION

(a) Upon the Consultant's acceptance hereof, the Company agrees to pay the Consultant according to the following schedule:

(Insert compensation rate or fixed fee and any allowance for or schedule of allowable expenses, if any.)

(b) In the event that the Company desires, and it is mutually agreed to by the Consultant, the Consultant's services may be used in the conduct of training/consulting programs not specifically identified in paragraph 4(a). In such cases, the Company agrees to pay the Consultant on the basis of the following schedule:

(Insert compensation rate or fixed fee and any allowance for or schedule of allowable expenses, if any.)

(c) In the event of special circumstances, variations to the fee schedule of paragraphs 4(a) and 4(b) will be allowed as mutually agreed in writing by the parties hereto.

5. NOTIFICATION

The Consultant will be notified by the Company in writing to begin his participation in specific training and/or consultation assignments to which the fee schedule of paragraphs 4(a) and 4(b) applies. Such notification will include a statement of the time(s) and places(s) of the intended training/consultation involvement with other necessary information.

6. EXPENSES

The Consultant, as an independent contractor, shall be responsible for any expenses incurred in the performance of this agreement, except as otherwise agreed to in writing prior to such expenses being incurred. The Company will reimburse the Consultant for reasonable travel expenses incurred with respect hereto.

(A specification of "reasonable" may be inserted here.)

7. METHOD OF PAYMENT

(a) The Consultant shall be paid as provided for in paragraphs 4(a) and 4(b) hereof, on the basis of a properly executed "Claim for Consulting Service" form (sample attached).

(b) The "Claim for Consulting Service" form is to be submitted at the end of the calendar month during which consulting services are performed. Exceptions to this arrangement are allowed with the written approval of the Company.

(c) Payment to the Consultant will be made by check, delivered by certified mail postmarked no later than _____ days subsequent to receipt of the "Claim for Consulting Service" form as provided for in paragraphs 7(a) and 7(b).

8. COPYRIGHTS

(a) The Consultant agrees that the Company shall determine the disposition of the title to and the rights under any copyright secured by the Consultant or his/her employee on copyrightable material first produced or composed and delivered to the Company under this agreement. The Consultant hereby grants to the Company a royalty fee, nonexclusive, irrevocable license to reproduce, translate, publish, use, and dispose of, and to authorize others to do so, all copyrighted or copyrightable work not first produced or composed by the Consultant in the performance of this agreement but which is incorporated into the material furnished under this agreement, provided that such license shall be only to the extent the Consultant now has or prior to the completion or final settlement of this agreement may acquire the right to grant such license without becoming liable to pay compensation to others solely because of such grant.

(b) The Consultant agrees that he will not knowingly include any copyrighted material in any written or copyrightable material furnished or delivered under this agreement without a license as provided in paragraph 8(a) hereof or without the consent of the copyright owner, unless specific written approval of the Company to the inclusion of such copyrighted material is secured.

(c) The Consultant agrees to report in writing to the Company promptly and in reasonable detail any notice or claim of copyright infringement received by the Consultant with respect to any material delivered under this agreement.

9. DRAWINGS, DESIGNS, SPECIFICATIONS

(a) All drawings, sketches, designs, design data, specifications, notebooks, technical and scientific data, and all photographs, negatives, reports, findings, recommendations, data, and memoranda of every description relating thereto, as well as copies of the foregoing, relating to the work performed under this agreement or any part thereof, shall be subject to the inspection of the Company at all reasonable times; and the Consultant and his employees shall afford the Company proper facilities for such inspection; and further shall be the property of the Company and may be used by the Company for any purpose whatsoever without any claim on the part of the Consultant and his employees for additional compensation, and subject to the right of the Consultant to retain a copy of said material shall be delivered to the Company or otherwise disposed of by the Consultant, either as the Company may from time to time direct during the progress of the work, or in any event, as the Company shall direct upon the completion or termination of this agreement.

10. CONFIDENTIALITY

(a) It is understood that in the performance of his duties, the Consultant will obtain information about both the Company and the Company's client, and that such information may include financial data, client lists, methods of operating, policy statements, and other confidential data.

(b) The Consultant agrees to restrict his use of such above-mentioned information to the performance of duties described in this agreement. The Consultant further agrees to return to the Company and to the Company's client upon the completion of his duties any and all documents (originals and copies) taken from either organization to facilitate the project described herein.

11. NONCOMPETITION

The consultant agrees that he will not perform his professional services for any organization known to the Consultant to be a client of the Company unless the Company has employed the Consultant for the provision of such services to the client. This restriction shall remain in effect for a period of two years after the termination of this agreement. For the purposes of this section, "client" is defined as any organization, which during the said period of restriction, has engaged the Company to promote: (Provide a list of all the services/products provided by the Company.)

12. APPLICABLE LAW

The parties agree that this agreement is to be construed according to the laws of _____ (state jurisdiction).

13. ASSIGNMENT

The Company reserves the right to assign all or any part of its interest in and to this agreement. The Consultant may not assign or transfer this agreement, any interest therein or claim thereunder without the written approval of the Company.

14. INTEGRATION

This agreement, executed in duplicate, constitutes the entire contract between the parties and may be canceled, modified, or amended only by a written supplemental document executed by each of the parties hereto.

IN WITNESS WHEREOF, the parties hereto have accepted and executed this agreement this _____ day of _____, 20__.

_____   _____

John Smith, Consultant   ABC Trainers Inc.

by: _____
(Authorized signatory)

TABLE 4
DETAILED CONTRACT CHECKLIST
(Commonly used for government contracts)

GENERAL

1. Date of agreement

2. Identification of client and consultant, including transfer of responsibility to successors (If the client is a public body, the authority under which it acts and the source of available funds should be specified.)

3. Review of the background and brief definition of the project

4. Scope of the assignment, including references to any detailed description incorporated in appendices

5. Effective date of commencement of work, when different from (1), and estimated or stipulated time for completion

6. Designation of individuals in client and consultant organizations responsible for policy decisions

7. Work statement containing a description of the requirements in detail (The description should include the problem to be solved or the objective of the investigation, the approach or method to be used, and the extent or degree of work to be undertaken. The proposed statement of work should be sufficiently descriptive so as to become a usable yardstick.)

8. Provision for changes in the work requirements

9. Provision for arbitration of disputes

10. Provision for termination by either party for "cause" or "convenience"

RESPONSIBILITIES OF THE CONSULTANT

1. Specify a project leader, professional help, services, and information to be supplied

2. Work schedule to be maintained

3. Personnel to be supplied (may be detailed in appendix)

TABLE 4 — Continued

4. Availability for conferences with the client

5. Reporting, including the schedule and nature of reports

6. Ownership of designs, blueprints, reports, etc., to be specified in the contract

7. Safeguarding of information supplied by client

8. Guarantee of performance, where required

9. Limitation of liability of the consultant with regard to loss or damage of reports, third party use of reports, errors or omissions or professional negligence (this provision for the benefit of the consultant)

10. Right to cancel the contract upon written notice of (x) days, provided that nonperformance of the other party can be clearly documented and provided that the defaulting party has been given (x) days to make good non-performance

11. Provision for disposal of any or all materials used in the performance of work

RESPONSIBILITIES OF THE CLIENT

1. Information, services, and facilities to be provided

2. Availability for conference with the consultant

3. Number of days of staff support by client agency staff

4. Prompt review and approval of reports and products

5. Termination by reason of events beyond control of either party

6. Provision against delays

TABLE 4 — Continued

FINANCIAL PROVISIONS

1. Total financial commitment by the client
2. Method and schedule of billing by the consultant
3. Method of payment
4. Currency or currencies of payment and conversion rates
5. Guarantee of payment by the client
6. Payment of interest on delayed payments
7. What are patent requirements? Who has copyright in reports and other products? Who has publication rights and under what circumstances?
8. Payment shall be made within (x) days of billing, billing to be by arrangement
9. Allowable costs or expenses to be billed separately from labor costs shall include but not be limited to:

   Telephone

   Postage and courier

   Travel

   Accommodation & miscellaneous

   Photocopying and printing

   Graphics

   Special typing support

   Translation

   Miscellaneous special materials

   Computer costs

   Subcontractual services

Generally you need not explain to your client that you are using subcontracting services unless your client specifically asks. Sometimes a client would like to have the qualifications of a subcontractor clarified. All services performed by any subconsultants are performed under your consulting company's name, and you are ultimately responsible for the quality of their work, so you must be very selective of who you hire and should monitor and approve all work they perform. In all outward respects, the sub-consultants are your employees under your direction. For example, all correspondence pertaining to the project should be printed only on your stationery.

Your subcontracting agreement should clearly spell out that the relationship of the sub-consultant to you is one of an independent contractor. You should also seriously consider a noncompetition clause in the contract that restricts the subcontractor's taking advantage of access to your clients to sell consulting services directly. A noncompetition clause or restrictive covenant can vary depending on the circumstances and the laws of your jurisdiction. Legal advice should be obtained before you complete any contract so you can be certain that the noncompetition clause would be reasonably upheld as fair and appropriate if it were contested. The clause normally states that the sub-consultant shall not perform professional services independent of your firm to any of your clients past or present. The exception would be if the sub-consultant performs such services under your direct employ as an independent contractor. A two-year time period for the restriction is fairly common. The restriction covers a wide or narrow geographic base depending on the nature of your services.

A summary of the standard clauses that should be considered include:

(a) The parties to the contract

(b) Independent contractor status of sub-consultant

(c) The responsibilities of the subconsultant fully specified

(d) Term of the contract

(e) Amount and method of payment for fees and expenses

(f) A cancellation provision in case the contract is canceled

(g) The method and amount of remuneration to be paid to the sub-consultant up to the point of cancellation

(h) A confidentiality provision stating that all the client information accessible to the sub-consultant is to be held in strict confidence

(i) All documents obtained by the sub-consultant are to be returned to the consultant or client

(j) Provision that the contract cannot be assigned or duties delegated without the written consent of both parties

(k) Other "standard" or "unique" provisions

The format of Sample 21, which shows a consultant contract, can also be used for a sub-consulting contract.

4.5 Agency agreement

An agency agreement is a contract that would be prepared if you were acting for a client as an external agent: for example, if you were selling a product on behalf of a client, or negotiating on behalf of the client with the government for funding purposes. The clauses in this type of contract vary considerably. Generally the client prepares the agreement for you to sign.

4.6 Letter of retainer agreement

This is an agreement that you outline in a letter. One form of retainer relationship is when you are available "on call" at the request of a client based on need of your services. The consultant charges the client for being "on call" and available, even though the consultant may not be used.

Another form of retainer relationship is if you provide a service on a periodic basis, for example, monthly or quarterly.

5. PREPARING YOUR OWN CONTRACT

You should consider having several standardized contracts with variations depending on the different types of consulting services you perform. Space can be left in the contract for inserting the unique features of a specific consulting project. If your contracts are stored on a word processor or a personal computer with word processing capabilities, each contract can easily be personalized in an original format for each consulting job.

The process of preparing your own contract is not difficult. Try to obtain as many sample forms of contracts as possible from your competitors and from contract books that are available from your local library or law school. Then refer to the various headings listed in this chapter or shown in the sample contracts or checklists. Outline the areas that you feel are important for your particular type of consulting services or problems. As soon as you have completed this exercise, expand on the points in a de-

scriptive paragraph and then sub-divide into clauses in a format appropriate to your needs and in a style you prefer.

Take your draft contracts to your lawyer to evaluate. It is to your benefit to save your lawyer's time and your money by preparing the documents yourself. You are most familiar with your work and the important factors of your projects. Your lawyer can review your draft contracts and rewrite them or add additional clauses if required.

Major companies or government frequently have their own standardized contracts and send them to you for signature. In some cases there is room for negotiation; in other cases, no negotiation is possible. If you are presented with the contract, you should review it thoroughly yourself and mark the areas that cause you concern. Also, note the areas that are not in the contract that you would prefer to have covered. Then discuss the contract with your lawyer. If you have any doubts about the required provisions of the contract, it is best to either negotiate to remove those provisions if possible, or turn down the project. If a contract is not completely to your liking, the degree of risk or dissatisfaction on your part or your client's part is high.

If a client wants to make changes to your contract, it is better to make them yourself rather than have a client make up his or her own contract. A client-prepared contract could have clauses or conditions you do not want.

In summary, attempt to prepare all your own contracts. This will establish the client-consultant relationship on your terms. Your initiative and leadership in preparing the contract should have a positive effect on the dynamics of the relationship with your client.

Chapter 19
TIME MANAGEMENT

Like any other valuable resource, time can be managed. The better it is managed, the more productive and profitable your consulting business will be. All the other acquired skills you possess will lose much of their effectiveness if you are disorganized. As you probably will not have the time to attend to all the matters requiring your attention, you must ensure that the important tasks get done. Prioritize activities that generate continued profitability and future growth. By using some of the following proven techniques, your efficiency, productivity, and satisfaction will be increased considerably.

1. KEY STRATEGIES

1.1 Set priorities

Based on the goals you have established for your business, set your high, medium, and low priorities. Write them down. High-priority items are those that are vital to the business, have a deadline affixed to them, and usually need your personal attention. Medium-priority tasks are necessary to the business, but may not require your immediate attention; perhaps some of these tasks can be delegated. Low priority items may be postponed to a more convenient time, or not done at all.

Keeping a "to do" list provides a source of satisfaction and feeling of progress as items are crossed off. It can also alleviate the stress that results from trying to remember everything that has to be done.

Dealing with the high-priority items first is a particularly effective timemanagement technique. By handling a critical task early in your day, you have the reward of feeling a sense of accomplishment. Often this provides additional motivation and drive to maintain the productivity momentum. If there are unexpected interruptions, or minor problems arise, you are able to devote attention to them knowing that you have already dealt with your top-priority item. If on the other hand you defer your high-priority item until the afternoon, chances are that problems will arise that prevent you from getting to that high-priority task. As there can be a daily stream of unexpected interruptions, some people operate day after day in this time trap, never getting to those critical tasks.

In order to accomplish your high priority tasks, it will be necessary to have a block of uninterrupted time. Hold all calls for the first hour of each day. Schedule other blocks of time necessary to fully complete a priority task.

Avoid procrastination. If one of your critical tasks doesn't have a built-in deadline, set one. In this way you will ensure that it gets to the top of your priority list. Perhaps you are having trouble starting a major project because it appears to be massive and you don't know where to begin. It is helpful to divide the major project into manageable stages. For instance, when preparing a bank loan proposal, one day's task may be to make a list of all the items you will include in your proposal. The other stages will be preparing each of the items on your list: sales projection charts, net worth statement, marketing concept, and loan rationale. Handling a large project in this manner of bite-size pieces, it is conceivable that the task could be accomplished within a week.

1.2 Be organized

If you make a habit of writing everything in your day timer or diary as soon as you become aware of an event, you will avoid double-booking appointments or forgetting them. You may decide to schedule your appointments for the afternoon whenever possible, to allow your morning to be a free block of time during which you can accomplish items on your "to do" list. When scheduling your workday, allow yourself some flexibility and leeway, as things don't always go according to plan. Allow sufficient time so that each task can be carried out in a thorough, unhurried manner.

Having an up-to-date and efficient filing system will enable you to find your files quickly. On the other hand, keeping every piece of paper that comes across your desk in an escalating stack, or in overstuffed files, only creates frustration and delay when you are trying to locate a piece of information. Of course you will need to keep a copy of your important correspondence, proposals, and bookkeeping records. But filing space is expensive. Before filing a piece of paper you need to ask yourself: Will I ever have to refer back to this? Can I get another copy of this if sometime in the future I need to refer to it?

There is much to be said for the person who is able to keep a tidy workspace. While many defend their cluttered desks by saying, "I know exactly where everything is," it is well known how much time is wasted shuffling papers. The hidden time waster is the distraction created by a cluttered work area. Instead of having a clear train of thought when working on the critical priority items, a casual glance at a the clutter may trigger numerous reminders of things that must be done. This could create unnecessary delays in completing the immediate task, as well as cause extra stress and a feeling of being overwhelmed.

Being prepared for meetings and appointments saves time otherwise spent in prolonged discussions. Before the meeting you should review your file, make notes, prepare an agenda, and stick to it. Anticipating potential problems will enable you to have an action plan ready to implement, rather than merely reacting to events as they occur.

1.3 Delegate

As your company expands, you may need to increase staff, contract out for employees, or have consulting associates. It will be necessary for you to delegate to others some of your responsibilities. At times, it will appear easier to do it yourself than to train, supervise, and check someone else's work. Delegating the authority builds staff morale, competence and motivation.

Learn to say no. You may receive a request, for example, to participate in a community activity that will require taking time from your business day. Knowing your daily workload and having the ability to say no is important to your time management.

1.4 Be decisive

Preciseness in identifying problems and decisiveness in the actions to be taken will save time in your workday. Similar to the technique used with large or insurmountable tasks, by breaking a problem down into different parts you can see more clearly the root of the problem. To resolve it, list the various alternatives and rate the degree of effectiveness of each. Practicing this technique will help you develop the ability to go through this process quickly in your mind. This will enhance your effectiveness in resolving small problems before they escalate into larger ones.

The art of speaking and writing concisely is a time saver for you and your associates. It will also foster improved communication between you and your staff, and customers. The effective use of e-mail and voice mail messaging can greatly enhance your time management.

2. AVOIDING TIME WASTERS

2.1 Using voice mail effectively

Voice mail allows customers to send messages to you directly. It creates a better impression than a telephone answering machine, and is far more versatile. A full 75% of all business calls are not completed on the first attempt. The effect is an incredible amount of wasted time and energy. Here are some prime examples of the benefits of voice mail:

- *Reduces telephone tag.* Lets people communicate the complete message without regard for confidentiality or complexity of the information. More accurate and private than pink slips. Messages are in the caller's own voice, with all the original intonations and inflections.

- *Saves time and money on long-distance charges.* When messages are left on voice mail, calls are invariably shorter, as the caller gets right to the point.

Live communications encourage less chit chat, thereby wasting time and money. When you are out of town, you can call into the voice mail to receive your messages in the evening when the long distance rates are lower.

- *Eases the time zone/business hour dilemma.* No more waiting until noon (or rising at 6 A.M.) to call the other coast. This will save a lot of time and inconvenience.

- *Increases productivity of staff.* Instead of staff answering many phone calls or taking messages, staff can be more efficient and do additional tasks or provide more personal service to callers who wish to bypass the voice mail and speak directly to a receptionist or secretary.

- *Cuts down on paging and holding times.* The caller can go directly to a voice mail box rather than waiting on hold.

- *Voice mail/auto attendant works 365 days a year, 24 hours a day.* You can phone in any time from anywhere to receive your messages, with a confidential access number. The voice mail system can route callers to appropriate voice mail boxes, take messages, play customized greetings depending on the time of day or evening, offer other mail box menu selections for specific information, and perform many other features, as noted below.

- *Automatic paging of all voice mail messages.* Your voice mail can be programmed to call you as soon as messages are left on the service. You can leave instructions as to where calls should be directed (cellular,

pager, home, or associate's number) as they are received.

- *Fax response option.* This means that a caller can phone a voice mail box number, input his or her fax number, and instantly your fax message is transmitted to the caller's fax machine. You can store any number of pages on the computer to be transmitted automatically upon request.

2.2 Using e-mail effectively

Similar to voice mail, but in the written form, e-mail can be a great time saver when used effectively:

- Communicating with others in different time zones is greatly enhanced with e-mail. The business day virtually becomes 24 hours.

- Costs are considerably less as there are no long distance telephone charges. Messages are briefer and to the point. The formalities typical of business letter writing are omitted and replaced by informal greetings and sign-offs.

- Formatting is simplified and expedient, with less time being spent making it look nice for the reader, as with business letters.

- When receiving an e-mail message, it is quick and easy to send a brief acknowledgement or reply by selecting the "reply to" option on the e-mail program menu. The recipient's address as well as your own is automatically inserted for you.

- It is easy to send a copy of the message to other parties for their information, action or response by adding their e-mail addresses. In this way, you can receive group feedback on a proposal within a short time frame.

2.3 Too many telephone calls

Ensure that written and verbal telephone messages are complete. Knowing not only the name and phone number of the person calling but also the purpose of the call enables you to deal with the response quickly and effectively, often delegating the response to someone else. Bunch your calls before lunch or towards the end of the day when people are less likely to chat. Use fax, e-mail, or voice mail messages instead of a telephone call where one-way transfer of information is all that is required.

2.4 Overscheduling/too many things to do

Concentrate on important items and disregard the trivial. Use your diary to plan your day and prepare a priority list of tasks. Learn to say no. Delegate.

2.5 Too much paper

Deal with each piece of paper only once. If it is junk mail, throw it out. Request to be taken off the distribution list of unknown faxes and junk e-mail. If it is for the file, file it immediately. If it requires a response, a handwritten response or a telephone call may suffice. Or delegate routine matters to another staff member. By handling your morning mail in this manner, you will avoid tomorrow's task of dealing with the paperwork you set aside today.

2.6 Scheduled meetings

Be certain they start and end on time, and follow the agenda. Keep on topic. Ensure that a summary is given, noting any action to be taken after the meeting and by whom.

2.7 Perfectionism

Striving for excellence is healthy, gratifying, and attainable. However, aiming for perfection is frustrating, neurotic, and a waste of time.

CHAPTER 20
EXPANDING YOUR PRACTICE

There are many ways to acquire clients. The simplest way is to keep your existing clients happy and nurture the present and past clients well. Studies show that over 70% of a consultant's business is based on repeat business or referral business from existing clients. A marketing formula shows that the average person has over 200 contacts including friends, relatives, and associates. By carefully developing this client potential you can expand your practice rapidly.

For example, from one satisfied client you could obtain numerous projects — sufficient to keep you busy on an ongoing basis. If your client gives you repeat work on a regular basis and also recommends you to ten other business associates in the same industry, and if five of those ten become clients, your business will grow. Former employees of the first client or referral clients may go to work for other firms in the private or public sector. If they enjoyed working with you, they will request your services again or refer work to you. The possibilities are limitless.

An effective way of keeping your clients satisfied is to create client dependency. The more the client relies on you because of your specialty, the more repeat business you will generate. The more your client respects you for your knowledge and leadership, the more the client will look to you for guidance.

It is important that the client feel in control at all times. You must maintain your image as a unique commodity. Your role is to complement staff. You do not want to be perceived as just another person on staff.

If there are particular tasks that the client does not enjoy, and if you have the skills and ability to perform those tasks and fill the void (and if the situation seems appropriate), you can create further dependency. If the outcome of a project is particularly successful and considerable positive feedback occurs, make a point of having your client share the glory with you. A satisfied client will appreciate your value and provide you with more consulting contracts.

There are other ways of developing your practice. Expanding your line by adding additional services that are natural extensions of your first service is an effective method. If you have clients that retain you for one service, you are creating a potential two- or three-fold growth pattern with all your clientele. Because you already have credibility with the clients for one project, it will be much easier for you to market your skills for the other services.

Subcontracting is another way of expanding your practice. You can locate subcontractors from your network and through referral. They can be effectively used to increase your earnings by providing depth and greater capacity for your business. You would be in a position to make proposals for larger or more complex projects using past, present, or future clients as your base. If a client has been satisfied with your service on a smaller project or a particular service line, and you have additional service lines and a greater depth and capacity, the prospects are endless. Naturally, subcontracting will involve more administration for you, but the independent contractor status of sub-consultants will allow you flexibility to hire them on an as-needed basis.

Other ways to expand your practice are to review all aspects of your operation on an ongoing basis, note the weak areas, and develop a specific plan for dealing with them. Improvement in areas such as self-promotion and more efficient follow-up on leads can also enhance your clientele base.

APPENDIX 1
CONSULTING AND OTHER ASSOCIATIONS (UNITED STATES AND CANADA)

To find general or specialty consulting associations to join, or to locate other associations that relate to your area of practice interest, review the directories below. They are updated annually and are available in most public libraries.

1. UNITED STATES

Consultants and Consulting Organizations Directory. Gale Research. (**Note:** also includes Canadian listings).

Encyclopedia of Associations. Gale Research.

National Trade and Professional Associations of the United States. Columbia Books.

2. CANADA

Associations Canada: Directory of Associations in Canada. Micromedia Inc.

APPENDIX 2
FREE OR NOMINAL COST BUSINESS PUBLICATIONS

There are many sources of small business or tax publications to assist you in your planning. Here are some of the key ones. Look for the contact numbers in your local telephone directory.

1. UNITED STATES
- Internal Revenue Service
- Major banks
- Major international certified public accounting firms
- Small Business Administration

2. CANADA
- BMO Bank of Montreal
- Business Development Bank of Canada
- Major international chartered accounting firms
- Canada Revenue Agency
- RBC Royal Bank

APPENDIX 3
PROPOSAL EVALUATION CHECKLIST

1. GENERAL FACTORS

(a) Has the bidder responded with an appropriate technique or is he or she trying to fit the problem to a favorite technique?

(b) What priority will this project receive from the consultant? How important will it be to his or her firm?

(c) Does the proposal meet the terms of reference and the intended scope of the study?

(d) How useful or capable of implementation will the end product be?

(e) What degree of originality is present in the proposal?

(f) Are the submission of progress reports and presentation of interim briefings required? What progress reports and interim briefings are planned?

(g) What degree of direct consultant-client liaison is proposed? Does the consultant-client relationship include a training component for the client's personnel? What type of training is proposed?

(h) Is the proposed content of progress reports in accordance with the requirements of the client? Will progress reports contain a monthly statement of costs incurred, commitments, and, if necessary, a revised estimate of total costs?

(i) When the project is complete, how does the consultant intend to hand over the project?

(j) What degree of follow-up and/or debriefing is proposed? To whom do the relevant data belong and what happens to them when the project is completed?

2. PERFORMANCE

(a) Is the usual business of the consultant closely related to the proposed work?

(b) Do the references to past experience include activities specifically related to the requirements of the proposed study?

(c) Has the bidder been honored by professional societies because of the performance in a specific professional area?

(d) What reputation does the firm hold in the area of the proposed study?

(e) Has the firm worked for this client before, and if so with what success?

(f) Are the statements of past performance worded in a meaningful way so you can identify what work was actually performed?

(g) Are there aspects of past performance that indicate particular weaknesses or strengths?

3. SCOPE OF WORK

(a) Has the proposal demonstrated an understanding of the problems to be solved?

(b) Is this research area new to the company?

(c) Has the bidder made an accurate assessment of the problem based on an interpretation of the requirements put forth in the work statement?

(d) Has the bidder presented an approach that will achieve the stated objectives?

(e) Is the proposed approach supported with justification of why it should achieve the evaluation objectives?

(f) Do you think the suggested approach will work?

(g) Has the bidder introduced unanticipated events which may result in a project overrun or an expanded scope of work?

(h) Does the proposal differentiate between the simpler and the more difficult performance requirements?

(i) Does the proposal convincingly show a depth of understanding of the problem?

(j) Are the technical problems clearly delineated or are they merely "parroted" from the proposal request?

(k) Have the limits of the problems been specified to show that the proposed study will be restricted to an appropriate scope?

(l) Is there a concise but adequate review of literature? Is the literature review an annotated bibliography or is it a scholarly critique?

(m) Are the specific objectives of the proposal clearly stated? Are these goals realistic in view of time, equipment, budget, and professional experience of the principal investigator?

(n) Does the plan, in fact, permit an unequivocal test of the stated hypotheses of research questions?

(o) Does the proposal represent a unique, imaginative approach?

(p) Is the technical program fully responsive to all written requirements and specifications?

(q) Are there any apparent discrepancies or omissions?

(r) Are the "products" clearly defined and presented?

4. PERSONNEL

(a) Is it clear which tasks in the study will be assigned to specific personnel and for what amount of time?

(b) Are the personnel assigned to specific tasks qualified by training and experience to successfully perform the tasks?

(c) Is there a clear organization chart depicting project management? Is the apportionment of personnel level and time to specific tasks realistic?

(d) What assurances are made concerning the availability of personnel proposed? Was a contingency plan requested if certain personnel become unavailable?

(e) Have enough time and personnel been included to provide adequate administrative management of the study?

(f) Is the author of the proposal one of the key personnel?

(g) Does the success of the project depend, to a large degree, upon personnel not directly associated with the prospective firm?

(h) Do biographies relate specific experience of personnel to the specific needs of this project?

(i) Does the proposal show the capabilities of the management to handle a project of the size contemplated?

(j) Is the position of the program manager in the overall organization and the limits of his or her authority and responsibility shown?

(k) Are the type, frequency, and effectiveness of management controls and method for corrective action shown?

(l) Does the task organization integrate the overall organization in terms of effective integration of research, development, design, drafting, technical writing, and, where appropriate, test functions?

(m) Is it clearly demonstrated that top-level management will continue a high level of interest and assume responsibility for successful accomplishment of the program?

(n) Is the proposal dependent on recruitment of key personnel?

5. PLANNING AND MANAGEMENT

(a) Has the work schedule been specified clearly, and is it realistic in terms of time and money? Does it fit with available personnel?

(b) If the time of performance is important and is a competitive evaluation factor, is the proposed schedule supported by the technical proposal?

(c) Is the planning realistic? Does it follow recognized and accepted procedure?

(d) Does the proposal show that the delivery schedule will be met and how it will be met?

(e) Is sufficient detail regarding master scheduling, programming, follow-up, and other like functions given to reinforce the foregoing assurance?

(f) Are the various technical phases of the project detailed and realistically scheduled?

(g) Are effective review, evaluation, and control provided at specific checkpoints?

(h) Has the bidder allowed for all necessary clearances (e.g., OMB (United States), Statistics Canada (Canada))?

6. FACILITIES

(a) Are the facilities and equipment needed for successful completion of the study specified in the proposal?

(b) How does the bidder intend to access facilities not at the contractor's site?

(c) Does the use of facilities outside of the contractor's firm require a subcontract? If so, is the proposed subcontractor specifically mentioned, along with an explanation of its required qualifications?

(d) Is the planned use of facilities, such as printing, data processing, etc., realistic?

(e) If computer services are required, are there controls built into the processing so corrective action can be taken at intermittent points if necessary?

(f) Is any government-furnished equipment needed?

(g) Are the proposed laboratory and test facilities adequate for the requirements of the technical scope?

(h) Are resources overly committed?

7. COST

(a) Is the overall cost within range of your (the contracting agency's) budget?

(b) What is the relationship between the cost figures and equivalent items in the technical proposal?

(c) Are the personnel costs reasonable according to the tasks to be performed?

(d) Are the appropriate personnel assigned to perform the appropriate tasks?

(e) Have expenditures been set aside for subcontracting requirements such as data processing?

(f) If a large-scale questionnaire must be mailed, has an adequate sum been set aside for postage?

(g) Have costs for development of instruments and purchase of materials such as scoring sheets, etc., been included?

(h) Does the travel seem reasonable when compared to the tasks to be accomplished?

(i) If consultants or experts are included, is their daily rate reasonable and within the proper financial range? Is the proposed time reasonable?

(j) Is an appropriate type of contract requested?

(k) Is the schedule of payment acceptable?

(l) Have appropriate procedures been used to estimate costs?

BIBLIOGRAPHY

1. CONSULTING AND SMALL BUSINESS — GENERAL

Gray, Douglas A., and Diana L. Gray. *The Complete Canadian Small Business Guide.* McGraw-Hill Ryerson, 3rd edition, 2001.

Holtz, Herman. *How to Succeed as an Independent Consultant.* John Wiley & Sons, 3rd edition, 1993.

James, Jack D. *Starting a Successful Business in Canada.* Self-Counsel Press, 16th edition, 2004.

Kelley, Robert E. *Consulting: The Complete Guide to a Profitable Career.* Charles Scribners Sons, 1981.

Kishel, Gregory, and Patricia Kishel. *Cashing in on the Consulting Boom.* John Wiley and Sons, 1985.

Schiffman, Stephan. *The Consultant's Handbook: How to Start and Develop Your Own Practice.* Adams Media Corporation, 2nd edition, 2000.

Tepper, Ron. *Become a Top Consultant.* John Wiley and Sons, 1988.

2. CONSULTING — MARKETING

Conner, Dick., and Jeffrey Davidson. *Marketing Your Consulting and Professional Services.* John Wiley and Sons, 3rd edition, 1997.

Holtz, Herman. *The Consultants Guide to Winning Clients.* John Wiley and Sons, 1988.

_____. *The Consultant's Guide to Proposal Writing.* John Wiley and Sons, 3rd edition, 1998.

Kemppainen, Rudolph C. *Power Consulting: Using the Media to Expand Your Business.* John Wiley and Sons, 1988.

Marcus, Bruce W. *Competing for Clients: The Complete Guide to Marketing and Promoting Professional Services.* Probus Publishing Company, 1986.

Tammemagi, Hans. *Winning Proposals.* Self-Counsel Press, 2nd edition, 1999.

3. CONSULTING — SPECIALTY

Kaye, Harvey. *Inside the Technical Consulting Business: Launching and Building Your Independent Practice.* John Wiley and Sons, 2nd edition, 1993.

Simon, Alan R. *How to Be a Successful Computer Consultant.* McGraw Hill, 4th edition, 1998.